Couple, Family and Group Work

First Steps in Interpersonal Intervention

Couple, Family and Group Work

First Steps in Interpersonal Intervention

Hugh Crago

Open University Press

Open University Press
McGraw-Hill Education
McGraw-Hill House
Shoppenhangers Road
Maidenhead
Berkshire
England
SL6 2QL

email: enquiries@openup.co.uk
world wide web: www.openup.co.uk

and Two Penn Plaza, New York, NY 10121-2289, USA

First published 2006

A catalogue record of this book is available from the British Library

ISBN-13: 978 0335 21688 8 (pb)   978 0335 21689 5 (hb)
ISBN-10: 0335 21688 9 (pb)   0335 21689 7 (hb)

Library of Congress Cataloging-in-Publication Data
CIP data applied for

Typeset by RefineCatch Limited, Bungay, Suffolk
Printed in Poland by OZGraf. S.A. www.polskabook.pl

Contents

Acknowledgements

This book owes much to the students I have been privileged to teach at three Australian universities (Griffith, New England and Western Sydney), and at a private training college, the Jansen Newman Institute (Sydney). My colleagues, supervisees and former students have taught me a lot, and the discussions we have had about their clients and their professional challenges have been a major source of material for *Couple, Family and Group Work*. A number of these people have also supplied invaluable comments and suggestions on draft chapters of the book. Among them, I would particularly like to thank Penny Gardner, Lê Hoang, Tracey Popham, Adam McLean, Jacqueline McDiarmid and Jane Quayle. I have also learned a great deal from consulting to the Hunter Child Protection and Family Counselling Team, the Central Coast Children's and Young People's Mental Health Team, the staff of the Cyrenian House drug and alcohol rehabilitation programme, Sydney, when it was led by Michael Doyle, and subsequently Michael's staff at Foley House, Sydney.

I also owe a great deal to those who have taught and trained me over the past twenty-five years, and I particularly thank my first trainers in Australia, Bet Roffey and the late John Roffey. In the USA, I remember with gratitude David Singer and Sarah Pearlman, then at Antioch New England Graduate School, as well as the chance to listen first hand to a few of the 'greats' of early family therapy: Gregory Bateson, Murray Bowen and Carl Whitaker. Much of what is best in my counselling derives from Maureen Crago, my life partner and for many years my co-therapist. What I do now often reflects what I saw her do twenty years ago, although I am ashamed to say that I often failed to realize its full worth back then. She has read the entire manuscript of this book, as she has read everything I have written, offering encouragement, suggesting many helpful references, and quietly correcting errors.

The late Margaret Topham introduced me to the dynamic family therapy style she had learned from Virginia Satir, and encouraged me to believe that I could do it; Nancy Miller, Maureen's and my first supervisor, supplied steady, continuing support, gentle challenge and enormous practice wisdom. Max Cornwell provided mentoring and encouragement to contribute to the community of Australian family therapy. Within that community, I would especially thank Brian Stagoll, Moshe Lang, Catherine Sanders, Liz Mackenzie, Melody Krok, Chris Lobsinger and Carol Boland, all of whom have provided inspiration, encouragement and friendship, as has (from Canterbury, UK) John Hills.

Above all, my clients over nearly a quarter of a century have not only provided the material on which I have based the case vignettes, but also enriched my life with all those inspirational, mundane, challenging, frustrating, and joyful experiences that make a therapist's life such a surprising and satisfying one.

Hugh Crago
Sydney, Australia 2005

Introduction

Couple, Family and Group Work is a beginner's guide to 'interpersonal intervention' – that is, to working therapeutically with more than one person at a time.
It deals with couples, families and groups: unfortunately, there is no space in a
small book to deal adequately with intervention in organizations, communities
and temporary social systems such as conferences and workshops, which share
some common features with the more 'clinical' areas of interpersonal work.

Couple, family and group work have all been extensively written about, at
levels from the most basic to the most sophisticated. Oddly enough, though,
there do not appear to have been many attempts to bring these different areas
together in a single text (in fact, I know of none). They have established themselves as largely separate areas of study and professional practice.[1] While some
individual therapists also see couples, and many family therapists also see
couples, few individual therapists regularly see families. And while some professionals do both individual and group work, they rarely combine it with
family or couple intervention. Of course, there are worthy exceptions to all of
these generalizations, but they are true for the majority of practitioners.

These divisions are reinforced by the way jobs are organized, and the way
mental health professionals are trained. Most psychologists and psychiatrists,
and most of those who call themselves counsellors, receive basic training
only in individual (one-to-one) forms of intervention. Social workers may be
required to study group work and (sometimes) family work in addition to case
work, but typically these subjects are taught by different lecturers, who set
separate textbooks for their individual courses. Training programmes in family
therapy rarely address the skills and principles common to both family
'groups' and groups of unrelated individuals.

To my mind it makes overwhelming sense to introduce students, as well
as experienced one-to-one practitioners, to *all* the main varieties of clinical
interpersonal intervention in a single volume, so that both the real differences,
and the real similarities, can emerge. Anyone trained solely in one-to-one
counselling and therapy will probably feel a certain level of anxiety and

discomfort at the thought of exposing themselves to the multiple, interacting tensions of 'people together'. Even the prospect of seeing a couple – two adults in a relationship – can elicit that feeling of panic, and even more so a whole family or a group ('Wow! All those people in the room!'). This anxiety is not unjustified. Working with two or more people simultaneously *is* different, it *can* be hard work, and you *cannot* simply do what you do with an individual client – or rather, you can, but it will not be all that effective, and you may buy yourself major problems. It should help to know from the outset just what you need to do if your work is to be fruitful, whether that be with a couple, a mother and child, a whole nuclear family, or a therapy group of unrelated adults.

Of course, each of these client units requires from us somewhat different ways of being, and different skills, and this book will make some of those variations clear. But at the same time, we can actually use what works with therapy groups to help us be more effective with family groups; we can see how the same process that governs the opening sessions of couple work also manifests in the opening phases of a therapy group, and so on. Writing this book has made me aware of things I had only glimpsed before, and introduced some intriguing possibilities that I had never thought of.

My hope, then, is that this will be a book with something to offer to anyone who already possesses baseline skills in one-to-one counselling and therapy, but who is relatively new to interpersonal work in any form. Obviously, this means students who have already completed a year or two of training in the microskills of counselling, and who are beginning to find their feet with seeing real clients under supervision. But it should also be useful to more experienced practitioners who are widening their scope to include couple work, to those who wish to supplement their individual practice with a therapy group, to those who have trained as family therapists, but who are under pressure to run groups for their agency, in order to cope with long waiting lists, and so on.

Perhaps it is grandiose, but I would like to think that, elementary though it is, the book may also have something to offer to experienced, sophisticated practitioners in couple, group or family work – if only by inviting them to 'go back to basics' and think about what they do in new ways, or within different contexts. Finally, I would hope that reading this book might inspire some people outside the helping professions to realize that they may be ideally fitted to one or more of the modes described here, and to pursue training in interpersonal work – especially since interpersonal intervention typically requires a more extraverted, active and flexible style of relating than one-to-one counselling and therapy.[2]

Some of my older readers may remember the term 'primer', which meant a beginner-level textbook (*A First Latin Primer*, etc.). I would have called this book a 'primer of interpersonal intervention' but the term now seems hopelessly old-fashioned. Instead, I have chosen the phrase 'First Steps . . .', which means much the same thing. This is a book that gives you *some* basics, *not* a complete or comprehensive guide to all aspects of interpersonal work. Desperate to be inclusive, authors sometimes end up writing textbooks which carefully describe so many exceptions, special cases, and complications that they obscure the basic principles they originally set out to teach. I have tried to avoid this temptation.

In order to get the fundamental principles established clearly, I have written mostly about voluntary clients, people who are prepared to seek help because they know (or one of them does) that something is going badly wrong. I have said little about clients who are forced by the legal system to attend counselling sessions, or group therapy. I have not attempted to deal with the special challenges of couples where one uses violence to intimidate the other, or families where children are abused physically or sexually. Keeping children or adults safe from violation requires some modification in assessment, and in how sessions are conducted, which I have not described;[3] but even if I did, no textbook can substitute for good supervision in the early stages of learning a new field of practice. And, although there are some differences in working with abusive systems, most of the principles and understandings outlined in this book still apply.

I aim to present readers with a simplified map of the territory of interpersonal work. To assist you in negotiating this territory, I will offer you some principles that I have gradually come to accept over my working life. Most of them I have learned from other people; some I have worked out for myself. I will give examples of what to say in various situations (but bear in mind that my examples are only templates, which you must adapt to your own ways of speaking and your own clients' needs). To bring the principles to life, I will provide clinical vignettes – glimpses of particular clients and particular situations requiring intervention. Most of these are based on past clients of my own, with names and identifying details changed; some blend details from several cases that have similar features.

Over many years as a teacher (not only of counselling, but also of literature and of human development) I have realised that if I cannot spontaneously explain a complex concept in simple language, or find an analogy that helps others to understand it, then I don't really understand it myself. My plan is that this book will contain plain-language explanations of complex matters (and some simple matters). If I have to fall back on repeating the technical language of those who originated the theories, then I will have failed, so this book will have some gaps, corresponding to the concepts in psychotherapy and systems theory that I am personally still struggling with.

There was another reason for using the phrase 'First Steps' as part of my subtitle, and this is that the image of a child learning to walk also fits with the developmental metaphor which I have frequently used in the chapters that follow. In other words, I have used the 'stages of life' ('growing up' from infancy to adulthood, reproducing oneself, reaching maturity) as a way of explaining the way that couples, families and groups evolve over time in an ongoing therapeutic process. This metaphor is not, of course, a new one; indeed, it is one of the oldest there is. But it has proved particularly useful and illuminating to me. I can still remember the revelatory impact of reading, some twenty years ago, Bennis and Shepherd's classic article on the stages of group development.[4] Here was something that helped me to understand the otherwise baffling way that my therapy group was acting, how it could be so different from one session to the next. Here was something that showed me what to expect, and how to handle it.

Not only groups, but also couples, families and organizations (and even temporary social systems such as conferences) predictably go through 'stages', and, if properly assisted through each of them, will evolve towards 'productive autonomy', just as children, if properly parented, normally grow into adults who are capable of running their lives and nurturing children of their own. Ever since Freud, we have known that adult clients in therapy are quite capable of becoming childlike in their relationship with the therapist, and that part of the work of long-term therapy is to assist them to 'grow up' within that relationship – with consequent gains in maturity in their significant relationships outside of therapy. Similarly, there are ways in which we can assist couples, and larger groupings, to grow up and take more responsibility for their lives. Conversely, it also helps to know that human beings in relationships and groups may also 'grow down'[5] – in other words, revert temporarily to more dependent, less mature behaviour as the result of various forms of stress and anxiety.

Partly because I have conceived it as unfolding organically from the earlier chapters to the later ones, this book is best read continuously from beginning to end. Some readers may want to confine themselves to the chapters dealing specifically with their particular interest, and they can certainly do so, but they will miss out on some things, since I often refer back to principles explained in earlier chapters, showing how they must now be modified in a new context.

So far, I have mostly been speaking of 'principles' rather than 'theories'. As you read the opening chapter of this book, some of you may be wondering what happened to the imposing bodies of theory you were supposed to master as a student. Where are behaviourism and cognitive behavioural therapy in this book? What about psychodynamic therapy (with all its different 'schools'), systems theory (with all *its* different 'schools'), person-centred therapy? Where is Narrative therapy, or other variants of the social constructivist approach? In fact, I have drawn upon several theoretical traditions in this book, but they do not occupy the centre of the stage, as they so often do in standard textbooks. Why not?

Those who originate particular therapeutic approaches often invent novel and impressive terminology to emphasize the differences they perceive between their work and what has gone before. Yet in practice, much of the history of counselling and psychotherapy over the past century has been the rediscovery and 'marketing' (under new 'brand names') of things that have been known and practised for years. Thus, cognitive behavioural therapy has in recent years discovered the body of knowledge about the client–therapist relationship that psychoanalytic therapists call 'transference'. Cognitively-oriented therapists don't call it that, but that is what it is.[6] And self psychology, a newish school within the psychodynamic tradition, seems to have rediscovered the power of what Carl Rogers half a century before had called 'empathy' and 'unconditional positive regard'.[7] Recently reading an account of the work of Ignacio de Loyola, the sixteenth-century founder of the Jesuits, I discovered that his *Spiritual Exercises* contained a series of instructions for using 'positive imagery' that would sit comfortably (except perhaps for its overtly spiritual content) in any modern self-help text. There is far less that is new under the sun than most therapists think. A particularly striking case is the recent development of 'interpersonal psychotherapy', which has, within the individually oriented realm of treatment for depression, reinvented some of the principles that family therapy has been using for fifty years.[8]

Rather than theories, I have written this book around *principles that govern practice*. Some of these principles do derive from a single body of theory (or at least, from a body of practice wisdom within a particular theoretical tradition). Thus, the principle of asking 'Why *this* problem? Why *now*?' (see Chapter 7) is derived from the British object relations school, particularly the work of the Tavistock Clinic. The principle that 'people spontaneously warm up to the work they may need to do' (see Chapter 4) derives from the sociometric theory of Jacob Moreno, inventor of psychodrama. The principle that 'the more people there are in the room, the greater the need for structure to be provided by the leader/facilitator/therapist' is my own, but I doubt if anyone working with interpersonal systems would have failed to come up with a similar 'rule of thumb'. I have drawn on such principles throughout this book, and they are collected and summarized in the final short section, 'Principles of interpersonal intervention.'

My debts to theory can be found throughout, but particularly in Chapters 2 and 6, which I think of as 'why?' chapters. These chapters cover some understandings that help me (and hopefully my readers) to appreciate the complex, multi-determined nature of couple and family dynamics. My position is that while we (as counsellors and therapists) need these understandings, they do not necessarily translate directly into 'principles for intervention' – the latter are contained in the 'how' chapters which make up the rest of the book. In writing Chapters 2 and 6, I have made my own synthesis of several relevant bodies of theory, principally psychodynamic theory, attachment theory and the early intergenerational theories of Bowen and Boszormenyi-Nagy. Where possible, I have noted the overlap between these and the insights of behaviourism and sociobiology. To some (particularly some contemporary family therapists) my synthesis will probably seem quaintly 'modernist', but these are the ideas that have worked for me, over the past quarter century, and have shaped my own understanding of personality and human interaction.[9]

You have already seen (and probably ignored) a few superscript numbers, indicating a note. These refer to notes which I've collected at the end of each chapter, and I have tried to avoid referencing in the main text. I want *Couple, Family and Group Work* to be read and pondered without the tedious, intrusive chatter of bracketed references. Readers can ignore superscripts much more easily than they can a Harvard-style reference. Those who do wish to consult the endnotes need to know that where there are a number of things to be referenced in a given paragraph, I've normally kept the superscript numeral until the end of that paragraph, and the note will then contain all the references, often with a linking commentary. A few longer notes are designed as mini-essays that do not just list, but *introduce* articles and books which can take readers further.

Just as with theory, so with the selection of clinical content. I have attempted, as far as possible, to write mainly about things that I feel I actually understand from direct experience. I have already explained that my intent in this book is not to write a 'complete' account of every interpersonal modality. Some presenting problems, and some types of clients, receive little or no attention here, simply because my own experience is insufficient to say much about them. I have attempted to acknowledge diversity through writing about clients from different cultural backgrounds, socioeconomic levels, and sexual preferences, but these examples reflect my own clinical experience, and so inevitably, there will be omissions.

Moreover, my intention throughout is to write about ways of working that (other things being reasonably equal) hold good across a wide range of differences. I do not believe that a counsellor must necessarily share the cultural or class background (or gender, or sexual preference) of a client in order to do successful work. Logically extended (and some would be happy to do just that), this principle would mean that only ex-alcoholics could work with alcoholics, only those sexually abused as children could work with child sexual abuse survivors, only those who have experienced a psychotic episode could work with the mentally ill, etc. This reflects a misunderstanding of what empathy is, and in my experience, many clients will deliberately seek a counsellor outside of their own culture or subculture, just as others will insist on seeing one who shares it.

What is vital, however, is an attitude of respect for difference, and a willingness to ask about what one does not understand. An interpersonal therapist cannot be shy about admitting ignorance, or scared of acknowledging the obvious. The other vital thing is to have explored one's own pain, one's own particular suffering or damage. To know it, to be able to feel it, and yet to be sufficiently detached from it not to be overwhelmed by it – this is what is required of us if we are to empathize with a wide range of client feelings, which may originate in very different *experiences* from our own, but which generate *emotions* that are common to all human beings.

We can in fact identify larger categories which subsume some of the 'differences' that cultures (and mental health professionals) emphasize. For example, the 'traditional male' in white, Western cultures today may have more in common with the males of some non-Western cultures than he does in common with the (white, Western) woman he lives with! Similarly, families in Britain, Australia, or the USA who live in rural and remote areas may preserve a way of being and thinking characterized by fatalism, hierarchy, the positioning of power and responsibility outside the self, and a stress on obligations and loyalties (rather than rights and freedoms) – all of which are typical of non-Western cultures. Somewhat similar beliefs and behaviours can sometimes be observed in those (Western) families who are born to poverty, or who are burdened with mental illness and disability. In other words, where life is governed by a need to survive above all, earlier ways of thinking and relating continue to prevail, embedded within our educated, high-tech, urbanized, democratic society.[10]

I have used the term 'intervention' in the subtitle of this book, because it can imply both 'counselling' and 'therapy'. And pragmatically, I have used 'counselling' and 'therapy' almost interchangeably throughout, except where the term 'therapy' is now so entrenched that to refer to a 'counselling group' or to 'family counselling' seems odd. While a real distinction can and probably should be made between 'psychotherapy' (which works with the unconscious, via the client–therapist relationship) and 'counselling' (which mostly addresses problems at a conscious level) the terms are now hopelessly confused in the minds of lay people, and even many professionals. For what it is worth, I personally regard most of the practices in this book as 'counselling', but it would be unfortunate if they were, therefore, relegated to some 'lower' level of expertise and significance: in fact, most of them demand considerable self-knowledge, and sophisticated clinical skill.

Most readers want to know something about the author of a book, although textbooks do not always provide such information. So what can I say? That I am a middle-class, heterosexual male, born in Australia of British descent on both sides. This information 'positions me', as academics say these days, in relation to my intended subject matter, and thereby (at least in theory) indicates some of my potential biases and 'blind spots'. Yet does it really? Let me supply some additional details, and then judge for yourself.

Has my comfortable, middle-class background meant that I have little appreciation of deprivation or marginalization? A sensitive and intense child, I lacked key social skills for Australian males (such as how to trade aggressive but good-humoured insults with other boys), and I grew to be extremely tall and thin. At school I suffered a great deal of teasing and some minor bullying, all of which drove me further inside myself, so that my private fantasies and intellectual interests flourished at the expense of my ability to get on with other people. Scarcely a day goes by, even now that I am middle-aged, without some teenager giggling knowingly at me in the street, or yelling at me from a passing car, simply because of what I look like. I have learned to live with this, and to recognize the ways in which my own behaviour has increased the likelihood that others would notice my differences. For me, the choice of counselling as a profession was in part a way of learning to connect with others, and learning to make better use of the 'other side' of my personality, less in evidence in my schooldays – my humour, expressiveness and ability to inspire others.

Quitting a secure academic position at the age of 32 in favour of retraining as a counsellor meant several years in which I, my wife, and our two young children lived on a very low income – below the official 'poverty line'. In this respect, I have some (limited) understanding of what it is to deny one's children some of the things that their peers enjoy, and to be treated as a 'non-person' by those in secure employment. And although things have improved greatly since then, I have enjoyed less job security than most of my age cohort. Of course, much of my marginalization has come about through my own obstinate choices, and this is very different from being born to poverty, or having marginalization thrust upon one by the colour of one's skin, or one's religion.

When, in my thirties, I was studying family therapy, I began to realize how little I knew about the family into which I had been born – my 'family of origin'. This led to a lengthy quest for knowledge and insight, in which I interviewed middle-aged and elderly relatives, and pieced together many sad and fragmented stories into a coherent narrative of repeated family experience over several generations. Sections of this narrative can be found in Chapter 6, as illustrations of common family processes. I discovered then that I belong to a family typified by fairly sensitive, vulnerable individuals, many of whom had, just like me, felt 'different' both at school and at work. As I have grown older, I have been less in denial of my own suffering, and the suffering I have unwittingly caused others. Going into therapy in middle age has greatly assisted in this process, and has been slowly but profoundly transformative. All of this, I think, has enhanced my ability to empathize with clients who feel guilty, shamed, inadequate, afraid, disempowered, angry and bitter.

Has my gender condemned me to automatic sexism? Both my own parents were educated professionals. There was no sense in my family of origin that men 'counted more' than women, or that they were more 'rational', or more intelligent, or entitled to dominate the household. My father shared domestic tasks with my mother. I exhibit the (gendered) female preference in our society for 'talking things out' rather than 'practical problem-solving'. Of course none of this means that I understand the deeper aspects of what it is to be female, to carry a child within one's own body, to give birth to it, to feed it, and then to see this child, once part of oneself, grow up. Nor have I ever had to endure the humiliation, intimidation and disempowerment that so many women have felt, at the hands of fathers, brothers, lovers, husbands, male employers. And although I have often been seen as 'weird', 'different' and threatening, I have not suffered the denigration and discimination that gay and lesbian people must often put up with, even in these (relatively) enlightened times.

So now you know more about me. Do your new impressions match those you formed on the basis of my initial 'positioning of myself'? Probably not. And if I were to tell you more, your judgements would change yet again. Most of us start by stereotyping those we do not know (or even those we think we know!) In coming to know them better, we modify those stereotypes. 'Different' becomes 'same', and 'same' becomes 'different'. That is, in part, what interpersonal work is about.

Notes

1   Within the systemic family therapy tradition, couple work is often considered alongside family intervention, especially as many 'family' presentations convert into ongoing couple therapy for the adults.

2   I do not mean that *only* personalities of this type can do good interpersonal work, and I personally know of several exceptions, people who are quiet, serious, and strongly bounded. But in general, I've found that more extraverted types are more readily drawn to interpersonal work, simply because they both require higher energy, and 'give back' higher levels of energy and stimulus, than individual work. This is certainly the view of Shirley Gehrke Luthman and Martin Kirshenbaum, therapists on the Satir model, which flourished in the late 1960s and early 1970s (see Luthman and Kirshenbaum 1974, esp. pp. 209ff.; see also Crago 2003).

3   The basics of this are well covered in Lukas (1993: 101–11) and in Chapter 7 of Bobes and Rothman (2002). See also MacKinnon (1998), which is excellent.

4   Bennis and Shepherd (1956).

5   This delightful term was, as far as I know, coined by Epston (1989). In many of his early papers on work with 'problem children', he plays humorously with the whole idea of maturation, suggesting that 'growing up is a difficult decision', and that children have control over whether they 'grow up' or 'grow down'.

6   See Grant and Crawley (2002: 68ff.).

7   Rogers (1951).

8   See Markowitz (1998).

9   A good, clearly written summary of psychodynamic principles in practice can be found in Jacobs (1998). If you are new to attachment theory, you will be

very well served by Karen (1998). The best introduction to Murray Bowen's work is Kerr and Bowen (1988), largely written by Michael Kerr during Bowen's final years. Ivan Boszormenyi-Nagy's own writing is dense and difficult, even for those sympathetic to his ideas. Probably the best way in is via the very clearly written application of his concepts to family work with the elderly in Hargraves and Anderson (1992). Of Boszormenyi-Nagy's own works, the most approachable is the one co-authored with Barbara Krasner, *Between Give and Take: A Clinical Guide to Contextual Therapy* (1986). The behaviourist principles I describe in this book are the most basic ones, covered in any introductory psychology textbook: operant conditioning, in the form of positive and negative reinforcement (originated by B.F. Skinner), and social learning theory (Paul Bandura). Sociobiological approaches go in and out of fashion, and are certainly not favoured by contemporary family therapists, but I share with Murray Bowen the conviction that many of our 'human' behaviour patterns are in fact versions of behaviours we share with virtually all mammalian life, and even with 'lower' orders such as reptiles, birds and fish. In recent years, 'evolutionary psychology' has put a new slant on sociobiology. For a recent survey of evolutionary psychology, see Siegert and Ward (2002). Also of relevance here is the work of Maturana: see Maturana and Varela (1992).

10   The anthropologist Louis Dumont (1977) observed that Western (European) culture began to diverge radically from the rest of the world in the early modern era, giving rise to a society typified by an emphasis on individuality, individual rights, freedom, 'growth' (both economic and personal) and change. Dumont contrasts this with the societies of the rest of the world (and also with pre-modern European societies), which emphasized the collective responsibilities rather than rights, loyalty and obligations rather than freedom, and preserving the existing order of things, instead of changing it. I would add to this a view of the world in which 'spirit' or holiness is inherent in nature, land, or community, not in individuals, whereas Western societies have increasingly located spiritual agency and sanctity within the 'enchanted interior' of individuals. Western culture is thus, in the wider context of time and place, an aberration, yet it is an aberration which has imposed itself increasingly on the rest of the world. Many of the characteristics that Dumont found in non-Western cultures are also those that survive, to some extent, in marginal subcultures within Western nations: rural and remote areas, the urban poor, the mentally ill. The transpersonal psychologist Ken Wilber (1986) supplies a somewhat different perspective on this same phenomenon, suggesting that earlier stages in the evolution of consciousness survive within societies that, overall, have moved to more advanced stages. Many of the ways that 'mentally ill' individuals think and speak reflects what Wilber would call the 'Typhonic' level of consciousness (in which spirit and power reside in objects and places external to self); similarly, many people who have lived lifelong in small, remote communities, or in communities restricted by extreme poverty and

lack of opportunity, think and act in terms that Wilber would see as typical of the later 'Mythic Membership' stage, where the collective is far more important than the individual, and life is seen in fatalistic, deterministic ways. Again, I would contend that these different ways of thinking, feeling and acting are *not* unique to people raised in non-Western cultures, but exist also *within* Western cultures – albeit only in pockets. I would also argue (though it is not currently popular) that despite obvious differences, most non-Western cultures are alike at this fundamental level. They share a 'deep structure' that is profoundly different from our own, and *this* is the 'difference that makes a difference'. Of the various books and articles dealing with cross-cultural issues in counselling, the vast majority fail to see these 'deep structures, and focus instead on specific differences, often portrayed as unique to *one* particular non-Western culture, when in fact they, or features very similar, can often be found across many. The most intelligent guide to cross-cultural issues that I have found to date is written by a therapist who is also a social anthropologist, Inga-Britt Krause. Her *Therapy Across Culture* (1998) offers a far broader and deeper perspective on its subject than books written by those who are primarily counsellors/therapists, and whose knowledge of other cultures is derived mainly from secondary sources.

1 A necessary discomfort
From individual to relationship work

The comfortable alliance

Psychotherapy began as a one-to-one relationship – doctor and patient. From Freud's psychoanalysis through Carl Rogers' non-directive counselling[1] to today's cognitive restructuring much has changed, but what has often remained unquestioned is the assumption that a one-to-one relationship is the way that human change is effected. A client consults a counsellor or therapist in the privacy of an office. Their conversations are confidential. The client learns to trust the professional and, within that trusting relationship, change becomes possible. That is the paradigm on which most of us work.

By the time they have completed their training, most new counsellors are starting to feel comfortable in a relationship with an individual client. They are becoming confident in their ability to help the client feel at ease and talk freely. While the occasional client may be hard to like, it is not too difficult to feel 'unconditional positive regard' for the majority. The more our clients lower their defences and disclose painful and conflicted aspects of their lives, the more we tend to feel confirmed in our empathy for them. Moreover, most of them (admittedly not all!) respond positively to our interest. They like us listening to them, and they are happy to have more of it. To engender this sense of safety and trust in another human being, whom initially one did not know, can be a very affirming experience. As newly qualified counsellors see more clients, they repeat this experience, and gain even more confidence.

When we meet with the same client over a period of months, or even longer, most of us find it easy to experience a reassuring predictability: we know how that client will be in the room, what her/his issues will be, what mode of response will soothe, what is needed to provoke insight or behaviour change. The 'therapeutic alliance' should also, of course, permit confrontation and allow the client to express anger or disappointment in the therapist. So it will not always be comfortable or confirming for the therapist – or for the client. But by and large, it is the sense of an intense, trusting relationship with one person that therapists enjoy, and this is what makes one-to-one work the overwhelming favourite of most of those who go into the helping professions.

At its worst, the therapeutic alliance can be a cosy collusion, in which the client invites the counsellor to 'side with' him or her against significant others. And while we all know we are not supposed to do that, it is hard not to fall into the trap. As one supervisee of mine pointed out, 'Your therapist sort of *has* to take your side, to some degree – if she didn't, you wouldn't fully trust her or believe in her.' And, I might add, if your therapist *didn't* take your side – or at least appear to – on at least some issues, you wouldn't put up with her confronting you on others! Even if we don't *intend* to take our client's side – against a partner, a parent, a child, a boss – our client will often simply *assume* that we do, and interpret our words accordingly.

Let me introduce a provocative analogy, which may nevertheless shed some light on what happens in individual therapy. Don't many *affairs* start with a third party who seems willing to listen and take our side, while our nearest (and supposedly dearest) cannot? While sexual attraction and 'romance' are certainly important components, aren't many affairs initiated and sustained at least as much by the experience of intimacy and sympathetic listening? And isn't part of the attraction a sense that you have each other only for a short period of time, in secret? But aren't sympathetic listening, closeness, limited times together, and secrecy also part of a relationship with a therapist? In other words, when individual therapy works, it works partly because it embodies the same 'dyadic process' that characterizes any close two-person relationship, including both friendships and affairs – a process in which, as personal qualities and values common to both are selectively reinforced, appreciation tends to grow stronger, and a sense of precious, shared experience bulks larger.

When the client is not one person, but two, however, it is no longer easy or natural for this process to take place. Now the 'comfortable alliance' must stretch to accommodate two people. It will typically take longer, and require more effort on the part of the third party, the 'listener and carer'. And the connection that is forged will be both harder to maintain, and more easily fractured, because if the counsellor achieves too close an understanding with one, the other is likely to be alienated.

Out of the comfort zone

Counsellors who have found their feet with individual work rapidly lose their sense of skill and confidence when they are asked to see a couple. Over and over again, what I hear is:

'Why do I feel so drained after a session with a couple? I don't feel that way when I've seen one of my individual clients!'

'I like to listen really well, and just respond to what my clients say. I like the initiative to come from them. But with a couple, I find that I can't do that. If I do, we just go round and round in circles.'

'I don't think I can ever be a couple therapist. I know I'm supposed to stay neutral, but I always end up siding with the woman, and if I pretend that I'm not, I'm not being true to myself!'

Yes, being with a couple can be difficult, exhausting, sometimes ungratifying and (at least at first) unpredictable. You feel like you're starting to get through to one partner, and suddenly the other one interrupts and takes the conversation off on another tack, so that the apparent progress is lost. One says something hopeful, but the other contemptuously dismisses it. One talks all the time, battering away at the other, who sits in sullen silence, refusing all your best attempts to get him or her to participate.

Most counsellors new to couple work sense that their normal set of skills is insufficient, and this is often expressed in a wish for 'formulas'. What do I do in a first session with a couple? How do I know when I need to intervene? Are there some exercises or structured activities that I could do with them? While none of these requests is illegitimate in itself, collectively they point to two underlying issues which really need to be considered before the requests can be meaningfully answered.

The first is the counsellor's own sense of being deskilled or drained *simply by being in a room with two people in a conflicted relationship*. (The same discomfort often occurs in a social situation, where a couple separate, and their friends start inviting to dinner only the one they're more sympathetic to. There doesn't seem to be *room* for the other.) This feeling of being deskilled or drained somehow needs to be held onto and thought about, rather than evaded by a search for anxiety-dispersing 'recipes for therapy'.

The second issue is that the counsellor's feelings while in the room with a couple will also reflect the couple's *own* sense of discomfort and unfulfilment. The demands that the counsellor feels are, in part, the same demands that each client partner feels from the other. The sense of impotence or deskilling is similar to the feeling of 'What more can I do?' or 'You're asking the impossible' that the two partners feel, in various ways, when they experience each other's disappointment, rage or frustration. The wish for 'something structured' in the counsellor points to the couple's need (usually unvoiced and often unconscious) for someone to provide something to 'hold' them both, in their state of unsafety with each other. And that something will not usually be exercises or activities, but clear, fair rules, and firm boundaries – maintained by the counsellor.

Like it or not, being in a room with two people in an intimate but conflicted relationship is not going to be smooth or easy. Why?

First, any two individuals in a conflicted relationship will have two different views of what happens between them. In fact, they are going to have two different *realities*, two different *worlds*. A couple counsellor has no choice but to engage with *both realities*, something that is far harder than simply adjusting to the reality of *one* other person.

Second, where an individual client may initially fear the counsellor's judgement or criticism, this can in many instances be overcome relatively rapidly. When a couple present for therapy, however, each may fear not only the counsellor's condemnation, but also the judgement and criticism of his/her partner. There is thus a double hurdle to be leapt before trust can be built, and before each can feel safe enough to speak their truth in the presence of the other. Some couples never reach that level of safety, no matter how good the counsellor may be.

Third, couple interactions generate great intensity. Counsellors feel they are in the presence of something powerful and persistent, something they cannot modify simply by interacting 'therapeutically' with either partner. Indeed, such an interaction with one partner is often greeted by an automatic disqualifying move from the other. There was an old cliché about falling in love: 'this is bigger than both of us'. Well, the couple process, too, is bigger than both of them, and often defies logic and conscious understanding. This is probably what marriage counsellors meant when they used to talk about there being 'three clients: the two partners, and the relationship'.

Fourth, in the presence of a conflicted couple, it is very easy for counsellors to feel either like a parent faced with two quarrelling children, or (worse) like a child faced with two quarrelling parents. Depending on the roles we played in our own families of origin, we may be invited to regress to the feelings that we had as a child, or to the feelings that our *parents* had when confronting us and our siblings. These feelings may well be ones of impotence, frustration and inadequacy – or occasionally, in extreme cases, of fear and distress.

Separate worlds

As we have already suggested, the longer the one-to-one therapeutic relationship lasts, the harder it is for counsellors to avoid some degree of bias. However much we strive for neutrality and objectivity, we become drawn into seeing the client's significant relationships from the client's point of view. Even in the first few interviews, the subtle process of being 'inducted' into our individual client's world view begins. Here is an example:

> Mario feelingly complains about his wife's lack of affection, her 'freezing him out', her willingness to get involved in work, but not in talking with him. He offers multiple examples of his wife's conduct, which seem to support what he is claiming. In the room, he relates straightforwardly to the counsellor, and there is no sense of manipulation or playing for sympathy. He is willing to own that he himself may have contributed to the relationship breakdown, but his strongest feelings remain ones of hurt and alienation.

What sort of guesses are we likely to make about Mario's wife? How will we picture the interactions between them? The client's presentation of his relationship constrains our own view of it. To the extent that we trust him, we will also be inclined to trust his account of his wife. We will pay attention to the things he has highlighted for us, and we may not immediately consider other possibilities – because he has not mentioned them.

Hopefully, however, we are aware that Mario may be offering us an incomplete picture of his wife, that he may have 'blind spots' in relation to her. We act as good therapists should, showing empathy without necessarily 'agreeing' with the client's perceptions:

> 'She seems to shut you out so completely . . . her work seems so important to her, and she doesn't seem to care nearly as much about you.'

Mario responds with more intense feelings of exclusion and aloneness. Our carefully 'neutral' response, which focuses on the client's own feeling state and does not explicitly agree with his perception of his wife, produces in him an assumption that we share some of his values, that we 'see it his way'. And in a way, we do. If we were to blatantly challenge his view, or even ask him what he thinks his wife may be feeling, would he come back for another session? We might lose our chance to work with him.

Let's look now at how this situation might look if we had in the room not our original client, but the client's 'significant other', by herself.

> Leonie, Mario's wife, presents initially as a power-dressed, efficient, corporate woman who fits the picture he has drawn for us. However, twenty minutes into the interview, she is crying bitterly and saying that she only works so late because she feels there is nothing to come home to. Mario doesn't welcome her with affection when she returns from her job, he doesn't seem to value the money she contributes to their household, he shows no interest in her professional life or ambitions, so she has given up trying to share her working day with him. She says that she longed for children, but that Mario was dead set against having them yet, and that

this has produced a major conflict, in which her own parents take her side, and won't come to visit if he is there. We are surprised and shocked. This woman is just as sincere as Mario, her examples are just as compelling.

What has happened? We have been confronted with the phenomenon that two people in a relationship can each have a reality. Each partner experiences the relationship a certain way, and tells it to a third party in a way which is true to that reality.

Not Judge Judy!

A simplistic, 'courtroom' view of relationships would assume that one party is 'right' and the other is 'wrong'. Or, at least, that one party has 'more of the truth' or is 'more reliable' than the other. I call the latter the 'Judge Judy' line. (Judge Judy Schendlein is a feisty 'grandmother-with-a will-of-steel' who presides over a TV courtoom ('real people, real cases') in a widely syndicated US series. She listens to a parade of aggrieved litigants, questions them aggressively, interrupts them, and tries to get at the reality behind the tangled web of accusations and counter-accusations. That's her job, and she does it well – with a shrewd eye to dramatic appeal.)

For those of us who work in a counselling capacity with people in relationships, however, the Judge Judy line on 'truth' or 'evidence' is inadequate. How can we possibly say that one or the other party has 'more of the truth' or is a 'more credible witness'? The fact is, *both* are highly credible witnesses *to their own truth*. The truth of *the situation that encompasses both* is of another order. The more we explore its complexities, and understand its interactional nature (both parties contribute to it), the more impossible it becomes to think any longer in terms of 'right' and 'wrong'. There can be no 'judgement' in the case of Mario and Leonie, no 'ruling'. Human relationships do not conform to the justice system. There is no final 'truth' to be established. Rather, each person has his/her own reality, and the interaction of those realities, those truths, creates the interpersonal world in which they live.

If we were in a courtroom, what would we notice about the 'evidence' presented by each of the conflicted parties in 'Mario v. Leonie'? When we hear Leonie's testimony, for example, we would realize that Mario has totally omitted the issue of children – clearly a major cause of distress for Leonie. And he has made no mention of the involvement of other family members, a stressor that she is acutely aware of. Does Mario leave these things out because he wishes to conceal them? Perhaps, but probably not. This is not a case of 'lying' or intention to deceive. Rather, he tells his counsellor *what matters most to him*, and fails to mention things that to him seem peripheral or less important. He does not fully realize how strongly Leonie feels – or he doesn't allow himself to realize it. Like most of us, he is bound up in his own world, and his own hurts are foregrounded. For her part, Leonie too may be unaware of the distress her behaviour is causing to her husband. She has paid attention to all the times that Mario seemed bored or irritated by her attempts to talk about work; she has not necessarily read between the lines and recognized his pain at being excluded. Why should she, when his words at the time conveyed something else?

A different kind of truth

What we can say, without a shadow of doubt, is that once we have heard another version of each story, a much fuller and more complex truth has emerged. In turn, this more complex 'truth of the situation' offers us more possibilities for understanding and intervention. No longer are we drawn inexorably into siding with our client against a hostile interpersonal world. We continue to feel for her, or him, but we begin to feel for others in the situation as well.

Hearing the two separate 'testimonies', it is easy to see the way that Mario and Leonie actually contribute to a joint situation, which is painful for both of them. Leonie *expects* that Mario will not want to hear about her day at work, so she does not offer to tell him about it. Mario *expects* that Leonie will live a work life which totally excludes him, so he acts towards her with the coolness which he feels. She, in turn, then feels cool towards him, and his belief that she is 'freezing him out' is confirmed. As we shall see in Chapter 6, it is the study of these painful, self-confirming sequences in human interactions that led to family therapy, and to the development of new ways of intervening that offer hope of interrupting those sequences.

Each participant naturally tends to assume that the other party is 'to blame' (although sometimes a participant may assume all of the blame for the situation, and exonerate the other, which is equally unrealistic). But 'blame' and 'guilt' are part of the framework of individual truth which participants impose upon a far more complex situation.

So at this point, let's pause and summarize:

1   Each party in a close relationship has his/her own 'truth' or 'reality', which automatically dictates the selection of facts, feelings and interpretations that he/she will tell to a third party.
2   When we meet with only one of these parties, we will inevitably tend to see the entire situation through their selective presentation of it, and thus be drawn into 'alliance' with them, to some degree.
3   The fact that this occurs can make it hard for us to appreciate the

extent to which our client may be inadvertantly perpetuating the very process he/she finds so distressing.

4   When we meet simultaneously with both parties in a conflicted relationship, a 'broader and deeper truth' is available to us. We have more resources to draw on, and more possibilities of intervention. Hence one of the 'rules of thumb' of family therapy: *if you get stuck, invite more people in!*

5   Although individuals in a conflicted situation often act as if they are in a courtroom (launching a 'case' against each other, or 'pleading guilty' to avoid a worse judgement), it is not useful for us to join them in this set of assumptions. In fact, it is not even accurate. Moral judgements are things that human beings *impose* on problematic interactions, but the interactions themselves have little to do with morality. In most cases, people get 'stuck' in certain behaviour patterns, without wanting to, or meaning to. The moral judgements they make simply entrench those patterns, rather than helping them escape from them.

Worlds in collision

When two people in a relationship come for therapy together, their two separate 'truths' or 'worlds' collide. Sometimes the collision is obvious, as when a couple openly spar with each other; sometimes it is quiet and subtle, where one remains silent rather than directly contradict the other's reality, or offers superficial compliance that masks inner anger or sadness. Whatever form it takes, though, there are going to be areas in which the two are in disagreement, and if they attend a joint session, then those areas are going to be exposed.

For the rest of this chapter, I shall try to lay out how we, as professionals, need to behave in order to create conditions that are potentially growthful for two unrelated adults in a committed relationship, and specifically, what we need to do that is different from what we would do were we to be working with either member, in the absence of the other.

> Mario becomes increasingly angry as Leonie talks feelingly to the therapist about how little interest he shows in her daily work. He interrupts her and begins an aggrieved justification of his own position, swinging between defensiveness and blaming: 'That's really hard to believe, Leonie! Why wouldn't I be uninterested in your day, when I kept trying and trying all those years, and you just brushed me off? How can you sit here and say that I'm cold towards you when *you're* the original ice maiden!'

In response, Leonie begins to cry, and turns again to the therapist:

'See – this is what happens at home every time we try to talk about this. He just can't listen to what I'm feeling without picking on me and attacking everything I say. Frankly, I think it's too threatening for lots of men to just listen. It's their male egos. And of course with Mario it's worse, because I earn most of our income, and I think he feels jealous of me, deep down.'

I could easily continue this dialogue for page after page, and probably by now, you could too! We are all familiar enough with the way that angry, hurt couples blame, defend and counter-attack, moving rapidly from one area of vulnerability and distress to another, so that no resolution occurs, and no real listening occurs either. Mario and Leonie's worlds are in collision. Each experiences the other's reality as too threatening, too overwhelming, to really take it in. Each of them has only a limited capacity to sit with the other's truth, and try to understand it. If we, as counsellors, simply listen respectfully to the interaction, it will probably escalate into greater levels of distress (or alternatively, fizzle out into sullen silence and despair on both sides). So what do we need to do instead?

'They've got a communication problem!'

Many neophyte counsellors, faced with behaviour like Mario and Leonie's, readily 'diagnose' the fact that this couple have a lot of trouble listening to one another: they have a 'communication problem', perhaps stemming from their 'low self-esteem' which causes them to employ 'defence mechanisms'. Such labels may help the counsellor to feel more secure, but they are of little help to the couple. The next step, for many beginners, is to 'rectify the deficiency' by coaching the couple in how to listen better, communicate more assertively, or whatever. Again, this is confirming for the counsellor, putting him or her in the comfortable position of 'teacher' of 'skills' which he/she learned in his/her training, and which it seems natural to impart to clients. And many clients, at least in the first session or so, will apparently go along with such 'teaching', even tell the counsellor that it was 'interesting' or 'beneficial'. But while such an intervention may be useful later in the counselling process,[2] it is unlikely to be useful now.

Offering 'skills' in a first session with a couple is a bit like offering 'advice' in the first session with an individual client. In many cases, the 'advice' or the 'skills' will simply be ignored, or even 'not heard' at all in any meaningful way. (Try asking clients at the end of therapy what they remember of the first session!) Couples, like individual clients, need to feel fully 'heard' and validated by their counsellor before they are going to be open to listening to such advice, and even then it may miss the mark. In the case of couples, too, each partner probably needs to feel heard by the counsellor, before he/she can start to hear, and be heard by the other partner. This may take a few sessions, or many sessions. It is not likely to have happened yet!

Secondly, if the counsellor too rapidly offers 'skills' and 'teaching', this is tantamount to saying to the couple, 'I am uncomfortable with the level of tension between you, and I want to avoid it'. While at a superficial level the couple may accept the teaching of skills, they are going to feel unsure about whether their deeper feelings can be heard and validated within the counselling relationship.

So, if we don't rush quickly into diagnosing and prescribing, what do we need to do?

1   We need to interrupt the sequence: in other words, we need to *take some control, in the interests of allowing the clients more control over their own interactions.*

2   We need to show both clients that we are interested in, and care about, their reality, without obviously entering an alliance with either. In other words, we need to *side with their legitimate feelings, not with their 'case' against the other.*

In doing this, we will be starting to create a space where the two can feel safe enough to voice a fuller version of their own truth, and begin to appreciate the truth of the other. Whatever we offer to one, we will also offer to the other – although not necessarily immediately, or in a rigid and obvious way. This is the principle of *balance*. I sometimes think of it as the couple version of the 'holding environment' in individual therapy. When it is experienced, clients will say things like 'We think you're very *fair*'.

Together, the two factors listed above are probably the most basic skills of interpersonal work. I have set them out as if they are separate skills, but in fact each depends upon the other. And perhaps 'skill' is not the most appropriate word either. 'Skill' suggests some sort of technique that can be learned in a mechanical fashion, whereas what I am talking about is (in Carl Rogers' eloquent words) 'a way of being'. The way of being we need to exhibit with a couple or a family is well expressed in my colleague Sophie Holmes' phrase, 'to sit, in a firm but kindly way, with the uncertainty in the room'.[3]

There may be much more that we need to do to help a couple like Leonie and Mario, but we will be unable even to get to square one unless we do the fundamental things listed above. They sound simple enough, but in fact they are far from easy. However, with time and practice, you will find that you do them almost without conscious thought, just as you learn a complex skill like driving a car in traffic so that it becomes virtually automatic. For the remainder of this chapter, we will concentrate solely on how to put this 'way of being' into practice.

The counsellor must be in control

When working with a couple, a counsellor must sometimes (often) act like a 'traffic cop', blocking one flow of traffic in order to let another get through – but in such a way that in the longer term everyone gets a fair deal. Interrupting and directing the flow of conversation is *ensuring balance and fairness in the interaction*. Such balance is essential to a couple's sense that this is a safe space for them *to be together* (as opposed to a space that feels safe for one, but not for the other).

It is often the case that in couple sessions, one partner (usually the more talkative or overtly demanding one) can take up a great deal more time than the other (who usually has a more passive style, or may experience difficulty in articulating thoughts and feelings). The counsellor must make sure that the quieter partner has unpressured time, and sufficient conversational 'space', to respond as she/he wishes, and to explore more fully the implications of what he/she first says. Sometimes, the more talkative partner will cooperate with the counsellor on this enterprise. Often, though, the more talkative one will be too anxious to allow his/her partner's process to unfold, and will interrupt verbally, or through non-verbal signs like foot tapping, turning away, audible sighs, and so on.

In the event of such interruptions (overt or 'undercover'), two things need to happen. First, the counsellor needs to 'protect' the other partner's right to talk. Second, the counsellor must do so in a way that does not give a dismissive or disrespectful message to the interrupting partner. Depending on the personalities involved, how much the counsellor has gained the couple's trust, and the counsellor's own 'style' for handling confusion or conflict, there are a number of options that can be employed:

- The counsellor can simply make a handsignal, a headshake, or some other gesture, to indicate to the interrupting partner that they cannot break in yet.
- The counsellor can turn to the interrupting partner, and say something like 'I know you're having some strong feelings about what he's saying. Can I ask you to bear with me for a little, so he can finish, and then I'll be interested to hear what's been going through your head now.'
- The counsellor can overtly apologize for blocking the interruption: 'I'm sorry I have to stop you just for a moment. Both of you need to have your say, and it's my job to make sure that what happens in here is different from what you usually do!'

Clearly, any of these might be crashingly 'wrong' for some couples and for some counsellors, while perfectly acceptable for others. Some individuals are highly sensitive to perceived slights, and may react with visible irritation when asked to hold off. But most, however sensitive or egocentric, will pay at least lip service to the rule of 'both sides having their say', and it is not difficult to gain couples' adherence to the *principle* – even if, in practice, they find it hard to sit and let each other proceed uninterrupted.

How often, and how crudely, the counsellor needs to 'police' interruptions will depend not only on the individual personalities involved, but also on the stage that the couple work has reached. In the first few interviews, we may need to intervene frequently, and overtly, in order that a workable dialogue can occur at all. Later, as both clients have come to feel safer with us, and with each other, intervention may be unnecessary, or need take only a subtle form. After a while, even quite volatile and impulsive individuals will start to 'self-censor' and joke about their need to 'push in' on their partner's conversation. I often use humour from the beginning, to defuse what a couple may potentially perceive as a 'power play' by me as the professional.

> 'Look, I have to stop you here. Sorry about this, but you don't want to pay me money just so you can do what you'd do at home for nothing, do you?'

Humour works for me, with most couples (with some, I wouldn't dare!), because it is part of my nature, and comes unfeignedly and without any 'put down' quality. For a counsellor whose nature is different from mine, such a tactic might seem forced, and perhaps give the wrong message. As with most counselling skills, it is a matter of finding what works for you, not slavishly following the formula that this book – or any other 'expert' source – offers you.

I have just been writing as if counsellors always need to intervene in order to stop interruptions. Let me now backtrack and state some of the exceptions!

To begin with, in a first session (and perhaps even in a second) it is important to allow the couple's interaction to unfold in its 'natural state' for some time, before the counsellor attempts to intervene and pick up the reins. That may take 10 minutes, 15 minutes, 30 minutes, or even more, depending on the individuals concerned and the nature of their interaction. The counsellor needs time to listen, observe, and start to make sense of the pattern, before intervening too forcibly. (Educational videotapes sometimes show celebrated therapists interrupting a couple within a minute of two of the session's commencement – a daunting, and perhaps misleading model to follow! They can do so, and get away with it, because they are experienced enough to trust their instinct and, probably, because their high reputation buffers them against client shock and hostility.) Because couple patterns are normally entrenched and rigid, however, it is not usually necessary, even for less experienced counsellors, to wait for most of the session before intervening, and stepping into the interaction in some way or other may in itself be an important sign to the couple that 'something different is going to happen here'.

Secondly, there are going to be times when a partner's interruption *needs* to be permitted, because it will lead to something important or different – for example, if the quieter partner tries to interrupt the more voluble partner, thus acting more assertively than usual. And of course, partners are going to interrupt each other anyway, at times, without the counsellor being able to stop them! Some of these interruptions may allow the counsellor to focus on some aspect of immediate process – how each is feeling here and now, in the room – which may lead to new information becoming available to both. Needless to say, it becomes a matter of the counsellor's judgement whether to 'block' an interruption, or let it proceed. Sometimes it is simply trial and error, until, with time, the clients and their characteristic interactions become predictable and the counsellor can sense when it might be important to let one interrupt, or when the interruption is just going to be 'more of the same'.

Finally, I have up to now been writing as if all couples presented with a high level of talkativeness on the part of at least one partner, and as if there were often a high level of volatility in the room. I have focused on one very common situation – but there are others, and an alternative to the 'attack/defend' couple is the one where *both* sit silent, reluctant to speak out, reluctant to risk saying what is going on for them. In such cases, the counsellor's 'taking control' does not mean intervening in an ongoing, intense, overlapping interaction. Instead, it takes the form of actively engaging with both, in an attempt to make it safe for each to speak, turning from one to another and saying things like:

> 'What do you think about that, Jim?
>
> 'Is that the way you see it, Lahnee?
>
> 'I'm guessing that your experience is probably different from that, Sue – am I right?

It is not sufficient, with a 'passive couple', to simply sit and wait for them to speak. Once a reasonable, and respectful, silence has been left, and yet there has been no response to what the other has said, the counsellor needs to intervene, naming what is going on. For example:

> 'I'm aware that you're not wanting to say anything right now, Jim. Could you tell me what that's about?'
>
> 'Could you say what makes it hard to talk at present?'

If the client still finds it hard to speak, I sometimes resort to offering 'guesses' as to what is going on for him/her, and asking for agreement or disagreement. This is dangerously similar to the 'closed question' which of course we are not supposed to ask, but it has its place. For example:

> 'John, when I've seen other men in your position, and their girlfriend's been saying more or less what Julie's been saying about you, they've told me that they've felt so resentful that they just couldn't be bothered saying anything. They just thought they'd get their heads bitten off. Could that be how you're feeling?'

Or:

> 'John, is it OK with you if I make a few guesses about what you might be thinking right now? You don't need to say anything, but if you think my guess is near the mark, could you let me know somehow?'

Even though this type of counsellor activity seems very different from the 'traffic policing' we discussed earlier, the underlying principle is the same: by actively taking charge, the counsellor is signalling to the couple that something is going to happen in the session that is different from what happens outside it. Counselling is not going to be simply a replica of the couple's normal pattern of interaction.

Balance: supporting each partner without taking sides

In order to take control of a session in the ways that we have been discussing, counsellors need to have credibility with each partner. This credibility is gained, just as in any other form of therapy, through showing the client that we are listening carefully, that we can summarize his/her concerns clearly in our own words, and that we are sensitive to his/her particular distress. Responding empathically to each partner after he/she has finished stating a position is as vital in couple work as in any individual counselling session. But, in couple work, the empathic paraphrase serves an additional purpose, related to the structuring of the session.

In individual work, the counsellor's empathic paraphrase typically prompts the client to 'go deeper', to elaborate, to give examples, ot to explore further aspects of his/her situation. As Rogers used to explain it, the actual experience of being heard and validated, in a way that reflects genuine interest, propels the client to uncover new 'layers' of meaning, or to supply some element that was missing in his/her original statement. 'Walking with the client' thus becomes the way that the counsellor assists an ongoing process of uncovering and clarifying central concerns.

In couple work, this can, and does, happen with each client on many occasions. But when there are two clients in the room, the empathic para-phrase must sometimes be employed differently: to indicate to each partner that the counsellor has understood, *and to temporarily 'close off' that person's part of the interaction*, while the counsellor turns to the other and invites their contribution. So I prefer, in the context of couple work, to speak of an 'empathic summary'. The difference is not great, in terms of actual wording, but the function is somewhat different. In a couple session, each must wait while the other has his/her say. In order to wait, each must feel confirmed in the counsellor's attention and respect for his/her position.

> 'So, Leonie, it seems like what actually happens for you each day when you get home is that you feel so pushed away by his lack of interest that you lose energy for telling him about work. And that's deeply disappointing for you, because you'd actually like him to share that interest.'

Having heard this, assuming that it accurately represents her position, Leonie will be more prepared to tolerate the counsellor turning to Mario and engaging with him in a like manner.

Of course, Leonie may take the counsellor's empathic statement as a signal to go further, and the counsellor may need to listen and respond once again, perhaps this time overtly signalling the intention of 'closing off' the inter-action for now.

> 'And that disappointment that you're talking about is deeper, isn't it, because for you there are other disappointments too, to do with the conflict over whether or not to have children. And I know that's pretty central for you, and we're going to need to come back to it a bit later on. But is it OK with you if I ask Mario now about how it's been for him listening to you talk?'

Clients will rarely refuse permission, if asked respectfully, and (as indicated above), the counsellor should already have accumulated enough 'credit' (trust, or respect) to put such a request, and have it granted.

Where two people have very different worlds, and these worlds are in collision, the counsellor's position is difficult. How to avoid 'taking sides' with one, and losing credibility with the other? The psychoanalytic therapist's aim is to remain neutral with regard to patients' *internal* conflicts (e.g. by refusing to side with either their self-condemnation or their self-indulgence). The couple therapist, on the other hand, aims to display the same evenhandedness and non-partisan quality in relation to the matters of *external* conflict – that is, the matters over which the couple themselves are in dispute.

But of course, that is easier said than done, and in practice many couple counsellors and therapists end up taking a position which is perhaps less strictly 'neutral', yet which still, from a structural point of view, positions them as midway between the conflicted partners. They tend to do this by forging 'temporary alliances' with first one partner, and then the other. Salvador Minuchin would align himself quite clearly with one, on one issue, but then with the other on some other issue, so that the overall balance was maintained.[4] I am now (after 25 years!) confident enough to do the same.

In practice, what we as counsellors need to do is to indicate strong sensitivity to the pain each client feels, and strong support for their entitlement to something better, while avoiding entering into their blaming of the other, or their self-blame. In mediation practice, a distinction is made between a client's *interests* and his/her *position*. The mediator must align with and validate the client's *interests*, but not necessarily the client's *position*.[5]

> 'So, Shumaila, you feel really distressed at how nobody seems to look after you, or care for you. And that feels much worse, because you spend so much time looking after your kids, and your husband, yet none of that care comes back to you. And that's a very unbalanced situation, it's not very fair, is it?'

In Shumaila's world, she is surrounded by ungrateful people to whom she gives her all, without receiving any love or consideration in return. In the response above, the counsellor restates the client's perception that her interpersonal life is 'out of balance' between giving and taking, making a strong statement in support of her sense of entitlement to a more balanced outcome. This is siding with her 'interests'. But notice that the counsellor does not support Shumaila's location of the whole responsibility for this situation in her husband and children, nor does the counsellor at this point challenge her by pointing out that she herself contributes to the unfairness of the situation by refusing to ask for what she needs. That can come later, preferably after Shumaila has felt safe enough, and validated enough, to begin to admit her own complicity in the situation without being prompted.

The counsellor must 'hold' the couple before they can 'hold' each other

By discussing the need for the counsellor to take control of the couple interaction, while also acknowledging and validating each partner's reality, we have already gone a long way towards elucidating the 'way of being' that permits a couple to feel safe in the counselling room. The counsellor moves freely from one partner to the other and back again, encouraging interaction, but also halting it if it becomes unproductive. Each partner in turn is acknowledged and validated, leaving each with the sense that he/she is valued and important to the counsellor, but not at the expense of the other. The message is that both count, that both have rights, but that neither will be permitted to abuse or invade the space that is rightfully the other's.

A potentially misleading, yet still illuminating, analogy would be that the counsellor operates like a parent with two children, each of whom wants the parent all to him/herself, and resents the presence and demands of the other. In this situation, the parent or 'good authority' figure[6] must make some rules, and take some control in the interests of fairness to both. If the parent simply lets one child crowd the other out (as animals often allow one or more of their multiple offspring in a single litter to 'crowd out' the weaker ones), she is not doing her job. Yet if she simply imposes her own rules without listening to the genuine distress of both, she is not doing a good job either. Those children will grow up with 'discipline' but without a sense of being loved and valued for themselves. She must balance the legitimate needs of both, and at times place restrictions on both, so that they can be enabled to grow to a healthy aware-ness of others' needs as well as their own. And, as most of us know, when a parent sets reasonable limits, even on 'aggressive' or hard-to-control children, the limits, and the parent's willingness to police them, are felt not as bullying or imposition, but as a relief. There is a sense of safety, because children feel deeply unsafe if they can get away with anything, and actually need to feel that there are boundaries to their freedom.

In much the same way, a counsellor needs to balance the twin forces of empathy and control, setting limits in order to create a 'safe space', a place where there is a sense that whatever they need to say is going to be OK, at least here, now, in this room, and that whatever they do say will be received by the counsellor (although not necessarily by the partner) with respect, understand-ing and sensitivity. (Of course, these principles must be modified in the case of couples where the counsellor suspects that violence is present, and where one partner may not, in fact, feel safe to say what is really going on, for fear of reprisals outside the session. References which show how to assess for violence and how to proceed if it is present, can be found in the endnotes to the Introduction.)

Of course a counsellor is not a parent, and cannot treat clients as if they are children. That is not what I mean. But just as individual therapy, when it proceeds to any depth, and lasts any length of time, often leads to a situation where clients will perceive the counsellor on the model of a parent or some other authority figure from the past, and behave in relation to the counsellor as they did to those figures ('transference' in psychodynamic terminology), so too does couple therapy tend to recreate a situation where two people 'compete' for the attention (love?) of a powerful, parental figure. If we can sufficiently balance respect for their individual, painful realities with limit setting that requires them to respect each other, they will feel a degree of the same relief that siblings do when a parent takes control and straightens things out. And they will in all likelihood be prepared to come back and see us again, and risk going a little further.

It may not feel, at the end of a few sessions of this sort of thing, that we have done very much at all. After all, we have given them no new 'skills', no brilliant interpretations of what their behaviour means, no emotional catharsis. But we have actually given them quite a lot. We have tolerated the discomfort that they themselves cannot tolerate. We have resisted the pressure to judge or take sides. We have recognized their separate realities. We have remained non-anxious (or at least, *less* anxious than they are!) in the presence of their anxiety. It has not been as comfortable as one-to-one work, but the discomfort has been necessary. On this foundation, something may in time be built. Without it, nothing can.

Notes

1 This was the term Rogers used in his early publications, such as *Counselling and Psychotherapy* (1942). Perhaps recognizing that no counselling or therapy can ever be truly 'non-directive', his approach is better known today as 'person-centred therapy'.

2 The Sydney therapist Jacqueline McDiarmid often coaches couples in 'island hopping'. She uses this metaphor to convey the idea of being able to temporarily leave their own 'reality' and put themselves in their partner's position. She then systematically teaches them the skills of empathic paraphrasing, practising them in-session so that each can eventually learn how different it feels to be *listened to* properly, instead of argued with (McDiarmid, personal communication, 2005).

3 See Rogers (1980) and Holmes (2002: 137).

4 See Minuchin (1974: 148–9). Another pioneering family therapist, Ivan Boszormenyi-Nagy, expressed a somewhat similar idea in his concept of 'multidirected partiality'. For Nagy, each member of a family, each individual in a couple relationship, will have his/her own sense of fairness and entitlement. And inevitably, these 'entitlements' or 'rights' to happiness, co-operation, care, and so on, will clash with those of others in the family. So, he argues, counsellors need to be 'partial' (biased) in the sense that they acknowledge the reality of the 'rightness' of what each family member feels is due to him/her, while not necessarily agreeing with the actual demands he/she may make on others. In this way the counsellor will 'side with' each individual

in turn, while in the overall picture siding with none (see Boszormenyi-Nagy and Krasner 1986).
5   See Lidchi (2003).
6   'Good authority' is a term used and explained by Pitt-Aikens and Thomas Ellis (1989).

2 Attachment and disenchantment
Why couples lose hope and seek help

In my experience, couples do *not* come for counselling to improve a relationship that feels good to both, but just needs 'a bit of fine-tuning'. One partner
(usually a male) might initially present their situation that way, but most often
this will turn out to be face-saving: things are actually much worse.

Couples come to us because their trust in each other is faltering. A half-
unconscious, multi-determined web of need, illusion and real shared history is
starting to unravel. Though couples will more often speak of anger, frustration
and disappointment in each other, the unravelling of an adult attachment
bond is actually *frightening* for many people. When previously reliable signs
of love and care start to disappear, a kind of existential anxiety is aroused.
When a partner walks out, without a clear indication that she/he will return,
panic (often expressed as anger) is a frequent reaction in the other partner. It is
important for us to know why these things are so: what draws people together,
why they choose each other and what that means, and why the erosion of
their bond feels so threatening.

While *we* may need to know this, couples themselves usually don't.
Indeed, if we attempt to explain these factors to them, or engage them in a
search for understanding ('What attracted you to each other when you first
met?'),[1] they will often see our questions as irrelevant, or supply answers
that lead nowhere. What this tells us is that attraction, partner choice, and
the formation and destruction of attachment bonds are partly *unconscious*
processes. Life is living us, not the other way around.

I have placed this chapter here, after the chapter on the counsellor's first
engagement with a couple, because of my belief that we need to have a 'map'
of attraction and disenchantment, before we get far into working with two
people in a relationship. Otherwise, we are too easily pulled off course by the
language in which couples typically give meaning to their experiences.
'Because we loved each other' is not an explanation of why a couple committed to each other, nor does it explain why the same relationship is ending to
say, 'I stopped having feelings for him/her.'

In the same way, we need to have some clear ideas about *difference and similarity* as they apply to a couple who have chosen to be together. For example, why do couples typically say, 'It can't work because we're just too different', while we know (and so, if they are honest, do they) that it was those same differences that drew them together in the first place? When faced with this common presentation of why a relationship appears to be breaking down, it actually helps me to know that, however different a couple may appear, there are underlying similarities, similarities that are actually very powerful, although usually out of awareness. It probably won't help the couple much for me to explain any of this, just as it is unlikely to help them if I try to engage them deeply in understanding why they fell in love in the first place. But it helps me to stay on course, while I try to navigate a couple's clashing realities, and avoid being blown off course by their mutual recriminations.

When love is not enough

Everyone knows how it goes. For a while, miraculously, just being together is sufficient. Sex is exciting and affirming. Being in love is a wonderful feeling, and as long as it lasts, you feel filled with hope and confidence. Nothing seems too hard: with this person by your side, you can make up for the shames and disappointments of your childhood, achieve your artistic or business dreams, give up drinking – anything at all. Then, after a while, the 'in love' feeling fades, and each of you starts to feel dissatisfied and disappointed, at least in some aspects of the relationship. Your partner's faults, which you graciously tolerated while you were in love, now get on your nerves, and you start to comment sharply on them. And you get angry or sullen when your partner does the same to you. The feelings of hope and confidence diminish, as the two of you face the realities of living together, in which external pressures – such as children (when they arrive), or the children you already have by earlier relationships, or the children you both desperately desire but can't seem to have – inevitably get in the way. Very quickly, for some couples, and much more slowly for others, a point is reached where each starts to question whether this relationship was such a good decision. There is a terrible feeling of being abandoned, as if something vital to your survival has been removed beyond your grasp. It's like being kicked hard in the stomach. The person who made you feel so good, who seemed to accept you just the way you were, is now the person who makes you feel bad, and nags at you to change. Gradually, for many couples, anger replaces disappointment, and a fierce wish for justice replaces the hope of perfect love. You want to salvage something, at least, from the wreck of your dreams. If your partner won't listen to you or accept you any more, then so help you, at least you're going to make him (or her) suffer! The divorce lawyers profit from our need for 'justice' and 'retribution', needs as fierce as once our love was.

Why does all of this happen? Most people believe that they 'picked the wrong person'. If only they had chosen more wisely, they wouldn't have had these problems. Others place the responsibility, not on their own poor choice, but on the other partner, who has 'let them down', 'lied to me', or 'turned out to be someone completely different than who I thought she was'. These explanations are reassuring, because they offer people the hope of doing better next time without any soul-searching on their part. They simply need to 'make a better choice', or find a person who is 'won't suddenly change on them'. But these 'explanations' don't explain enough.

Why is it that we always feel (at least for a while) as if our partner is vital to our survival? When we are 'in love', why do we need so strongly to be with him/her all the time, feel so bereft if we are unable to be together? When we start to fall out of love, why does her/his disapproval or emotional withdrawal hurt so fiercely? 'I can't live without you', say a thousand popular songs, 'I'm nothing without you', 'If you go, it's the end of my world'. Popular songs are not popular for no reason: they echo what people themselves often feel, only they say it more eloquently.

What really happens when people fall in love and commit themselves to a live-in relationship with a single partner? For some, the bonds are forged in the incandescent crucible of desire, a state in which, at least for a time, two adults really do feel as if they have merged into one, cannot live without the other's presence, and are daily renewed by their closeness (as one woman said in response to a 1970s sociological survey, 'Sex is perfect. He only has to touch my hand and I want him'). For others, falling in love is a much quieter process, a slow drawing together of two individuals for whom being together 'feels right'. Sex may play a minor part for some couples, yet the sense of 'we belong' is still strong. In both cases, a choice has been consciously made to be with a particular person – yet the full dimensions of that choice, and its meaning in terms of the past and future of both, can never be known at the time.

There is a third category, where people end up living together, marrying, or having children together, without a real choice having been made by either. Not so very long ago, pregnancy would force a marriage between two people who had nothing in common beyond a single impulsive sexual encounter. In the affluent, developed West, the shame attached to unwed pregnancies has now greatly diminished, marriage is no longer a 'given' of social respectability, and single motherhood is no longer as great a stigma. But the shame of out-of-wedlock pregnancy is still something to be reckoned with in many non-Western cultures – the same cultures where, traditionally, the choice of a partner for one's offspring was made by parents or other senior members of the extended family, rather than by the couple themselves. Until the gradual rise of 'love' as the determinant of free marriage choice, arranged marriages were also, of course, the norm in sectors of our own society.[2]

The 'unequally yoked' couple may also be the result of marrying in order to escape an abusive or stifling family, or marrying an unsuitable partner because of strong pressure from others ('We get on OK, and at least he doesn't hit me', said one young woman of her long-standing boyfriend, whom her hard-working, traditional Asian family expected her to marry). Or, some partners in 'forced choice' relationships may always have been aware that they were attracted to the same sex, yet committed to a heterosexual relationship because their actual sexual preferences were socially unacceptable.

In forced choice couples there may never have been an 'in love' experience, yet the sense of disappointment in the partner may still be strong, carrying with it a weight of anger and bitterness at having trapped oneself into something that was never felt to be right, even at the very beginning. One might imagine that in such relationships both partners would feel relief when the relationship starts to come apart, yet quite often the shared history of good times and bad times still constitutes a bond, and its rupturing feels like a loss.

Most of this chapter will concentrate on couples who start off with a sense of 'love', or at least free choice, because in them the tension between attachment and disappointment is most noticeable, but it is important to remember that not all couples who seek help from a professional will have begun their relationship in this way, and may require something different from the counsellor like acknowledgement, in front of an outside 'expert witness', that the circumstances of the original marriage were unfortunate, and that nobody is to blame for what has gone wrong as a result).

It is also important to remember that every choice is a road not taken: commitment involves giving up. For some individuals, it isn't so much the disappointments of the partner, but the fact that somewhere, outside the relationship, another life once existed, and could still exist, and now they cannot have it. For some, there's an acute sense that they've closed down options, for others, a conviction that they've committed too soon, and denied themselves an important stage of life that they ought to have had first. Obviously, this often goes along with 'forced choice' relationships, but it doesn't have to be confined to them. Even some 'love matches', where both partners feel like they 'freely chose', can end with one partner, or even both, feeling somehow cheated of the carefree life of 'raging' and one-night stands they could have had, that first boyfriend/girlfriend they could have married, that person they were always secretly attracted to but never dared to pursue, or that promotion opportunity they turned down in order to follow their chosen partner. Regret for what has been lost *outside* the relationship is as important, for these people, as regret for what has been lost *within* it.

So, what is 'love' actually about? What is going on when we 'choose' a partner? Much of what I shall explain here is not new: many other writers have said much the same, though their language may have been somewhat different, and my preference for the level of 'biological knowing' will be obvious.[3]

But I have tried to put it all together, so that Bowlby's attachment theory, the psychoanalytic notion of child–parent attraction, and Bowen's theory of differentiation of self are layered one upon the next, into a single complex formation, like successive strata in a cliff face laid down unimaginably long ago.

A matter of survival

We have only to observe lovers in a public place to realize that what is happening between them is *adult attachment*. They sit close, they look into each other's eyes, and in many cases they are in constant physical contact: touching, holding, stroking, playing – in a way which is sensual, and yet curiously innocent. In fact, the only other time that we observe such behaviour in humans is between mothers and their babies, and this is the clue to the true nature of what is going on. Attachment in infancy is a biologically driven process by which the infants of many species instinctively bond with the adult who cares for them. When ethologist Konrad Lorenz's baby geese learned to waddle after him, for all the world as if he was a mother goose, they were demonstrating 'proximity behaviour': stay close to the caregiver, for your own survival.[4] Gaze up at the caregiver, and crowd up close to her (or in this case, him), because she/he is the source of food and safety.

When adults choose a partner, they are replicating (on an adult level, and in adult ways) the same process that they once displayed as infants in response to their mothers. Only now, 'attachment' has another, more complex meaning. Part of what we call 'love' is a sense that *our emotional safety* (rather than our physical safety), *our need for emotional nurturing* (rather than our need for food or shelter or grooming) *depends on this one person*. Our survival is tied to her (or his) existence. We are dependent upon her (or him); *she (or he) has power over us*. We instinctively conduct ourselves so as to call forth the compassion, trust and affection of this person – in part, to ensure our own emotional future. The Chilean biologist Humberto Maturana points to how most of us instinctively feel when we see a kitten: In his words, '*Ah! Little cat!*' The kitten 'elicits' an incipient attachment bond from us: we feel for it, and reach down to stroke it. How much more powerfully does a human infant – especially if it's our own child – elicit that bond! Love is a biological necessity, Maturana concludes.[5]

That is why couples who start their relationship with some form of 'love' and some sense of 'choice' are likely to feel so vitally connected to each other that any threat to the relationship seems like *a threat to their own survival*. It is as simple as that. And for a couple, a 'threat to the relationship' may take the form of harsh words, guilt-inducing nagging, angry quarrelling, or sexual rejection – as well as violence, lying and sexual betrayal (which many couples still call 'unfaithfulness', indicating that it has more to do with *trust* than with sex in itself). For a surprisingly large number of people, it is the lover's promise of constancy, the undertaking to 'be there' no matter what, that counts most of all. Weeping, a client in her thirties recently told me after the breakup of her four-year relationship, 'When we first met it was so wonderful. *He told me that he'd take care of me.* I've never forgotten that.' Attachment is about *being able to rely on someone.* When attachment is threatened or fractured, that sense of reliability – a basic trust in the goodness of the universe – temporarily disappears. No wonder we react so strongly!

For this reason, I've gradually come to realize that true empathy for couples whose sense of basic trust has been violated may require responses from me like:

> 'When he said he'd take care of you, it felt so incredibly special. Like something you'd longed for all your life.'

Or:

> 'Just thinking that maybe he isn't going to take care of you after all makes you feel as if you can't really trust anything any more.'

These are strong words, and may strike some readers as over-dramatic. My excuse for using them is that *this is what it actually feels like inside*, when a primary adult attachment bond, deepened and intensified by a history of sexual intimacy, is threatened.

Desirable differences

In the formation of adult relationships, the attachment level is primary, the foundation on which all else is built. Yet there are other levels which we also need to know about, and which strongly influence the way couples act and feel in relation to one another. A baby 'attaches' to a mother instinctively, at a time when it has no concept of 'self' as we would understand it, and so does not realize it is turning for preference to an 'other'. But by the preschool years – when a child is between 3 and 5 years of age – the child will have an awareness of itself as a being separate from its mother, a distinct, individual little person. *Little*, because its mother, and other important people in its world are (it realizes) a lot *bigger*. The adults who surround the child are also distinct people, and *different*, from the child itself, and from each other. Gender differences, height and strength differences, and even differences of temperament ('Mummy's calm; Daddy gets mad'), are all becoming real to the child by this stage. And what often happens (though perhaps not quite as often or as predictably as Freud thought) is that a child tends to consciously idealize one parent and begin to prefer her (or him) to the other. This is actually something that *needs* to happen. It is part of 'individuation', the process by which we come to understand and enact our own uniqueness. But it often comes at the cost of loss. When we recognize our difference from (and attraction to) one of our parents, we simultaneously recognize our similarity to the other, and part of that recognition may be to deny it, or to struggle against it: 'I'm like Daddy, but I wish I could be like Mummy'.

The butt of many uneasy jokes, Freud's theory of the Oedipus complex (he was proud of his classical education) contains a fair bit of uncomfortable truth, and anyone who is honest in their observations of young children will see plenty of evidence of a distinctly coy quality in the way they make this shift of affections from one parent to the other ('To Pop: dump Mom, and have me' as developmentalist Karen Berger's eight-year-old daughter bluntly instructed her father, in a note left on his pillow).[6] Perhaps this form of attraction is the platform on which we later build our sense of our chosen partners as being 'desirably different' from ourselves.

This difference need not take the form of gender, although for many, that is part of it. Men are fascinated by women's pliability, by the soft curves of their bodies, by the gentleness of their voices and by how easily and naturally many of them seem to put others ahead of themselves and care about others' worries. Women are drawn to men's harder, more muscular bodies, to their (apparent) decisiveness and ability to take charge and make things happen. Stated so baldly, these are gender stereotypes, almost of Mills & Boon proportions, and of course there are many exceptions. There are plenty of women who are drawn to men because of their softness, and men to women who seem decisive and confidently self-promoting. Same-sex couples make the key issue clearer. Despite sharing the same gender, gay and lesbian couples are *also* drawn together by perceived differences, and this suggests that differences of attitude, personality and temperament may be more fundamental than physiological gender differences (as one client said of his partner, 'He's really looked after me; introduced me to people I'd never have had confidence to be around; I've never had anybody like that before. He's so much more outgoing than I am, and yet he really cares about me').

The folk psychology precept that 'opposites attract' contains a considerable amount of truth. We *are* drawn to those whose temperaments are dissimilar to our own, and we *do*, initially, find these differences appealing. We seem drawn irresistably to someone who is what we are not, and usually, we start off desiring to be more like them, and kind of hoping that the differences will 'rub off' if we stay with them. Of course it doesn't really work that way, but few of us *think* very much in the early stages of attraction. Perhaps, at the most universal, almost spiritual, level, all of us long for what is different from ourselves because we sense our own incompleteness (which the Greek philosopher Plato expressed in his myth of an originally hermaphrodite human being, subsequently cut in two, thus leaving each part searching for its 'other half').

Yet for nearly all of us, partner choice involves a far more specific set of discriminations than the simple longing to merge with a generalized Other. Nor is it simply a matter of 'assortative mating', the biological principle that in order to ensure a healthy genetic 'mix' in our offspring, we are instinctively 'pulled' towards potential partners whose genes are unlike our own. We humans seek out, not just Anyone who is different, but Someone *who is different in particular ways* – ways that relate directly to our own traits and characteristics.[7]

Thus the quiet, unassuming individual is 'pulled' towards the more confident person, the creative, erratic one is 'pulled' towards the stable, but less creative one, and so on. Furthermore, if we are honest, the particular mix that we are drawn to often turns out to be roughly the same *genetic* mix as that of the parent with whom we formed an Oedipal alliance in early childhood. Of course we don't see this in genetic terms, but rather, in personality terms, 'all my boyfriends are uncannily like my dad' or 'I'm always ending up with someone a bit like my mum'. The adult personality characteristics in fact depend upon the genetic temperament (the rudimentary 'personality' the baby is born with).[8] The same 'bundle' of temperamental traits (sociable, expressive, reactive, for example) may give rise to several somewhat different adult 'personalities', variations on the same theme, which helps to explain why we end up partnering someone whose personality, while having *some* traits in common with one of our parents, may not appear to be particularly close to his/her personality in others.

So the 'desirable difference' we perceive in our chosen partner in the early stages of attraction is likely to carry the resonances of long-ago devotion to a parent, of a hero-worship that must (if development occurs in a healthy manner) gradually give way to a more realistic appreciation of that parent's strengths and weaknesses. But at 4, 5 or 6 we tend to 'put on a pedestal' the parent we prefer, and as an adult in love we do exactly the same. Some degree of idealization is an essential part of romantic love, and this idealization, too, must give way to realism. But taking someone down from the pedestal is not easy or comfortable – either for us, or for the person we've placed there. It feels so disappointing, so distressing compared with the wonderful feelings of adoration we used to have, that couples equate 'the end of love' to 'the end of everything'. Those of us who began life securely attached can cope with the end of 'in love', and adjust to more modest expectations, but most of those we will see in the counselling room will not have started out with this foundation. Every loss, every abandonment, will remind them of the losses and abandonments of infancy, and it will be that much more difficult for them to 'see things in proportion'.

And as the partner comes down from that pedestal, it is the *differences* that we mostly notice, and to which we attach our feelings of disappointment – almost as if the partner had deliberately adopted those character traits in order to slight or distress us. The differences bulk so large because they remind us that the partner is not like us, not part of us, not under our control, and not capable of smoothly adjusting to our every need, as we once believed. So as young children we must learn to accept, first, that our adored parent is a person separate from ourselves, with needs and imperatives of her (or his) own; and second, that the parent we've given our allegiance to in that first great 'falling in love' in the 'play years', is not under our control either, is not a mirror of ourselves, and may not always live up to the adoration we've showered upon her (or him).

Freud had the courage to say what was unsayable at the time – that young children and parents have a *sensual* bond (as of course they do), and that mature, genital sexuality between adults builds upon this foundation.[9] Sex is an obsession of our society, probably more talked about than at any time in history, yet while we overvalue it, we also, curiously, *under*value it. Novelists excepted, we rarely speak of what sexual intimacy actually feels like and actually means to us. The experience of receiving a part of one's partner's body inside oneself or, conversely, the experience of *being* received within one's partner's body is not only very pleasurable, but also intensely meaningful. It is more than 'being close', it is 'being part of one another', 'being one flesh' in the Biblical phrase. Such is the intensity of feeling generated by the body's erogenous zones that we do not need genital penetration to experience this, nor do we need to be physically attractive, or young or able-bodied. Our bodies will feel it just as strongly.

Even in this time of relative carelessness about sex, to be offered this gift by another person, and to offer it to them, can be a wonderful experience. It is still (for many people) the ultimate form of trust. Sex with a partner we love and desire is a deeply significant transaction, which massively reinforces the 'survival level' attachment bond, and the sense of 'desirable difference' that originates with our 5-year-old adoration of a parent. It's hardly surprising, then, that when sexually based trust breaks down, it is felt as the ultimate betrayal, and for many people, intense love turns to intense hate, a wish to hurt, damage or even destroy the person who once made us feel so good (whom we *allowed* to make us feel so good!) but who now ceases to elicit that response. In Richard Wagner's opera *Das Rheingold*, the ugly dwarf Alberich lusts after the beautiful Rhinemaidens, who lead him on, and then spurn him. The mocking rejection of his desire leads him to renounce love for ever, steal the magic gold the maidens guard, and turn it into a ring of power, and a helmet of invisibility. Secrecy and aggression replace trust and shared delight. It is a bitter story many separating couples know all about.

Beyond difference: the similarities we don't see

There is a third, and final, level at which partner choice is determined. The first two (adult attachment and desirable difference) are easy enough to understand. They are compatible with our common-sense perceptions of what happens in couples. But the third principle is less obvious – more 'counter-intuitive', as scientists say. This principle is that each of us selects a partner whose level of basic selfhood – Murray Bowen would say, 'self-differentiation', which I'll explain shortly – is very similar to our own. This principle immensely complicates the 'opposites attract' principle, by introducing a new dimension entirely. In other words, the *differences* we commonly see in our own, or anyone else's, relationship may simply cover up more fundamental *similarities* at the level of emotional maturity.

As we have already noted, couples whose basic trust in their adult attachment relationship is starting to break down typically focus on the very differences that brought them together in the first place. Usually, each partner sees him or herself as more reasonable, and generally grown up, than the other. Hence the universal plea of almost every partner in counselling: 'If only he'd be more like me, we'd be fine'.

> 'I just can't stand how she won't even make the effort to get on with my friends. She knows they're important to me, but she isn't prepared to even try. She's really quite happy being so stand-offish, she doesn't see any need to change it – not even to save our relationship!'

All of us come to adulthood with varying degrees of what Bowen calls 'differentiated self' or 'solid self'. Solid self is not to be equated with 'self-esteem' or 'self-confidence', which are descriptions of how individuals feel within themselves. Solid self is a *relational* concept: it tells us, not just about how we feel within ourselves, but also *how we act within a close relationship*. In this sense, 'solid self' means having a reliable sense of who you are, and what is due to you, *at the same time as you have a reliable sense of who someone else is, and what is due to them*. That is what clearly distinguishes 'solid self' from the narcissist's overweening confidence in him/herself – a confidence which ignores the needs and rights of others. Secure attachment – the infant's sense of basic trust in the person who takes care of it, which later translates into a similar trust in self and others – is certainly the foundation for 'solid selfhood', but there is more to it than that.[10]

As infants grow into young children, they often give up (Bowen's word was 'trade') part of their early selfhood, in order to meet the needs of others (usually their parents). Without ever being aware of it, many children learn to be someone that others need them to be, rather than feeling able to be consistently 'themselves'.

> A young woman in her early thirties gradually realized that all her life, as long as she could remember, she had been trying to do what her mother and her elder sister seemed to want her to do, that she had up to now had no authentic life of her own, that she had never really 'chosen' anything; she had just followed the path she 'knew' was laid down for her. For this young woman, finding a 'solid self' proved a far from easy task; whenever she tried to follow her own instincts, she would feel extremely anxious, and 'feel like nothing' or 'feel empty'. Yet, if she set aside her own sense of what she needed, and acted the way she thought others wanted her to act, she would feel increasingly full of rage. Yet there was a sort of rudimentary self there, and as she has gradually allowed it to develop, her ability to 'hang on to herself', even in a conflict with her mother or her sister, has developed with it. Now she can feel proud of 'being me' much of the time without experiencing crippling anxiety.

In this example, the 'trading' of self occurred unconsciously, and very early. The example of sexual abuse (where an older person binds his child victim to secrecy with promises and threats) is an example, albeit an extreme and disturbing one, of the same process on a *conscious* level. The child 'knows' what has happened between her and her abuser, yet she cannot speak the truth, or bear witness to it. She must conduct herself as if 'nothing is wrong' for the sake of the person who has abused her, to preserve someone else from distress, or save the family from fracture. She has compromised her own truth in the interests of others, and feels no choice, no way out, often until many years later.

Murray Bowen's signal contribution to understanding relationships was his proposition that, almost inevitably, we choose to enter into a committed relationship with a person whose level of 'solid self' is approximately the same as our own. Those who are self-confident in the true sense tend to select partners who are similarly confident. We probably don't see too many of those in the counselling room. They are likely to form lasting and satisfying adult relationships, and even if they don't, they will typically handle the end of relationships without too great a level of mutual recrimination. Those who do not possess much 'solid self', however, find themselves irresistibly attracted to those whose level of unconfidence accurately matches their own.

For Bowen, few of us reach what he calls a fully 'differentiated' self – that is, a self that can remain in close and caring relationship with others, yet also think for itself, and not be swept along by the emotional currents that tear through families. Many of our clients will still be operating at what he would call a largely 'undifferentiated' position, that is, where the needs and emotions of others within the emotional system (family of origin, family of procreation) will automatically dictate their responses. Their chosen partners will exhibit a similar level of inability to thoughtfully separate their own needs from those of others, *even though they may display that inability in a very different way*. And that's the catch. We observe the surface differences, and fail to see the similarities underneath. That's what the partners themselves do, and too often, it's what we, as counsellors, do too.

For example, it's common for one partner to appear mature, calm and rational, and the other hysterical, childlike and emotion-governed. Since the first partner's behaviour looks just like what Bowen describes as 'solid self', and the second's actions look exactly like the 'undifferentiated' behaviour he describes, it's easy to fail to see what's underneath. In heterosexual couples it is often the man who will see himself as 'mature' and 'sensible', 'holding the show together' while his female partner 'drops her bundle' and acts like a silly teenager. The true levels on which both partners in this relationship function are displayed only when the roles are reversed: after years of 'selfless' putting up and 'acting responsible', the man suddenly runs away with a girl young enough to be his adolescent daughter. Now it's he who is 'dropping his bundle' and she, his wife, who is 'holding the show together'. His apparent maturity was indeed a 'show': as long as she remained dysfunctional and childlike, he could display his 'rational', caretaking self (a 'false self' that he probably developed in childhood in response to a needy mother who required him to act as a 'substitute husband'); but he lacked the confidence to express or act upon his own emotional needs within the relationship, until suddenly, swept away on a current of righteous anger at his wife, and middle-aged idealization of his new partner, he suddenly acts as irrationally as his wife has ever done!

Another example would be the couple where the wife is apparently super-confident, successful and outgoing in her political career, while the husband is unambitious, and seems to lack belief in himself, preferring to shine in her reflected glory. What Bowen would say, and what I have learned over and over again to be true, is that in such couples, the 'super-confident' one is (deep down) as unconfident as her partner. Her selfhood is not 'solid' at all: it can be sustained only as long as things are going well for her, and other people are doing exactly what she needs them to do. Suddenly deprived of admiration and smooth cooperation from others, or denied a promotion she convinced herself she was entitled to receive, this woman flies into rages, refuses to see visitors, and retreats into black depression. There is nothing solid inside of herself for her to fall back on, just an empty void, through which drift, wailing, the wraithlike shapes of her dreams of grandeur.

These are of course extreme examples, designed to dramatize the concept, but most couples exhibit such underlying similarities in less dramatic ways. I have gradually learned that what one partner does in one area of life, the other will do in a different area. They will never see the similarity, because their attention will always be focused on the arena where difference is apparent, never on the other. Years ago, I worked with a couple where the man was constantly irritated at his wife's untidiness around the house. He interpreted this as evidence of her disregard for his wishes, and of a basic lack of interest in what was so important to him. His picture of her was of a disorganized, careless, irresponsible person. Yet, in her career, she was capable of being highly organized and responsible; while he was untidy and careless in his attitude to his own job, which he valued much less than his aspirations to being a writer. He could not see her similarity to him, because he was looking in the wrong place.

Apparently 'fixed' personality traits are in fact far less fixed than we imagine, and depend heavily upon the roles that others play, the interpersonal environments in which we find ourselves. Consider the man who longs for an 'exciting' sex life, in which experiments are possible and risks are taken, and who feels bored and tied down by his staid, unadventurous partner. What happens when eventually, he breaks out of that relationship and finds another partner, whose attitude to sexual experimentation and risk is all he could wish for – and more? After a surprisingly short period of delighted mutuality, the man finds himself increasingly saying 'No, I don't feel like it', and increasingly resentful of what he experiences as being 'tied down' yet again – albeit in a very different way. He even finds himself longing for his original partner. It wasn't exciting, but at least it was reliable and there weren't any of these awful risks. He's done a complete reversal of roles from those he occupied with his original partner. Now it's he who is the 'unadventurous' one, and it's his new partner who is irritated by his conservative attitude.

It is these striking, 180-degree shifts that help us to realize that people are capable of behaving very differently from the way they commonly see themselves, and, provided the circumstances are different, are capable of behaviour that exactly parallels their partner's, and displays a similar level of selfhood. Gradually, I have come to see that if one partner is anxious, then most likely the other will be anxious also – except that typically the latter's anxiety will be 'masked' – somehow hidden from the view of both. If one partner is untrusting, then so will the other be.

The most often encountered example of the two different 'sides' of undifferentiated selfhood is the case of the couple where one chases and cajoles and nags, while the other refuses to talk and withdraws. In classic family therapy language, they are referred to as the 'pursuer/distancer' couple. The more the 'pursuer' tries to move in close ('Why won't you talk to me? Just tell me what you're feeling. I can't stand it when you go inside yourself like that!'), the more the distancer retreats ('Just leave me alone. I need some space. I'm going out for some air'.) Early family therapists referred to this as a 'couple dance', and indeed dancing is a good analogy: where one leads, the other follows, and by following, the other actually leads, and so on. Both are trapped in a repetitive, stultifying pattern of interaction.

To the outside witness, the 'pursuer' may look like the more anxious one: she (and it is often she, although, as we'll see a little later, the gender roles aren't fixed here either) can't rest without getting an answer from her taciturn partner, she worries, she frets, she rings her friends and asks for advice, she calls the counsellor. She follows her partner from room to room, even chasing him out to the shed where he's retreated, calling him up repeatedly on the mobile phone, or getting in her car and following him to his favourite haunts in the hope of finding him there. Anxious: yes. Possessive, yes. Controlling: yes. All of the above. But what about the 'distancer'? Is he really the calm, self-sufficient person he appears on the surface? Of course not.

He retreats into silence because of fear: fear of an out-and-out conflict with his partner, fear of raised voices and wounding words and tears. He's anxious too, but where she's anxious about losing contact with him, he's anxious about having too *much* contact with her. And where she displays her anxiety by moving in and trying to control his behaviour, he displays his by moving away, and thus very effectively controlling hers. Who is the 'powerful' 'manipulative' one? Both – or neither. She's 'possessive' because she fears losing him. His fear of losing her is much more deeply buried. And it may only finally surface when he *does*, definitively, lose her.

This very frequently encountered 'pursuer/distancer' couple in fact represents the two most common forms of 'insecure attachment' in infancy. The 'pursuer' is a classic case of 'anxious' or 'preoccupied' attachment: behind the adult woman who follows her partner from room to room trying to get him to 'open up to her' is the little girl who follows her mummy even into the toilet, because she's still scared that mummy might disappear unless she keeps her in view at all times. Behind the adult woman who 'nags' and pleads with her partner, lies the little girl who tugs again and again at her mummy's skirt, demanding 'Mummy, Mummy, Mummy!' until eventually she gets the attention she's been craving (and even if it's negative attention, that's a whole lot better than no attention at all). It is *fear of loss of the attachment figure* that drives this behaviour: in the child, in the adult. But the adult partner usually sees 'nagging' or 'attacking' rather than fear, for reasons that will become clear when we examine the inner world of the 'distancer'.

'Pursuer' adults are individuals who have never learned to cope with their own anxiety when a significant other withdraws. They didn't grow up with that solid trust that the other will still be around, or will come back, that trust which we think is part of 'secure attachment'. And a big part of therapy with such individuals in adulthood is to help them learn to tolerate the panic they feel when their partner temporarily retreats. If they can just *feel* it, without trying to take it away (by running after their partner and demanding a response from him) then it will probably start to diminish, sometimes quite soon. But most 'pursuers' never get to tolerate their panic for that long, so they never find out. And they never experience their own strength and self-reliance as a consequence. They are left feeling at the mercy of their partner, dependent on him for reassurance – a far cry from the 'attacking' aggressive figure they cut in their partner's eyes!

Behind the adult 'distancer', by contrast, lies the avoidant or dismissive style of attachment. As a very young child, this person turned away from his mother because she had (in his view, at least) proved unreliable or overwhelming. Either he needed her, and she wasn't reliably there, so he had to learn to manage on his own. Or she came in too close, and offered him a kind of attention that his temperament (with its low threshold for emotional stimulus) found too much to handle. He turned away, trying to retrieve a sense of his own boundaries. He was actually angry with her, back then, but his temperament wasn't the kind to wail loudly or thresh around, instead he stiffened as she tried to hug him, or turned away from her embrace. He just stayed quiet. The less he showed, the safer he felt. And in his own way, he got back at her. She didn't know what to do when he turned away from her, or resisted her attempts at affection. He could 'win'. It was a bleak kind of satisfaction, that win, but it would have to do because he'd never learned to trust that he could have any more reliable kind of security than the kind he could provide for himself. Now, as an adult, he experiences his partner as invasive and attacking, and totally fails to perceive her fear of losing him. Even if she were able to tell him, he wouldn't really be able to hear it.

When creatures experience a threat, they characteristically respond with one of three instinct-driven reactions: fight, flight or freeze. 'Fight' involves moving closer to the perceived enemy, 'display' behaviour designed to intimidate (erecting one's posture, uttering loud sounds), or an actual attack. 'Flight' involves literal running (or flying, or swimming) away. 'Freeze' is what hedgehogs do: staying very still, trying to make oneself inconspicuous, and withdrawing inside oneself. Quite clearly, these behaviours are the ones our pursuer and distancer are performing, too. The 'pursuer' manifests the 'fight' response, easier to see when overtly aggressive and blaming, harder to identify when overtly cajoling and pleading. The 'distancer' displays both the tendency to run away (wanting to leave the room, get away, drive off somewhere) and the alternative 'shutdown' and 'pull in' response.

Of course, there's a lot more to it than this, otherwise we'd be hedgehogs rather than humans. Being human, we have memories (conscious and unconscious) of our whole past lives as a (sometimes treacherous) guide to present behaviour. Being human, we have rational intellects as well as survival-oriented instincts – but all too often, as Bowen well knew, our rational intellects, proud products of that cerebral cortex that humans alone have evolved to its present level of extraordinary complexity, can lead us astray, because our rational intellects get overridden by those same survival-level instincts, or by archaic memories of childhood threats, or a combination of both.[11] That's precisely what Bowen meant by saying that intellect becomes fused with 'emotionality' (by which he meant, I think, 'instinct'). We cannot distinguish the one from the other, and so our resulting behaviour is 'undifferentiated', however calm and 'rational' it might sound.

Goodbye Earl!

So now, after what may seem a long detour, let's go back to partner choice. Why is it that there are so many pursuer/distancer couples? Because we choose to be with a partner who is *similar* to us in his/her level of selfhood (equally anxious, equally scared, equally unconfident) but *different* in the way he/she manifests it. At the level of 'desirable difference', anxiously attached individuals feel 'drawn' to the apparent calm and self-sufficiency of avoidantly attached people. Anxiously attached people wish they felt as self-sufficient, and so free from anxiety. At first, their partner seems to promise them a 'new beginning', a chance to have what they have never had. And avoidantly attached people, who have always found it difficult to reach out to others and tell them what they need, find that (at first) their anxiously attached partner can supply the words that they cannot, and bridge the gap on the other side of which they sit alone. Only later, as one partner's anxiety grows, does the early hope break down, and as one moves in to soothe her anxiety, the other moves away, in the pattern he learned so long ago, in order to soothe his. And so it goes.

When relationships break down completely, and couples separate, it is often possible to see early attachment behaviour return in its full force. Interestingly enough, while women tend to be the 'pursuers' within relationships, once the relationship is over it is often the man who takes over that role. Having previously, perhaps, taken her for granted, and certainly pushed her away when she came too close, now that she is gone, he becomes consumed with anxiety himself, and simply cannot let go. She asks for 'space' and he phones several times a day, sends flowers, and turns up on her doorstep; she says she needs to 'sort herself out', so he writes her twenty-page letters explaining (*logically*) why *she* was at fault in the relationship, and why things can be so much better now, if only she will come back and give him another try. The endless perseverating gives the lie to the claim of rationality.

All of which 'pursuit' behaviour ends up making her even angrier with him than she was to begin with, and destroys any chance that she might start to miss him, and feel more tenderly towards him in her loneliness. He won't allow her to be lonely: he keeps on intruding into her life, until eventually, she takes out a restraining order, just to keep him away. He may not have wanted a divorce, but his own behaviour has, unconsciously perhaps, ensured that he will get one. For her part, since the separation, she has largely occupied the 'distancer' role that previously was his, and her proud, angry isolation is made all the easier to maintain because he helps her to maintain it. This is what systemic family therapists mean when they talk about couples 'co-operating' to bring about a separation, even though at least one of the two consciously opposes the break-up of the relationship.

Relationships where one has a persistent pattern of violent behaviour exemplify how 'pursuer' and 'distancer', 'anxious' and 'avoidant' roles can switch around in dramatic ways. The 'cycle of violence' which is relatively easy to identify in such relationships involves one partner who intimidates, controls and physically attacks the other. These abusive partners (mostly, within heterosexual relationships, males) are still driven, I believe, by fear of losing their partners, but when you're being punched and kicked, you're not really likely to believe that. In response to his extreme possessiveness and invasiveness, his partner adopts extreme caution (the 'freeze' response), schooling herself to say exactly what he wants to hear, to avoid 'unsafe' topics, and eventually, saying nothing rather than risk arousing his suspicion and anger. Each episode of violence leads her to withdraw into herself, and to 'die inside' towards him; he then becomes a different kind of pursuer, and wants to 'woo' her back to loving him with affectionate words, gifts and flowers. As soon as she is securely 'back', he begins to worry again about losing her, and recommences his suspicious questioning and threats. So the cycle continues, until she 'finally gets the nerve to file for divorce'. While we rightly pay attention to the instances where such stands produce homicidal rage in the male partner, the Dixie Chicks' song, 'Goodbye Earl' provides a thought-provoking corrective: the women take the law into their own hands, and the violent man is quietly and effectively disposed of. The cheerful insouciance with which the song is delivered on stage gives it much of its edge.

I said at the beginning of this chapter that as counsellors we needed a 'map' of attraction, disenchantment, 'difference' and similarity, and I hope that I have gone some way towards providing one. It is a complex matter, and inevitably I've had to oversimplify some things that I've included, and completely exclude others, in order to make the main points clearly. But to my mind, what emerges is this:

- *'Falling in love' is a process that is nearly always temporary*, a kind of extended 'trance' which throws its cloak of invisibility over the real reasons why we are so powerfully attracted to a particular person. In this trance, we re-enter a state of infant bliss, full of wonder at another human being who can make us feel so good, and magically assist us to transform our lives.
- *Like chooses like*: we end up with someone for a good reason. Unless our union is 'forced' (and sometimes even then), there are always similarities, at a deep level, between us and our partner. Sometimes (not always) counselling can help people to recognize these deep

similarities, and thus offer couples a new reason for persisting in trying to live together in a way that offers dignity and emotional security to both.

- *Opposites attract:* we need to be with someone different from ourselves in order to expand and grow as individuals; yet being with someone with *these particular differences*, which often resonate with the personalities of one of our parents, means that

- *Disenchantment is inevitable:* part of growing to full maturity is seeing our parents (and our adult partners) for who they are, 'taking them off the pedestal' in order to honour them as ordinary human beings like ourselves. This is a painful process, and the more we have been prone to idealize our parents, the more we will be likely to feel deeply betrayed when our adult partners, too, prove fallible and human.

- *When disenchantment occurs, and 'love' fails with our adult partner, we are more likely to feel that our survival is threatened if our infant attachment was insecure.* Those who started life with less trust often continue to display coping strategies which will inevitably invite negative responses from most partners.

- *If we have never deidealized ourselves, never taken ourselves off the pedestal, then the failure of a strong adult attachment will hit us very hard indeed.* It is these couples, who still cling to an unrealistic idealization of self and other, whose primary goal now becomes to destroy the person who once meant so much to them, and for whom 'justice' and 'reparation' will replace 'love'. Woe betide any children who may have been born to this couple, for they will become helpless pawns in their parents' war of attrition!

Bearing in mind that most of the couples we see will not fall into this extreme category, unless we work for the Family Court or its equivalent, let's now, in our next chapter, see how we can, in practical ways, work with insecurely attached, disillusioned couples who still have some goodwill left towards one another.

Notes

1 Satir (1967: 118).
2 I have long been convinced that it would greatly assist counsellors and therapists to understand more of the history of 'love', sex, marriage and family life than most of them do. Knowledge of social history brings with it a broader perspective on institutions and values we would otherwise take for granted. Two very readable books, although now falling somewhat behind the latest research, are Edward Shorter (1975), especially pp. 125ff., and Lawrence Stone

(1977), especially pp. 325–404. More recent research, which suggests some modifications in Shorter's and Stone's conclusions, can be found in Casey (1989). Above all, I recommend Zeldin (1994), graceful, provocative, learned and witty! Zeldin deals with romantic love in the chapter 'How new forms of love have been invented' (pp. 74–85).

3   Hendrix (1988) explains a similar view of attraction and disenchantment in a popular, but not misleading, way. Somewhat more sophisticated, but gracefully written, is Shaddock (1998). Despite its age, Dicks (1967) remains a classic psychodynamic account of the complexities of partner choice. My own *A Circle Unbroken* (Crago 1999b) attempts to present some of the mysteries of 'biological knowing' and how 'life lives us' (rather than the other way around).

4   See Lorenz (1952: 41). (For basic reading on attachment theory, see p. 9 above, n. 9)

5   Maturana and Varela (1992: 246–7).

6   The details can be found in Berger (1988: 240).

7   My own sense of this intricate process is that we are instinctively drawn towards potential partners who replicate key segments of our own family's gene pool. Thus, we are attracted to a partner whose genes are sufficiently different from our own personal genes for them to be viable mates (the 'assortative mating' principle) while simultaneously similar enough to the genes held within our extended family, to ensure that family patterns of personality and behaviour will 'repeat' in the offspring that we and our partner may later produce.

8   On temperament research see Thomas *et al.* (1963) and Thomas and Chess (1980). An introduction can be found in Karen (1998).

9   Although English translations of Freud use the word 'sexual' (e.g. 'infantile sexuality') I prefer 'sensual', which in English has the broader meaning of 'appealing to the senses', and need not imply genitally-based feelings. Freud's classic statement on all of this, written in 1905, can be found in *Three Essays on the Theory of Sexuality* (see Freud 1977), but a much more approachable version, intended for a lay audience, is presented in *Introductory Lectures on Psychoanalysis*, Lecture 20, 'The Sexual Life of Human Beings' and Lecture 21, 'The Development of the Libido' (see Freud 1974).

10 Bowen's mature thinking on the 'differentiated self' is most accessibly explained in 'An interview with Murray Bowen' (originally published 1976) in Bowen (1978: 389–412).

11 Le Doux (1998).

3   What do you do after the third session?

The process of couple work

The 'third session phenomenon'

Over my years in practice I began to notice a certain regularity to the way couples behaved in their first few sessions. True, not every couple followed the pattern that I noticed, but the majority certainly did. And in fact, individual clients and whole families also followed this pattern, although with some variations in exactly how they did so.

Stated in its simplest form, the pattern went something like this: in the first session, couples would arrive in varying states of distress and, provided that I did a reasonably competent job, most would return a second time. Even though I had done little at the first session except listen empathically and exercise enough control to make it safe for both, clients would more often than not report at the start of the second session either that they had noticed some improvement, or that they felt some kind of hope. By the end of the second session, however, there would often be a plea for 'something to read that would help us' or 'some exercise we could do to make things improve faster'. After years of taking such requests at face value, I realized that it was generally premature to suggest activities or reading at such an early stage, and that if I did, they would mostly be swept away in the wave of anger and disappointment that was shortly to come. Instead, I realized that these requests were better treated as 'signs of disquiet', indications that the early hope was starting to wear thin. (In fact, the couple's wish for 'something to read' or 'some exercise' directly parallels the request for 'some exercise' or 'something to give them' from the therapist new to couple work, which we mentioned in Chapter 1. In both cases, the request for 'information' or 'direction' indicates doubt and anxiety.)

What followed was far more dramatic and easy to recognize. Whatever-it-was seemed to occur between the second and the third sessions. Some clients would simply not show up for the third session at all. They would phone in and report some kind of crisis, and say that they'd 'get back to me'. Very few ever did.

Those who did attend the third session were in a very different place from where they'd been in the previous meeting. Their faces would express sullenness, resignation, anger, disappointment, or tension – a range of feelings, but none of them positive. A few would question me with thinly veiled aggression ('How long do you think this is going to take?'). Most couples would attack each other, as if the fragile trust gained in the first two sessions had shattered in the intervening week. Usually, they'd report a major fight. Some would not attack at all, but indicate by their resigned demeanour that they didn't really expect anything to work anyway. Whatever form it took, the 'third session phenomenon', as I started to call it, seemed to signal the end of hope.

For some clients, the third session would be their last, regardless of what I did. It was as if these couples could last just one meeting longer than the ones who'd phoned in to cancel before the session. Many times, I found that the couples who gave up at this stage had also given up on their relationship, and had made a decision to split. They couldn't see much point in continuing with counselling once they'd come to this conclusion. My attempts to persuade them that it would be worthwhile to explore and learn from what had gone wrong mostly fell on deaf ears. Many couples unconsciously equate counselling with their relationship. Once the relationship is definitely over, so is the counselling. One partner may continue for a few sessions on his/her own, but only a few make a commitment to longer-term self-exploration.

But there was another category of clients, for whom what I did at the third session seemed to matter quite a bit. With these clients, what seemed to make a difference was how I handled their challenge to me, or to each other. If I got defensive and irritated in response to their attacks on my competence ('I was talking to a clinical psychologist who's a friend of mine, and *he* said that what *he* does with *his* clients is . . .'), the session went from bad to worse. If I started feeling anxious and over-responsible in the face of their renewed hopelessness and bitterness, and started giving them little lectures on what they needed to do, or how they had to allow some time for the process to work, then the session still went from bad to worse.

But if I could respond to their feelings in an open, non-defensive manner, then I would often find that the couple would make a significant shift. How would I do this? Probably I'd say something like:

> 'It must feel very upsetting to think that you've come along to see me, and so far, I haven't been able to help you at all.'

(I want to stress that this statement will be heard by clients as an unhelpful apology if it comes from an anxious, over-responsible space in me. But if it is spoken without anxiety, and with genuine empathy for their feelings, then it is unlikely to be heard that way.)

Sometimes one or both partners would agree. Sometimes they would politely insist that, of course, it wasn't up to me to fix them. Either way, however, there was generally a feeling of relief, because I had acknowledged what was so palpably in the room. Even though nothing had altered between them, there seemed to be the beginnings of an acceptance that the process might take some time, that things would not transform overnight, and that they could commit to a period of exploring their relationship, despite the very real uncertainty about whether anything positive would come out of it. Sometimes it also helped if I went further and added:

> 'I wonder if that's sometimes how you feel towards each other? You keep on hoping that the other one is going to do something to make it better, and it seems they always let you down.'

This intervention could help couples to link up their disappointment in me and the counselling process with their disappointment in each other. Again, relief often follows this acknowledgement.

These days, I see the whole three-session pattern as to do with magic, hope and despair. It is really another version of the 'falling in love/falling out of love' process that I summarized at the end of the previous chapter. This pattern has its roots in infancy, although most clients would quite understandably reject that interpretation as outrageous if I was silly enough to put it to them in those words.

In the previous chapter, we examined the primitive reactions of fight, flight and freeze which we share with 'lower' forms of life, and which somewhat correspond with the behaviour characteristic of various forms of insecure attachment. The psychoanalyst Melanie Klein believed that in fact all infants exhibit these responses to some degree, in the first few months of life. She considered that angry howls, fierce body twisting, and sullen withdrawal were part of the natural repertoire of children at this stage, even those we would now term 'securely attached'. Her term for these responses, 'the paranoid/schizoid position', corresponds roughly to the 'fight/flight/freeze' response.

What she went on to argue, though, was that if the child's development followed a desirable course, this automatic anger or automatic turnaway would gradually be replaced (somewhere between 3 and 6 months of age) by the child's acceptance that it cannot always have exactly what it wants, that its mother will not always get it right, and that (by extension) the world is not perfect. This acceptance brings sadness with it, a sense of loss – the loss of the infant's early belief that its mother is omnipotent, omniscient, and perfectly loving – but it also brings a certain calm, and a sense that although the world is not perfect, we can still make some of our desires come true, by our own efforts (rather than by the magical intervention of an adult caregiver). Klein believed that much of this development was inborn (we would say 'hard-wired' into the brain from birth), but clearly, how readily an infant is able to tolerate uncertainty and imperfection will have a great deal to do with how much its caregiver is able to *help* it to do so, remaining calm in the face of its distress, and comforting it when it cannot have exactly what it wants.[1]

What we see in our adult couples over three sessions is a kind of mini-recapitulation of Klein's developmental model. There is an initial burst of 'magical expectations' (as if clients somehow hope that coming to counselling is going to totally heal the relationship, and the therapist, like an infant's mother, is going to provide perfect care and love for each partner). The 'magic' produces unrealistic optimism, but by the end of the second session (usually), and certainly before the third session comes around, the 'magic' has worn off, and disillusionment and despair have set in.[2] The couple have 'fallen out of love' with therapy, and the initial idealized image of the therapist is abruptly replaced by one in which the therapist is disappointing, incompetent, or even destructive. Some couples 'fight' at this stage (attack the therapist or each other); others engage in 'flight' or 'freeze' (cancel the session, withdraw into miserable non-compliance). Couples who quit therapy at this stage are in effect reacting from Klein's paranoid/schizoid position: 'You can't help us, so we'll give up on you – and each other.'

But if the therapist can tolerate both types of reponse without overreacting – facing their anger squarely without the need to fight back, hearing their misery and despair without getting drawn down into it – then this will generally help. The couple now have the chance to make a shift – to a more mature, realistic appraisal of their situation: 'Yes, things are not good; yes, it's going to take some time to repair; yes, we must take responsibility for what happens to us, instead of expecting an authority figure to do so; yes, we must tolerate our anxiety that perhaps nothing *can* be repaired after all.' This is Klein's 'depressive position' in the context of adults in therapy.

Of course there are exceptions to the pattern I have briefly outlined here. Some couples cling to their magical expectations for far longer than a couple of sessions, refusing to recognize that the therapist is human and fallible, and continuing to hope for miracles 'from the outside'. Some couples proceed through their first three sessions with only a gradual deepening of intensity, and there is no obvious 'crisis': usually, these are the couples who enter therapy with more mature expectations in the first place, understanding that it will take time, and that the therapist is not a miracle worker. But for the majority, there will be some form of 'third session crisis' – mild, or dramatic – and if it can be negotiated successfully, then I generally find that the real work can begin.

So what does that 'real work' consist of? Let's start by looking at what we should *not* do, before coming to what we *can*.

What we shouldn't do: absorb the couple's anxiety

Faced with a new couple and their many, pressing concerns, it is easy and natural for us to become preoccupied with the couple's own agendas. These usually include some variants of: Can he/she change to meet my needs? Which of us should change first? Can our original feelings of love be revived, or are the feelings 'dead'? Should we stay together, or part? Who is most to blame for what has gone wrong between us, and how much should she/he be punished? Of course we need to listen respectfully to all of these, but to become caught up in them is to give up our hope of truly assisting the couple, for these are all questions that, ultimately, they must answer for themselves – however much they may wish to engage us as 'Judge Judy'.

Why do so many beginning relationship therapists become anxious about whether couples stay together or separate? There are two important aspects to this, one rooted in the process of the couples themselves, and the other in our own personal histories.

In the previous chapter, I suggested some compelling reasons why the potential break-up of a committed adult relationship seems a matter of emotional 'life' or 'death'. So powerful are the feelings involved as couples face this possibility, that it is impossible to sit in the room with them, and not feel it. *Their* anxiety easily becomes *our* anxiety. To recognize this process is the first step towards freeing ourselves from its effects. But it will be much harder to do so if our personal histories resonate with the couple's dynamics. Many of us become relationship or family therapists in part because as children we were the helpless witnesses of our own parents' marital struggles, and at some level longed to be able to help them. Even those of us (and here I am speaking about myself) whose parents stayed together, and quarrelled only sometimes, may still have felt the acute discomfort that sensitive children feel when parents suddenly lose their calm, their self-control, their air of wisdom, and instead yell at each other, or burst into tears, or fling wild accusations. Our stable universe suddenly starts to disintegrate, and we want more than anything for the storm to subside.

As children we may even feel in some dim way responsible for having caused the storm, or for not having been able to prevent it. We may come to adulthood with a burning desire to 'teach couples relating skills', a bright optimism about 'saving marriages' or 'preventing unnecessary break-ups'. But underneath these altruistic aims may lie a dark burden of childhood guilt at our inability to 'fix' our parents' own relationship. When we sit in the room with a couple, experiencing their feelings of disenchantment, anger, grief and despair, we are likely to feel all over again what we felt as children: anxious, responsible, and (perhaps) helpless. It will be all the harder for us to free ourselves from the couple's agendas, and to stick to our own.

There is another personal scenario, of a somewhat different nature, which is commonly involved in couple work. This is when we, *as adults*, have our-selves have gone through the break-up of a committed relationship, and often the divorce proceedings later. Inevitably, our feelings about this break-up, and how we handled it (or failed to handle it) will hover at the edges of our minds as we work with any ambivalent or separating couple. We may find ourselves anxious to help them to 'do it better than we did', and exasperated or disap-pointed when they fail to do so. Or we may find ourselves instinctively more sympathetic to one partner than the other, because that partner is playing on the stage of couple therapy the role that we played in our own separation drama. It can be very difficult to hold on to objectivity in these situations, however hard we may try.

If you find yourself drawn deeply, before you know it, into the anxieties of the couple you are working with, then it is particularly important that you talk to your supervisor, and begin to identify which elements of your enmeshment come from your own history, and which from the couple themselves. Some supervisors feel it is appropriate to ask you about your personal story, and help you make the connections in the supervision itself; others may prefer you to explore the connection in the arena of your personal therapy. Certainly, if it keeps happening to you, not just with the occasional couple, but with most couples, then you need to look in depth at what may lie unresolved or even unconscious within you.

Let's assume that you can manage, most of the time (nobody does it all the time!) to stay clear of feeling too anxious, too responsible, or too partisan in couple work. What should you be doing? If you aren't going to enter into their agendas, then how exactly are you going to help them? I am somewhat ashamed to say that it has taken me many years of seeing couples to actually feel clear about what I am providing for them, and how it can help them. Here is what I think I do. It is not prescriptive, and you may well feel that other aims are more important. This is simply what works for me.

How we can help: sticking to the point

The simplest and most fundamental way we can help couples is a logical extension of the 'traffic cop' role that we explored in Chapter 1: we need to 'slow them down' so that they can start to take in what is really being said, and confront the issue, instead of becoming detoured away from it. Few couples who come to counselling listen well to each other (if they did, they wouldn't be seeing us). Typically, they 'communicate' by focusing on their own hurt and anger, 'listening' to their partner only long enough to hear 'trigger words' that set them off on their own agenda once again, and screening out the rest. As soon as they start to feel vulnerable to a perceived attack, they shift ground to a different issue, on which they can 'counter-attack'. Thus the subject can move with bewildering rapidity from present to past, from minor to major issues, from practical to deeply emotional, within a few minutes. As I have grown older, I have found it harder and harder to keep up with these shifts, and felt more confident to interrupt couples fairly early on, with a statement like:

> 'I'm sorry, but I'm finding it really difficult to follow you. We started off talking about washing dishes, and now we're talking about something that happened ten years ago, and you've mentioned other things in between. I think it would help if we just stuck to one issue. Which one is the most important to you? Would it be OK if you let me interrupt you if either of you starts getting off the topic?'

The next step, then, is to try to 'slow-motion' the discussion so that each partner has a chance to say her/his piece, and get a real response from the partner. This is far easier to say here than it is to achieve in practice, and again, it calls for an active, interventive stance on the part of the counsellor. Again, it may involve interrupting one partner when he/she has made a significant statement, or interrupting the other, who wants to break in on the first. But, in the words of one of my individual clients who'd recently begun couple work with another therapist:

> 'It's a challenge! But it's really good, because she won't let me interrupt until Linda's finished talking! It's not like Linda's saying anything I haven't heard before. But it's different because I've actually taken in what she's saying. At home, I wouldn't do that, 'cos I'd just be thinking about what *I* wanted to say. It's very frustrating for me, but I'm prepared to do it because she's fair, and I know I'm going to get my turn, and Linda's going to have to listen to me the same way I have to listen to her.'

Sometimes the 'slowing down' can be facilitated by imposing the 'paraphrase rule', a technique invented by Carl Rogers, where both partners have to say back what they've heard the other say (to that partner's satisfaction!) before they are permitted to launch into their 'counter-attack'. Clients usually find this hugely irritating but, if willing to persist, find that it starts to yield results. It is, if you like, the first step in 'teaching empathy', and while it starts off seeming mechanical, tedious and artificial to both partners, it can lead to real empathy with some persistence and coaching on our part.[3] I would not usually ask my clients to engage in structured 'teaching of empathy', however, until the 'third session crisis' is past, and there is some evidence of willingness to persist with the process. Often, I will need to wait for many sessions more. Implemented too early, such strategies simply make clients feel misunderstood, the urgency of their needs dismissed. They have to believe that *we* can hear them before they will allow us to teach them anything about hearing each other.

How we can help: understand each partner more fully

Just as in individual counselling, *making the attempt to understand* is crucial, only this time it is *attempting to understand each in the presence of the other*. When nothing else seems to be working, and partners are locked in profound mutual incomprehension or antagonism, this is what I fall back on. If they shut each other out, then it falls to me to try my best to understand them, from my position as an outsider who is granted privileged access to their personal pain, and to articulate my understanding to them so that they can comment on it. Sometimes, indeed, this attempt at deep understanding is *all* I can offer.

In my view, 'understanding in depth' involves far more than the ability to empathically restate the position of each partner. It involves me in gradually working towards an understanding of their whole personality, the predictable ways that they see the world and react to people and situations. Here is an example of what I recently said to one man in a couple session:

> 'Selwyn, you seem to be the sort of person who sees the world in terms of right and wrong. You've told me often how important fairness is to you, and how affected you are when something unfair seems to happen. And so when Jane says that her son feels criticized by you, I think what you feel is how unfair that is. You've got a highly developed sensitivity to fairness, and sometimes that blots out any other issue that might be involved. After all, when you were a kid, and your dad treated you so unjustly, why would you bother to think about how *he* might feel, or what might be motivating him to act that way? It was natural for you just to feel how unfair he was.'

Some self-help books and popular psychological teachings have stridently maintained for many years now that we can choose who we want to be, and radically modify our personality through 'positive thinking', 'affirmations', 'future-focused imagery', and so on. I think this is facile, but it feeds many people's fantasy that everything would be fine if only their partner 'changed' in some key respect. As elaborated in Chapter 6, I believe that we all inherit a temperament – a 'bundle' of genetic traits which sets broad parameters for the adult personality we will later display. A person who is highly sensitive to both physical and emotional stress cannot magically become a cheerfully thick-skinned one, who shrugs off both flu viruses and sudden quarrels with ease. A quiet introvert cannot ever transform himself into a 'party animal'. By the time we reach early adulthood, we cannot *not* be who we are. I simply do not believe it legitimate for one partner in a relationship to demand that the other 'give up' or 'let go' of some core aspect of his/her personality, but this is what individuals in relationships often fear. A demand to change is felt as an attack on one's core being, a threat to who one is. (Of course, it is perfectly legitimate for each partner to ask the other to understand and appreciate them, and to make allowances for *their* 'core being'. That is very different, but in practice, the second often gets misheard as the first.)

I make a point of validating genetically rooted differences in personality ('Bill, you're telling me that you're quiet and thoughtful, and that's probably how you've always been. You're not going to change in that way. Leanne, you like to talk, and let your feelings out. That's probably how you've been ever since you were a baby, from what you say. That's your nature.') I make a clear distinction between what I see as 'non-negotiable' parts of the personality, and attitudes and behaviour that might be modified, if each really desired to do so.

What counts, for me, is the ability of each partner to *understand who the other really is*. Part of my hope, in working with almost any couple, is that slowly, and if I show consistent empathy for each of them, they may start to view their two different personalities as acceptable differences to be understood and worked around, rather than as positions each has adopted deliberately in order to 'punish' the other (which is the way many couples think).

A belief that we are shaped by a genetic temperament is not at all inconsistent with a belief that we are also significantly influenced by family of origin and by significant early events (although the two are often seen as somehow diametrically opposed and incompatible). Hence, for me, part of deeply understanding a client is coming to an understanding of his/her family-of-origin, its history, its customs, its values, and its range of personalities. If I have reason to think that family of origin influences may be particularly important, I may contract with the couple to spend at least one whole session, sometimes two, on the family of each of them. This may involve drawing up a formal genogram on a whiteboard or on a large sheet of paper that both the partners can see as it is built up, or it may simply involve my drawing up my own small genogram on my notepad, and using it to guide my questioning.[4]

In either case, what is most significant for the partner whose family is the subject of our exploration is that he/she is asked questions by an outsider, about things which he/she has usually taken for granted, or never questioned. For example, many clients have never wondered how their own childhood experiences (of feeling neglected, or feeling terribly responsible) might have been affected by events such as a parent's sudden illness, unemployment, move to another town, or forced migration to another country. So questions like 'So how do you think your Dad might have been affected by losing his job?' or 'How do you think your Mum might have been affected by that miscarriage?' can lead on to 'Well, if that's what might have been going on for him/her, and you were around 5 at that time, how do you think you might have been affected?'

It is not so much that any new facts are going to be uncovered (although they may be, if clients then go back to family and ask some questions about the 'gaps' the therapist has drawn their attention to) but rather that clients are going to be challenged to think in a different way about things they have simply grown up with, and accepted, often from a child's perspective that serves them less well as adults. This can lead to greater understanding of their own early experience, and (sometimes, but not always) more acceptance of it, and a more relaxed attitude to themselves in the present. Family-of-origin 'insight' does not magically change people's behaviour, but it can sometimes lift the burden on the individual by suggesting legitimate alternative explanations to the self-blaming ones that the individual may have clung to all his/her life.

Similarly, most adults come into therapy with fixed perceptions of other family members, often judgemental or fairly narrow. Many have never asked themselves the question 'How did my father come to be the way he was?', and even if they have acquired snippets of information about his history, have not *connected* that information with his behaviour towards them when they were children. If adults can broaden or deepen their view of parents beyond these fixed perceptions, then they are also, in effect, modifying their view of *themselves*, developing more tolerance and understanding of themselves, and in time this can sometimes flow on to a more accepting view of a partner also.

Of course, if there is deep anger and a sense of total betrayal by a parent (or other relative) – as there is likely to be where the client has been abused as a child by that family member – then this acceptance may be inappropriate, or impossible to achieve, and to keep offering opportunities for 'understanding' in such circumstances may be hugely unempathic. But sometimes there has been no obvious abuse, yet clients still prove incapable of modifying their view of family and parents, despite the sympathetic curiosity of the therapist. More often than not, these clients prove equally incapable of modifying their image of themselves – and their partner.

The key thing about all of this questioning around family of origin is that it happens *in the presence of the partner*. Often, partners have also developed 'fixed' views of one another's families, and it can be enlightening for them to have their own perspectives expanded along with their partner's. Alternatively, the 'outsider' can sometimes be more objective than the family member, and can experience delight or relief when presented with a fuller understanding of where the partner's apparently objectionable or incomprehensible behaviour comes from. Interviewing each partner in turn about their family may seem like 'doing individual therapy' within a couple session, but its effect can be enormously different from seeing each partner individually to do that work, or sending them off to a different therapist to do it. When the latter course is taken, many clients say little about the content of their individual sessions to their partner, and the partner never gets to witness the emotional impact of a particular question, or revelation. My wife Maureen points out that it's a bit like parents who send a child off to stay with relatives during a traumatic death, or a family crisis. In both cases, opportunities for joint learning are lost.

Luke and Naomi

Faced with his wife Naomi's lengthy outbursts of intense emotion, Luke would cease to listen after the first minute or two, his mouth curved down in an expression of scorn and disgust as he heard her 'raving on about some garbage'. Naomi felt very shut out by Luke's dismissive reactions, and typically tried to break through by speeding up and getting louder.

When, after quite a few repetitions of such fruitless interactions, we explored Luke's family of origin, he described two parents who had provided their children with a comfortable lifestyle and good schooling, but – as I saw it – very low levels of emotional support. Somewhat defiantly, Luke explained that he had soon learned that, as he was growing up, he must deal with his problems by himself, because nobody else would take any interest in them. In fact, it did not even occur to him as a boy that he could speak to his mother about what was bothering him, and his father worked such long hours that he was never available. An older brother with a developmental disability had bullied him regularly, but his fears were simply dismissed by Luke's parents: 'He's your brother, and he can't help it'. Luke's mother was an 'endless talker' who 'rabbitted on about some garbage' and, as an adult, Luke had learned to cope with this by 'turning off' and simply letting her talk while he 'thought about something else'. Luke described his father as opinionated, dogmatic, and uninterested in taking seriously any point of view other than his own.

As he told this story, over some two sessions, I attempted to provide a high level of support for Luke, emphasizing the distress he had had to bear on his own, the survival value of his coping strategies. Typically of so many males, he first minimized his own suffering, and felt my attempts at empathy as 'exaggerated' ('Well, it wasn't that bad. I just got on with things'). However, the consistency of my stance eventually helped him to see that he had, in fact, grown up in an emotionally neglectful, and physically abusive, environment. It was important that Luke should not feel criticized, and also that I should not be too critical of his family – *he* was allowed to be angry with them, but family loyalty made him wary of accepting my comments. The parallels between the way he'd learned to 'screen out' his mother and the way he now 'screened out' his wife were clear enough, but I chose to frame these as 'Well, now that you've told me about your mum, I can see how natural it is for you to "shut down" as soon as someone starts into a long rave . . . you've developed a habit over years and years of living with your mum, and it's pretty hard not to behave the same way with Naomi!'

For Luke, although he did not fully acknowledge it until the end of therapy, months later, the experience of seeing his family in a new light had led to a lowering of his defences, and a new level of honesty about himself and how he related to Naomi. For Naomi, the effect of the family sessions was instantaneous. She sat entranced, with shining eyes, as Luke and I talked, and at the end of the sessions, said how it had helped her to understand what had made him the way he was. Their relationship certainly did not transform overnight, but gradually both Luke and Naomi were able to stop taking personally behaviour which had developed long before they met. Simultaneously, I had been working with both partners to normalize their differences, something that also contributed to a favourable outcome:

'Luke, you and I both know that Naomi is the sort of person who needs to talk as soon as she starts to feel upset. Talking is how she deals with her feelings, and finds out what they're really about. She's told you that often, she doesn't know what's going on until she starts to "get it out". Now for you, it's different, right? You'd keep your feelings inside and mull them over, and you'd consider whether or not it was a good time to raise an issue with Naomi. That works for you, and there's nothing wrong with that. But she can't be the same as you, and you can't be the same as her.'

Normalizing differences takes them out of the *moral* arena ('You act this way because you know it hurts me') and into the arena of facts that need to be accepted. This avoidance of moral labelling is one way that the couple therapist strives to avoid the language of blame and shame, which is so much a part of dysfunctional couple interactions (and parent-to-child interactions, as we'll see later in this book).

How we can help: 'translating'

Part of helping couples understand each other better is ensuring that the real messages get through, instead of being missed completely, or misinterpreted. I was originally trained, like most relationship therapists twenty-odd years ago, always to get couples to talk direct to one another, and not to 'speak for them'. Generally, I found that higher-functioning couples could benefit greatly from such 'encounters', but that where there was a lengthy history of misunderstanding and felt betrayal, couples were better served if I mediated and translated, at least until they had demonstrated their ability to 'let in' – at least some of the time – what their partner was saying.

> I listened as Naomi wound herself up into one of her lengthy, dramatic outpourings. I would wait until Naomi finished, and then check with her whether I'd understood the essence of what she was trying to get across. If she agreed with my (much shorter) statement of what she most wanted to convey, then I would turn to Luke and ask whether that was the message he had heard or not. Often, it was not. He had stopped listening long before, failing to see the gleam of hidden gold amidst the dense forest. Why didn't I simply turn to Luke and ask him first what he thought Naomi was trying to say? Because I'd already tried that, and rapidly discovered that he had heard so little that his 'paraphrase' of her message simply served to infuriate her, and strengthen her existing opinion that Luke 'didn't care enough about her to bother to listen to what was most important to her'.
>
> When I felt that Luke had started to accept – albeit reluctantly – that he often didn't listen to Naomi, and we'd started to explore why (the family-of-origin work described earlier) I began challenging Naomi to try to say what she wanted to say just once, rather than five or six times over, in different words each time. I had to interrupt her, quite often, and say things like 'OK, Naomi, have you said it? Can you stop there, and let's get a response from Luke?' Again, I am not suggesting that I'd have used such directness with every couple. I had this couple's goodwill, they were serious about wanting their relationship to improve, and they were prepared most of the time to do what I asked. After quite some time, Naomi proudly reported that she had been trying outside of sessions to 'just say it in one' instead of many times over. This was a major challenge for her, because she actually felt a kind of elation as she rode her wave of words, and had to trade this sense of empowerment for the different reward of hearing that Luke had actually listened to her.

Finally, a key 'translating' activity is to reword potentially hurtful or destructive statements so that they have some chance of being received as constructive, at least in intention. In a way, this is simply another aspect of the avoidance of blaming and moralizing. It has also been called 'reframing'. Whatever we call it, it involves believing in the innate goodwill of most people in relationships, and trying to find a form of words that will convey that goodwill. Thus Naomi's 'Every time you don't bother to listen, I wither and die like a flower without water' might be restated as 'Luke, you're so important to her that she doesn't feel properly alive if she doesn't feel she's got your full attention'. (Now I just cheated there, as that's not actually something I said to that couple! I probably said something not so well worded, but it still created a space for Luke to think about the positive implications of Naomi's message, not just the negatives ones.)

Of course, like any other intervention, translating of a negative into its implied positive can be overdone, and done mechanically and slickly. If it doesn't proceed from genuine feeling for the clients on your part, and genuine goodwill isn't there on their part, then don't do it at all! Otherwise, it may easily seem like a belittling of your clients' pain.

How we can help: focus on process, not content

Couples will typically enter therapy presenting themselves as 'stuck' in an impasse around immediate, relatively specific difficulties of some kind. Why won't he help more with the housework? Why does he shut himself away playing computer games instead of spending time with her? Why isn't she (occasionally he) more interested in sex? Why isn't he ready to have children yet? These topics invite the counsellor to get caught up in the details and 'arbitrate' or 'negotiate'. Of course it is necessary to establish the nature and scope of the difficulties they perceive, but really, what I always come back to is that if there were an obvious solution to such practical problems, then the couple would have found it themselves, without professional help. No, as always in such situations, what blocks the couple is something that exists at an emotional, not a practical, level, something unconscious or irrational, rather than something they can consciously access and think about.

So my job is to direct their attention away from the details of the situation and the surface irritation of not being able to solve the problem, and to focus instead on what the situation actually *means* to each of them.

> Helgi, a skilled tradesman who was also a sculptor, and Max, a social worker, had been in a relationship for 7 years; they experienced themselves as very different from one another, and had fought and wounded one another often, but stayed together. Now, after much urgent pleading from Max, Helgi had finally agreed to move in with him permanently, and to give up the old family home, which his parents left him, and to which he had a huge emotional attachment. However, he fretted over the fact that Max's home was too small and cramped to house all his prized possessions, including many of his own bulky sculptures. 'There isn't even a single room in Max's house that can just be my space,' he said. Max

insisted that he wanted Helgi to have his space, and not to feel cramped, yet had a cogent objection to every proposal he put. If Helgi took over the spare bedroom, there would be no place for his own antique wardrobe, to which he was very attached, and so on. In turn, Max had suggested that perhaps they should sell his home and buy a new one together, in which there would be spaces for both of them, but Helgi wouldn't hear of this, saying that he thought Max's existing house was 'beautiful' and he didn't see any need to leave it.

After listening to this ongoing wrangle for the second time, I began to see that it wasn't really about how much space there was for paintings or wardrobes, but about fears that this new step towards commitment (Helgi selling his family home) would result in both of them losing their identities, having to give up some key aspect of themselves, and consequently feeling trapped and suffocated. I said something to this effect, and there was an immediate sense of relief, even though nothing had been solved at a practical level. In subsequent sessions, the couple reported that they had solved the problem in a way neither had previously envisaged as possible, and it disappeared from the agenda – at least, in that form!

This is an example of how presenting a 'practical' problem can be a couple's way of letting us know what is going on at a deeper, partly unconscious, level. If we can get the message right, and 'translate' it back into the language of selfhood and relationship, this in itself may be felt as helpful. It is also possible, and often necessary, to simply 'step aside' from *what* the couple are saying (it gets easier and easier to do this, as couples typically repeat the content of unresolved issues again and again, so there is little risk in stopping listening for a minute or two) and draw the couple's attention to some aspect of *how* they are communicating.

> 'Kalliope, I'm noticing that every time you reply to Athena, you say, "Yes, but . . ." and then you produce something she's done wrong, or something you feel resentful about. Of course those issues are really important to you, and it's your right to deal with them, but you never get to acknowledge what Athena's actually saying to you. I wonder what you imagine might happen if you actually listen to her all the way through instead of cutting in on her?'

This is also a confrontation, of course, but it is rooted in an observation of *process*. Notice how careful you need to be to 'balance' the statement, so that it doesn't just seem to Kalliope as though I am taking her partner's side against her.

How we can help: highlight progress (sometimes!)

It is a piece of practice wisdom in all strategic and solution-focused therapies that couples who are deeply steeped in dysfunction and despair tend to miss the indicators of hope, progress and competence, and we will describe this in more detail in the chapters on family work.

There are times when all we have to do, as counsellors, is to draw attention to the couple's successes in a way that they will find hard to dismiss. Let's return to Helgi and Max – a good example of a couple where real, positive development easily gets overlooked. Max is so worried that Helgi will push him away, or fail to be interested in him, that if Helgi fails to respond instantly and enthusiastically to everything he says, Max's face falls and he concludes that Helgi can't be interested at all. Since Helgi's natural way is slow, cautious and quiet, he doesn't very often give the only kind of response that Max desires. So there are ample opportunities for this couple to get caught up in little, repetitive cycles of disappointment. The 'bigger picture' is that they have made substantial progress over several years, starting well before they commenced therapy. They told me early on that they now fight much less than they once did, and that the fights get resolved much sooner. Now they are progressing somewhat faster – although it doesn't always seem that way to them, because they have come into counselling and made themselves more vulnerable as a result. When something goes wrong (as it does at least once a session) I acknowledge how difficult and hurtful it is, but then acknowledge their overall progress. With this couple, I can do so in a straightforward way, simply reminding them of what they themselves have told me in the past.

On the other hand, I have encountered couples where every attempt I made to praise them for what they'd achieved, or to highlight the changes that had occurred, has been greeted with either a flat denial, or a relapse into gloominess, with reports of some new crisis. With such couples I learned – and it was a hard lesson, because it seemed entirely counter-intuitive – that it was vital *not* to draw attention to the positive developments that were happening, or to draw attention to them within a *negative* 'reframe'. I learned to ask worried questions like:

> 'If things continue to improve, won't you be anxious that something bad might happen? What do you think is the worst possibility?'

Or:

> 'Seems like you handled that fight differently from the way you've always done in the past. But I wonder if you'll start feeling pretty uncomfortable soon, if you keep doing this? After all, you've been

used to really hurting one another, and that way, at least you knew that you were having a real impact. But now you're actually treating each other with respect, so I'm wondering – maybe you won't be able to feel that you've had an impact on each other any more?'

These statements from the therapist may look like clever tricks using 'reverse psychology' (the way lay people refer to what systemic therapists once called 'paradoxical interventions'). Instead, I see such interventions as giving voice to the very real ambivalence about change that many couples and families feel. It is simply that instead of the clients 'acting out' the ambivalence they feel (but don't speak of out loud), the therapist voices the ambivalence for them. And as so often in interpersonal work, this seems to be another case where it is a relief to have something named openly, instead of concealed. Sometimes, the consequence is that energy is freed up for the couple to actually embrace the change they have half-dreaded previously.[5]

Psychodynamic therapists speak of how the therapist needs to be 'the ally of both sides' of the client's ambivalence: the wish to change, *and* the resistance to change, the conscious goals, and the unconscious fears that may sabotage them. First-generation systemic therapists spoke of a couple's or family's 'status quo maintaining mechanism' or 'tendency to homeostasis', which sucked them back towards the 'comfortable discomfort' they'd always lived in, even though they desperately wanted to climb out of the quagmire. However we may describe it, the concept is much the same. And the principle of therapeutic leverage is similar too: with some couples (and families, and work groups) we cannot just ally ourselves with the clients' declared wish to change for the better, and expect that simply 'reinforcing' their advances will be enough. We will need to position ourselves so that we can *genuinely* see the pain and risk of change, as well as the comfort and reliability of the clients' current state (that's why I call it 'comfortable discomfort'). To do this genuinely, rather than as a glib bit of used car salesmanship, we need to be deeply in touch with our own resistance to change in key relationships. As Sal Minuchin memorably said some thirty years ago:

> In the measure to which I have learned to accept myself and to recognise areas in which I will never change, I have developed a sense of respect for the diversity of people's approaches to human problems.[6]

How we can help: listen to our own feelings in the room

The most powerful kind of 'process' intervention is when we directly use our own feelings, in the room, as part of a statement to our clients. This type of intervention is variously called 'immediacy' (if you speak the language of counselling microskills), 'using the here and now' (Irvin Yalom's term), or 'using countertransference in the service of the patient' (if you follow the psychodynamic model). These terms don't all mean exactly the same thing, but they converge on the same area. To be able to use one's own feelings in the room in a way which is ethical, and also calm and free from anxiety on our part, again demands that we know ourselves well. This is where, once more, personal therapy is so important. It should enable us to distinguish between feelings that we often have towards many people (and which are rooted in our own histories and personalities), and feelings which come up in us unexpectedly, and only in response to particular clients.

If I normally have no difficulty in sitting quietly and simply 'following' a client, then I will immediately notice it if, with a particular couple, I rapidly start feeling as if I am being forced to take a back seat, and can hardly get into the interaction at all. This is likely to be *information about them, not about me*, and after I have carefully observed it for a time, usually over several sessions, to be sure that it is not just a product of their state on a particular day, I might say something like:

> 'Carol and Peter, I'd like to tell you about what's been happening inside of me as I've been listening to you talking over the past few sessions. I've noticed that I felt very much on the sidelines, as if I had to put all my energy into listening to you, and had nothing left to think with. That worried me, because unless I can think about what I'm feeling, I can't be much help to you. I've been wondering what this might mean, that I can't seem to find time for myself in our sessions, and that I come out of them feeling sort of used up and exhausted – which isn't at all how I normally feel after seeing a couple.'

As a statement simply about how I have experienced them, this may be of some use to them. They may get a shock to realize how they come across, and it may raise their awareness of how they communicate in the presence of others. On the other hand, they may be tempted to dismiss my statement as long as it is simply about me ('Oh, he must just like the sound of his own voice'). It is when I invite them to link my here-and-now feelings with theirs that this kind of intervention becomes more powerful:

> 'Does anything in what I've said have any meaning for either of you? Is this how you sometimes feel with each other?'

When the information from me gets 'fed back' into the couple system in this way, as potential information about them, it can lead to a dramatic shift of energy in the room.

> Carol and Peter both immediately acknowledged that they felt 'sidelined' by each other, and that there was no room in the relationship for what was most important to them. They had not been able to say so directly, but had crowded and attacked each other instead, out of desperation. This led Peter to start talking about how he had felt unheard and unvalued as a child, and that he often felt the same way with Carol.

Needless to say, such interventions must never be self-serving; we cannot afford to give such feedback simply as a way of 'getting back' at a couple who have irritated us. And the intervention needs to be delivered calmly and respectfully, so that it does not carry the message that our own irritation dominates our intention. This is what Murray Bowen calls the 'non-anxious presence'; a by-product of the 'differentiated self'. It is the same presence that, as we saw earlier, the counsellor needs to have when acknowledging a couple's anger and disappointment in the third session.

When the Counsellor brings *himself* into the interaction in this direct way, then in effect, he has temporarily increased the number of participants from two to three. Of course, there are always three people in the room, but the counsellor's role is to stand *outside* the couple's dyad. Now, for a few minutes, he joints in on an (almost) equal basis. As we've seen, the results can be dramatic.

And if we do all these things, what happens then?

I hope it will be clear by now that the different processes I've been describing ('deep understanding', 'translating', 'attending to signs of progress', focussing on process, and 'paying attention to what our own feelings are telling us') are not things to be done in a particular order, or to any formula. I might do all of these things in a single session, or only one or two of them. In general, I would tend to do a lot more of the first two in early sessions, and more of the last two once therapy is well under way. Some well-respected relationship counselling agencies actually 'map out' what the therapist should do in the first two sessions, what should have been achieved by the sixth, and so on. I simply try things out, and if they work, I continue to employ them; if they don't, I put them aside to try later, or conclude that they are not appropriate for this couple at all. And here is another principle of interpersonal work (indeed, of all counselling or therapy of any kind) perhaps the most important of all: *Your best guide to how to intervene is how your clients react to what you do. Pay close attention to the responses you get, and use this to guide you as to what to say or do more of, and less of. Throw away the textbook (including this one!) if following it gets you persistently negative or uncooperative responses, and concentrate on doing those things which seem to get the clients 'on your side'.*

Of course, like all generalizations, that one too has exceptions (we aren't doing our job properly if we simply support highly dysfunctional clients in their blindness to themselves and others). Sometimes, it may not be until we listen back to a tape of a couple session, or even transcribe segments of inter-action, that we become fully aware of the feedback that our clients are giving us about how they perceive our interventions. To proceed in this way may seem very disorganized. 'But where is the counselling plan?' one of my stu-dents asked in dismay. My answer to that is: a tapestry looks pretty messy from the 'wrong' side (the 'back' of the tapestry). And it doesn't look very pretty when it's only a quarter done.

In handloom weaving, a pattern or design gradually emerges as each strand of colour or texture is filled in. And that is exactly like what happens in couple work. Patiently following each thread for as long as the couple are prepared to engage with it, then switching to another, and following that. Filling in a bit of one colour, and then a bit of another. At first, it seems a bit random, a bit disorganized, as if it's not going anywhere in particular. And if you look at the weaving-in-progress from the back, rather than the front, it will seem messy (all those threads hanging down), disorganized and lacking in meaning. *This is how the work often seems to clients in the earlier part of therapy.* But then, as the weeks pass, the pattern begins to show: first, it is the pattern of the couple's existing relationship: its repeated impasses, assumptions, inter-actions, projections. And then, as trust deepens and the couple 'drop down' into greater levels of honesty with each other and themselves, the pattern begins to change.

Every now and then, the therapist may contribute a new colour, or a new thread. That is one way of describing it. But remember: no therapist can influ-ence the couple's evolving design unless the couple themselves allow that to happen – and they only allow it to happen *because their relationship already contains the potential* for incorporating that colour or that thread. The therapist does not 'impose' anything on the couple. The couple sift through what the therapist offers, and accept or reject it, depending on what their relationship already contains, for their current present relationship embodies a number of alternative 'futures'. We are simply allowing one to gain attention, rather than another.

'Trust the process', the first generation of Gestalt therapists used to say: it's true. When we as therapists relax enough to be open to what a couple are telling us, and open to what our own reactions are also telling us, and non-anxious enough to use this information in the service of the couple (instead of trying to fit them into some predetermined plan or pattern that we think they ought to follow), then the tapestry will weave itself, a little more each day, in the way it needs to unfold. And, unlike Penelope's in *The Odyssey*, the weaving won't mysteriously get unravelled again overnight.

Notes

1 Melanie Klein's own term for this comparatively 'mature' stage is 'the depressive position' – see her 1952 essay, 'Some theoretical conclusions regarding the emotional life of the infant' (Klein 1975: 61–93). The phrase has unfortunate pathologizing connotations (suggesting 'depression'). But the idea of the 'normal sadness' that comes from recognizing that magic does not happen in real life is a valid and useful one. Klein's own writing is somewhat daunting for those new to her ideas. I first came across it in the literary criticism of Holbrook (1973), and found his casual incorporation of the 'bad breast' and 'the infant's wish to bite and destroy its mother' exaggerated and disturbing in the context of a discussion of C.S. Lewis' children's books about Narnia! Some thirty years later, I am less scornful about Klein, and more prepared to admit that perhaps Holbrook was right, even though his analysis threatened my childhood love for the magical world of Narnia by showing up its primitive emotional underpinnings.

2 There are many other examples of the same process from the world outside therapy. Those interested in politics and war, for example, can see the three-stage sequence displayed in the opening phases of many wars (the classic example being the Great War of 1914–18) where early euphoria and magical hopes of a rapid victory are replaced with a grim realization of what is really going to be involved. See Crago (1999a).

3 Rogers' 'paraphrase rule' is explained in his book *On Becoming a Person: A Therapist's Guide to Psychotherapy* (1967): 332.

4 On genograms, the best general guide remains McGoldrick *et al.* (1999). This comprehensive, authoritative text is also very readable, particularly because the authors have used the families of the 'the bold and the beautiful' to illustrate their points. The genograms of the Kennedys, the Fondas, the Freuds, the Jungs and the Windsors make fascinating reading. There are, of course, other ways of eliciting and using family-of-origin data. See, for example, Hoang (2005). Another recent, very different approach to genogram work can be found in Hildebrand (2004).

   Those who are inclined to 'action methods' may want to train in Bert Hellinger's 'family constellation' method. An English-language introduction to Hellinger's ideas can be found in Hellinger *et al.* (1998). Essentially, Hellinger's method employs classic psychodramatic techniques (group members are selected by the protagonist to represent various members of her/his family of origin) to produce powerful insights and shifts of perception towards significant others, present and past. An introduction to the method can be found in Stieffel *et al.* (2002).

5 Paradoxical interventions arose out of the realization of early systemic therapists that repetitive, dysfunctional behaviour patterns can often be stopped

in their tracks by asking participants to consciously do what they would normally do unconsciously. The principle is exemplified in the limerick about the centipede, which had no trouble walking, until asked which of its many legs it put first, whereupon it became unable to move at all. Another example would be the case of male sexual impotence, where nothing is physically wrong, but the man fails to get an erection simply because he has become anxious about getting one, or keeping it. Hence the idea that if someone *consciously tries to do something* that is both 'problematic' and (normally) unconscious, they may well find themselves (paradoxically) unable to act in the 'dysfunctional' way, and so gain a sense that they do, after all, have some control over what had previously seemed frighteningly uncontrollable.

6   Minuchin (1974: 120).

4 Facing difference, finding unity
How therapy groups begin

Attachment

Eight adults sit uneasily in their plastic stack chairs, trying not to stare at each other. The one person they seem prepared to look at is me, the group leader. Several of them smile at me, trustingly. '*You* will know what to do!' their eyes seem to say, or, complicitly, 'Poor things, the rest of them don't know what they're in for, but you and I do!' One or two look wary or even challenging ('Don't think you're going to make *me* do anything I don't want to!'). In the initial phase of virtually every group, it is the leader who is the centre of attention.

This has very little to do with what the leader does or says. I could start off by giving a lecture, laying down rules for the group, showing a videotape, or engaging the group in a structured exercise. If a leader begins in one of these ways, the group will probably feel some sort of relief and reassurance, and will settle back to enjoy the show. They won't have to worry much about themselves, at least not until they are required to contribute to a discussion, or share some personal experience as part of an exercise. But they will expect the momentum to come from the leader, and they will start silently evaluating how she is doing.

If, on the other hand, I begin by saying, 'It's up to you how you use this time. You can make up your minds what you want to get out of this, and how you're going to proceed', then an extremely anxious silence will generally follow, punctuated by nervous giggles, and random attempts to 'get something going'. I will still be very much the focus of the group's attention. Everyone wonders 'why he isn't doing what he's supposed to be doing'. Eventually, nearly everyone starts to get irritated or even angry about my failure to 'give some direction' or 'make something happen'.

So, whether the leader 'leads' in an up-front way that conforms with people's expectations, or apparently abdicates leadership, requiring the group to create its own structure, the leader remains central to the way the group thinks and feels and acts at this stage. That is precisely why this phase of the group's evolution has been called 'dependency'.[1]

In other words, a newly formed group orients itself to, clings to and looks up to its leader, just as Konrad Lorenz's baby geese did. Once again, we are observing a form of *attachment*. What the group members have in common with the infants of any species is a feeling of helplessness and incompetence. As an infant looks to the 'big person' in its confusing, overwhelming world, so do the adult members of a therapy group look to the therapist or facilitator, the 'expert' who knows what is supposed to happen, the person with the 'experience' to guide them. Like infants, they expect protection, care and feeding – although of course, these things will take different forms for a group of adults from the forms they take in infancy. In a group, for example, the leader might be expected to 'feed' the group members by solving their problems, teaching them useful skills, or offering them kind and supportive comments. 'Protection' might take the form of the leader making sure that group members observe the rules, and keeping things safe.

But wait a minute! Surely the group members are all rational adults (albeit with a few problems!), and all that's really going on is that they are sitting in a room together and not quite sure what to expect? Isn't it a huge exaggeration to describe this situation as a 'confusing, overwhelming world' such as a new-born infant experiences? Well, yes, if we're talking about what the group members will *consciously* experience, but just look at the levels of anxiety in the room in those first minutes, and then, as the group session progresses, just look at the odd and not-at-all-rational ways that *the group as a whole* finds itself acting (we'll see examples of this later)! Below the level of conscious awareness, the group does indeed behave like a small child in an alien, frightening world, and at that level dependency on its leader becomes totally explicable.

Approach and avoidance

Of course, this is not the only thing that is going on. Apart from observing the leader, and generating powerful expectations of him or her, the group members are also *orienting themselves to one another*. They are checking one another out non-verbally ('Is there anyone else here my age?', 'He looks like a real weirdo – I hope this group isn't going to be full of crazy people!', 'I'm willing to bet I'm the only gay in the whole group'). If the group leader remains relatively silent, then group members will have many opportunities to carry the 'checking out' process further through exploratory talking. Much of this talking may seem random or purposeless, even frustrating, to an outside observer, but group members are trying hard to offer 'safe' clues to who they are, and to deduce, from other group members' equally 'safe' disclosures, who they are going to feel comfortable around, and who they are going to avoid.

Jacob Moreno, founder of psychodrama, and a pioneer of group work in the early part of the twentieth century, would say that group members probably already 'know' who is safe and unsafe for them, even *before* the first group session begins. When they choose whom to sit next to (of course, for those who arrive later, this choice may be limited), Moreno maintained that these choices were dictated by gut-level awareness of individuals who seem 'sort of OK' and those who feel 'sort of risky', even an unconscious awareness of who resonates with their own emotional issues.[2] Every tutor and group facilitator knows that if she sits down first, the seats on either side of her will be avoided until there are no more left to take. The 'leader' is not perceived (initially) as 'safe' to sit next to (although, paradoxically, she will be expected to provide safety for others). Attachment will be demonstrated through 'proximity seeking' only later, when the group has achieved cohesion. Then, when something upsetting happens in the group, members may seek out the leader after the session, and attempt to engage him or her in an effort to quiet their anxiety.

Just as group members, consciously or unconsciously, attempt to identify other group members who might be 'simpatico', and keep their distance from those they feel instinctively uncomfortable with, so what they choose to say, at this stage, is dictated mainly by considerations of acceptability ('If I say this, people won't think I'm dumb'). This careful, risk-avoiding behaviour stems from the same source as the 'attachment' behaviour we noted earlier towards the leader. If the leader doesn't provide any obvious feedback on what it is 'right' to say, or rule anything 'out of order', then the group members must look *to each other* to provide that source of authority, and of course this is not an easy or comfortable process.

The hallmark of this phase is uneasiness, a search for common ground, and a desperate avoidance of conflict and difference. One member will raise a topic (generally of a fairly safe nature) and one or two others may respond, offering similar opinions, or relating similar experiences. Then the group will temporarily fall silent. These silences usually only last for seconds, a minute or two at the longest, but to group members they seem interminable and unendurable. This exemplifies the dependent, infant-like state that beginning groups seem to experience. If you ask group members later how long the silences lasted, they will often say 'Oh, for ever' or 'Nobody said anything for about fifteen minutes – it was just awful!' This is directly parallel with the experience of a baby, who has no concept of time, and to whom any painful or distressing state seems to be endless.

The group's first phase is a bit like a couple's first date. Two adults have to find out some basic things about each other, to establish how trustworthy each seems, and to find, by trial and error, topics of conversation which will involve both sufficiently for them to learn without too much risk the things they need to learn about each other. If they start to feel strongly attracted, each will have hopes and fears. Each will seize on any evidence that their partner shares their interests. Neither will be too keen to see evidence that their partner may not always conform to their hopes, or that what appears to be held in common may in fact be largely illusory. The disillusionment, as we saw in Chapter 2, will come later. Similarly with the group. Even though the purpose of the group is nothing to do with sexual attraction, the group members still follow a broadly similar path to the couple, checking each other out, trying to find subjects that will enable them to find out what they need to know, investing each other with hopes, and becoming anxious if it begins to seem that some of their fears, too, may be realized.

'Us' and 'them'

Generally speaking, those group members who have the least ability to tolerate silence and discomfort will be the ones to break the silence, and offer some other contribution which (they desperately hope) will 'get things going'. These group members will rapidly establish an (initially unspoken, but clearly felt) reputation in the group as 'the talkers' or 'the confident ones', and quieter group members begin to look to them to 'give a lead' or 'get us started'. In other words, these members get 'elected' by the group as 'unofficial leaders'. The leadership vacuum, left by the official leader's 'abdication' is rapidly, if temporarily, filled, *because the group needs it to be filled*. In the absence of a proper mother goose, even an adult male human will do for baby geese. So too, in the absence of a 'proper leader' who will 'feed' and 'protect' them, will group members 'attach' to whoever seems capable of fulfilling at least some of their needs, however imperfectly.

Typically, one of the 'anxious talkers' will explicitly suggest what the group should do. 'Why don't we go around the group and all say something about ourselves, to break the ice?' or 'How about everyone call out their ideas and I'll write them up on the whiteboard?'. Interestingly enough, however, *it is rarely possible for the group to actually follow these suggestions in any consistent or useful way*. A few people will nod, or indicate agreement, but usually nothing happens. Those who have been silent remain silent, and nobody feels able to ask them what they think (which breaks a social norm). In fact, some will disagree with the 'leaders', but they will not reveal this difference from those who have spoken. Difference is *suppressed*. So the 'plans' are not followed up, and uneasy silence recurs, only to be broken by another 'anxious talker' who proposes something different. Each time a new topic is raised, there is the (unvoiced) hope that 'this might unite the group'. The feeling of being united is called 'cohesion' in the language of group theory. It is the same powerful instinct for 'togetherness' that people feel in families (so much so that even when things in a family are unhappy or abusive, children typically cling to siblings and parents and do not want to be parted from them).

Occasionally, something more dramatic happens in this first phase. Sometimes one group member will launch into some story of personal pain or trauma that goes well beyond the safe, social level on which most of the group's conversation has so far been conducted. Often, this member will have had experience in other groups (where perhaps deep disclosure has been the norm), or is someone with little sense of social appropriateness, and undeveloped personal boundaries (a common consequence of violation of boundaries in early childhood). Such individuals may react to the high level of anxiety in the group by feeling driven to 'offer themselves' for the group's benefit, as a sort of sacrifice. Or, they may see early self-disclosure as a way to claim the group's attention and receive sympathy and support. Both may be true simultaneously.

Whatever the underlying reason, too early self-disclosure is generally unproductive for groups. It sends anxieties skyrocketing, and creates fears that 'the group is all going to be like this'. As I'll explain shortly, it is one of the leader's tasks in this phase to 'rein in' such anxiety-provoking events, so that they can occur later, when the group has reached a higher level of cohesion and empathy. (Is there a couple equivalent of 'premature self-disclosure?' Mostly not. In my experience, the established dyadic relationship seems to prevent either partner being so much 'out of step' with the other. The two partners may be very different in their level of early self-disclosure, yet in a curious way, the apparent reticence and withholding of the one will 'balance' the apparent vulnerability and openness of the other, so that neither actually 'rocks the boat' too dramatically.)

Being a good-enough mother goose: the first phase

In all of what I've said so far, I've been assuming that the official leader has 'sat back' and allowed the group members to find their own direction. The great value in looking at this scenario first is that it reveals the instinctive, unconscious reactions of group members much more clearly than if the leader provides structure and direction (we'll be discussing that scenario shortly). But even though the leader may not 'lead' in the way that group members expect, she can still do quite a bit to help the group along. Carl Rogers' word for group leader was 'facilitator', meaning 'a person who makes things easier'.[3] Here are some of the things I would personally expect to do in the first session (and sometimes in the second and third, too) to make things easier:

- Comment openly on how difficult the process is, how uneasy people feel, and how frustrating it is when things don't get going smoothly (*naming of here-and-now emotions*).
- Invite group members to think and talk about what makes it so

difficult, including feelings of irritation or even anger that I, the 'official leader', am not providing what the group needs (*modelling openness to feedback and negative feelings*).

- Tolerate, and react non-defensively to, demands from the group that I 'give them something to do' (*being 'non-anxious' in the face of anxiety*).
- Contain and minimize deep self-disclosures (*providing safety, by showing that I know how much the group can tolerate at this phase*).
- Indicate, by my general calmness and gentleness, that I don't share the group's high level of anxiety, and confidently expect that the group will in time evolve to a more productive stage (*again, being a 'non-anxious presence'*).

I don't expect that the group will respond directly to any of these initiatives. At this stage, it's more likely that they will be ignored. But at some level, I think that group members are reassured by how I act, even if only at a very basic level: 'We're all flapping around, but he's sitting still and he doesn't seem worried!' When people are anxious, the presence of someone who is much less anxious generally helps to calm things down.

If I can do these things reasonably competently, and not rush in and 'rescue' the group from its frustration and confusion, the group will start the difficult process of *taking responsibility for itself*. This is crucial, because it establishes right from the start that the leader is not going to simply nurture group members (at least, not in the way they expect), is not going to solve their problems (at least, not directly), but instead will expect them to take risks, put themselves forward, and participate actively in whatever work they want to do. In other words, they will need to be 'adults', not 'children'.

The group should also begin to get a sense of 'belonging together' ('cohesion'), if only in response to my frustrating and disappointing failure to 'lead'! Part of the frustration that group members feel in the first phase is that their accustomed ways of making contact with other people, and getting things done, seem not to be working so well in this new environment. Some group members may already have a sense that a different type of conversation is required, one that is less 'social', and more 'honest'. But at this early stage few, if any, group members will really feel ready for this. Even if one or two are prepared to 'go there', they will find it impossible to do so on their own. The group as a whole cannot progress towards this more 'advanced' behaviour until a critical mass of group members is ready to do so.[4]

This is one demonstration of a key principle: *a group is not just a collection of individuals (although group members will at least initially behave as if it is); it is an entity, a 'being' in its own right, and it will evolve its own patterns of behaviour, which may run counter to the behaviour of some individuals within it.* The 'early self-disclosure' which we mentioned above is a good example of this principle. You might imagine that this group member's action might 'model' self-disclosure for the rest of the group, and help others to respond similarly, thus taking the group to a deeper level overall. Later in the group's life, this will indeed be the case, but at this stage it rarely happens. Instead, the disclosure is greeted with frozen silence, or uncomfortable mutters of sympathy, or frenzied advice-giving, even though the self-discloser has not actually asked for help of any kind. Often, the session then starts up again as if nothing has happened, and nobody refers back to the episode at all. The group has not proved able to benefit from that one member's behaviour because the majority of its members have not yet established sufficient trust in the group as a whole, or felt sufficiently safe with the leader and with each other.

Interestingly enough, one of the key ways that groups evolve beyond the superficial level is through the open acknowledgement of differences. It seems that only when a conflict has been 'faced up to' can the group start to experience itself as a safe place. Facing up to differences risks conflict and pain, but risk-taking deepens trust. And the surfacing of conflict and difference is the 'work' of the second phase of the group's early development, even though the conflicts may only emerge briefly and not be fully resolved or fully understood. (Returning briefly to the couple context, some couples simply cannot tolerate the emergence of differences and conflicts between them, and actually split up as they enter the phase of 'disenchantment' which corresponds with this second stage of the group's early development. Rather than 'fight', they choose 'flight', and the same thing may happen to one or two new group members too. Sensing the beginning of a rough patch, they may drop out, or simply miss the next session in the hope that everything will be back on a more even keel when they return.)

Adolescent rebellion

This second phase can start as early as the second group meeting (occasionally, but rarely, it starts towards the end of the first). Some groups may spend several meetings in an extended 'first phase', still trying to feel cohesive 'the safe way' and getting increasingly frustrated in the process, until eventually the tension spills over into open conflict. Some groups show the conflict only mildly and in relatively passive ways. But it is always there. In an unstructured group, the second phase often revolves around the need for leadership. Typically, one or two members of the group get up the courage to be openly critical of, or aggressive towards, the leader. 'How can we get anywhere if you won't *do anything*?', 'What are you trying to do to us? Is this some sort of *experiment*?', 'Look, you're the "expert", we're the ones with the problems, but you're expecting *us* to solve it all ourselves!'

Often, though, the leader seems too risky a target for direct aggression. Instead, group members get mad at one another. Group theory says that this 'means' that they are really attacking the leader, but indirectly – for example, through focusing their negativity on group members who have taken the 'unofficial leader' role. Perhaps it would be more accurate to say that the real target is 'the leadership', whoever may be doing it. This targeting can take several forms. Sometimes, two 'leader' contenders may clash, each being critical of the other's approach or ideas ('Why do you keep imposing your ideas on the rest of us?'). Sometimes, the 'talkers' will complain about the 'non-talkers', indicating that they are not pulling their weight, or should contribute more. It is rarely possible at this stage for the anxious talkers to admit that lack of response from the 'quiet ones' fuels their own paranoia about how they may be being received by the rest of the group. (Anxious talkers are the group's 'pursuers' and 'The quiet ones' play the 'distancer' role.)

Sometimes one or more of the 'quiet ones' will retaliate, with unexpected bitterness, claiming that 'You guys keep on talking all the time and we can never get a word in. By the time there's a silence, everyone's already said what we were going to say and there's no point.' Few of them are ready to admit that, in fact, they sometimes feel relieved when the talkers spare them the limelight. Whatever form it takes, the second phase shows the group temporarily fragmenting, conflicted, and openly frustrated. It is as if the veneer of civilized conformism that governed the first phase has suddenly shattered, revealing quite primitive feelings underneath – a kind of *Lord of the Flies* scenario.

Of course, it need not be nearly as dramatic as the description I've just given. Many groups go through the second phase without too many fireworks, the aggression only leaking out in the form of sarcastic jokes or mild innuendoes, which can rapidly be denied if anyone challenges them ('Oh, I was just having a bit of fun . . . you're reading far too much into it!'). Attacks on the leader can be hinted at rather than overt ('Isn't it funny that nobody chooses the seat next to the him!'). But in all of this there is something slightly forced or self-conscious. The open or veiled aggression towards the leader (the 'parent figure' of the group), the sudden appearance of conflict instead of polite conformity – all of this reminds us of teenagers, keen to prove how grown up they are, while secretly still wanting and needing their parents' approval. This is not 'independence' – it is a *counter-dependency*, a *reactive* stance that is only temporary, but still quite stressful for all concerned.

Although group theory tends to focus on 'conflict' and 'storming' in discussing the counter-dependency phase, I suspect that 'acknowledging difference' is a more fundamental theme. If groups continued in the first phase, group members would continue to conceal their judgements of one another, ignore their wary or hostile feelings towards one another, and pretend that they had much more in common than in fact they did. This would mean that the group would never get beyond the superficial level of sharing ('the nail polish stage'). The counter-dependency phase must occur, in some form or other, if the group is to 'get real'. Sooner or later, group members must learn to be open about their less positive reactions to one another, if they are ever to achieve the kind of meaningful, honest communication that therapy groups, when they function well, should provide – a strong and very nourishing corrective to the pathetic 'niceness' or 'dirty' anger that most of us adopt in our normal social interactions.[5]

In this second phase of the group, the airing of differences and the open acknowledgement of conflict can be difficult, raw and even a bit hurtful, because group members have not yet achieved the level of cohesion and trust they need to deal well with such things. What is said may come across as critical or judgemental. But it will get easier later on. At this stage, the important thing is that the group should realize that conflict and difference can be survived – they are uncomfortable, but they will not destroy the group.

During this vital phase, there is not all that much (of a proactive nature) that the leader needs to do. However, there are definitely things that a leader should *not* do. Parents who feel deeply wounded by their teenagers' attacks, or who become furiously angry at their kids' 'ingratitude' – or, worse still, ignore it – often find that the aggressive behaviour simply escalates. Like good parents of teenagers, good group leaders must take their clients seriously, but not too personally, recognizing (but not saying) that this has more to do with the young people's developmental needs than with *them*. What generally works well for me at this stage of a group is to:

- Acknowledge the real feelings involved in the attack ('It must be just so frustrating when I don't behave the way you expect', 'I guess that when I just sit here without taking over, it might even feel like nobody is in charge, and anything might happen').
- Comment positively on the new behaviour that group members are displaying ('I'm noticing that several of you are a lot more up-front with each other than you were last week. Maybe you want to see what it feels like to be more honest in the group').
- Frame conflicts neutrally and non-judgementally ('When the two of you told the "quiet ones" that they got on your nerves, you were making it possible for the group to have an open discussion about these differences. And when the quiet ones said that they felt that their contributions got left out, they were giving you valuable information about how they feel in here. So there's a lot more clarity about what's really going on than there was last week').
- Recognize that conflicts cannot always be resolved straight away ('Right now it's upsetting that you and Mary've had a strong difference of opinion, and you haven't been able to resolve it').
- Make sure, when something strong or dramatic happens, that I ask all group members (including those who may not have spoken at all so far) to say how the event has affected them. This is particularly

important because it shows the group that a conflict is not just the 'property' of the two or three members directly involved, but that the way it touches others is equally important. It is not a 'play' that happens in front of an 'audience', who can keep their strong reactions safely to themselves: it involves everybody, and everybody can contribute something to it, and learn something from it. This sets an early precedent for what will occur much more often, and in more depth, in the group's maturity.

Just as in the group's 'childhood' phase, what seems to count most in the 'counter-dependent' or 'adolescent' phase of the group is that the leader can remain relatively non-anxious. Regardless of what I say, or don't say, I think my ability to remain calm is crucial. If I don't seem too alarmed, this provides some measure of 'baseline security' for the group members. If I display a level of tension comparable to theirs, then I feed the group's anxiety, and things either get worse or get stuck.[6] My calm behaviour *normalizes* what they are feeling: it is to be expected; it will pass.

The group grows up

If I can stay calm, and do at least some of the facilitative things listed above, I generally find that the 'counter-dependency' phase is shortlived. As early as the group's third meeting, sometimes, things have settled down. When a group member initiates something, she/he is more likely to get acknowledgment and follow-up from other members. Silences are less prevalent, and if they occur, less dire. Now that differences have come out into the open, they seem less threatening. A higher proportion of group members are now participating, although there are likely to be one or two who still aren't. There is a sense that the group is 'pulling together', and, oddly enough, the conflicts of the previous week seem to have brought members closer, rather than ripped them apart.

Just like a couple, groups rapidly develop a 'shared history', and a shared history of struggle can serve to bond members more strongly even than shared experience of good times. Now the group is 'really a group', and members will mark this by referring to 'our group' and 'the group' in a way they did not do before. Above all, the group now begins to have confidence in its own ability to do things without its leader's 'permission' or instruction – *independence*, rather than counter-dependence. This can be quite exhilarating. Group members begin to monitor their own progress: 'I think more of us talked today than ever before', 'I noticed that we seemed to get a bit deeper today'. They do not require me to *tell* them how they are doing. They are starting to 'feed' and 'care for' each other.

Paradoxically, the group also begins to take *more* notice of what I say! In the 'dependency' phase, group members might hang on my words, but then be unable to 'use' them. In the counter-dependency phase, group members might openly dismiss my remarks, or openly disagree with them. Now, it's as if I have joined the group – I have earned the right to participate in group discussion, and to offer interpretations or comments on members' behaviour, which will on the whole be respected and valued (though not automatically agreed with or complied with). In family terms, it is as if group members have 'grown up' enough to now have an 'adult-to-adult' discussion with their parents, seeing them as 'people' rather than solely as 'dad' or 'mum'.

Of course no group can really 'become adult' in just three or four sessions. The reality is that groups take many sessions to become fully mature, and there are several things that may cause them temporarily to fall back ('regress') to earlier phases (something we'll deal with in the next chapter). But in these first few sessions, unless something goes badly wrong, most groups will indeed go through a 'condensed evolution' from infancy to (tentative) adulthood. It is a process that will then be repeated and worked through more fully and slowly throughout the life of the group, but these first sessions provide an essential foundation. My rule of thumb is: if I can get a group through to the third phase at roughly the right time, then, barring accidents, the group will probably continue to evolve in a healthy, productive way thereafter. If the group gets 'stuck' in either dependency, or counter-dependency for too long, then we are in for trouble!

Once they reach 'adulthood' or 'independence', most groups can begin to sustain proper self-disclosure, and self-disclosure is the necessary prerequisite not only for deeper trust to develop between members, but also for 'here-and-now' interactions and the giving of constructive but honest feedback (see the next chapter). Group members have given up on trying to be 'just social' with each other, they have recognized that differences exist, and they have tested the group's strength in a 'trial' conflict. They have begun to experience trust in each other, in the leader and in 'the process'. They are ready to *work*.

So what happens when the leader provides more structure?

I am very aware that so far I have described a fairly confronting way of conducting a group's first few sessions. The unstructured model is suited to participants who are coping well with most aspects of their lives, and who are not in major crisis. It is particularly useful for trainee counsellors, who need to learn first hand how to be vulnerable (and cope with the vulnerability of others) in an anxiety-provoking environment. It is *unsuited* for participants with mental illnesses, and usually also for those who are intensely anxious or depressed, so sunk in their own misery that they cannot fruitfully interact with others. Most new group workers will probably opt for a less anxiety-provoking model, in which the leader will 'lead' in a more overt manner, providing the sort of structure that most participants naturally expect. And indeed, if a group is to consist of people who have never been in a therapeutic group before, and may not even particularly want to be there, then this structured group is the appropriate choice.

An example might be a group of parents who have for various reasons had their children removed from their care, and who have been told that they are more likely to get their kids back if they participate in a 'better parenting' group. These parents are officially voluntary participants, but they may well feel that they have little choice. Their motives for attending the group are likely to be pragmatic, and personal awareness and self-development are not likely to be high priorities for most of them. To subject such a group to the confronting model described so far in this chapter would be to risk high-intensity conflict at a very early stage, and, almost certainly, a high drop-out rate. In groups with semi-voluntary or involuntary participation, and psychologically unsophisticated membership, the development of a feeling of safety and trust can take a long time, and feelings of fragmentation are never far from the surface. In such circumstances, a more up-front leadership profile, at least until the group is well established, makes every kind of sense.

However, as I've already anticipated, even groups where leaders decide to initiate activities and run the group according to a preset programme of information-giving, discussion and activities (the 'psychoeducational' group), *still go through the stages outlined above*, at least in truncated form. Let me give some examples of how the stages might unfold in this type of group.

Let's imagine that the leader kicks off the first session with a short informational talk, or the showing of an informational videotape, and then invites some discussion. Who will respond to the invitation? Probably, the same group members who would tentatively have initiated proceedings had the leader sat back and invited the group itself to start. To be sure, these 'unofficial leaders' will contribute with more confidence, since we all learn in school how to respond to what a teacher has just presented. They will experience less anxiety, and the group as a whole will relax, sensing that things are happening in more or less the way they expected. But the 'quiet ones' will still, on the whole, remain quiet, and take little or no part in the discussion. And the whole group will still be 'checking out' the contributions from the 'talkers' to see what common ground there is, and to get a sense of similarities and differences (although these will matter a lot less if the group is never going to evolve into a free-flowing, participant-initiated format).

The group will still be deferential to the leader, and those members who do contribute will be unlikely (at this early stage) to offer opinions which directly oppose the leader's, unless a very direct challenge to members' values has been posed by the leader's initial presentation. The group will still avoid conflict, and attempt to orient itself to norms of behaviour – but these norms will be based on how the *leader* is behaving, and what the *leader* seems to want. The group will pay close attention to how the leader responds to each contribution – are some members' comments greeted with more interest or enthusiasm than others? Does the leader seem to 'favour' some members already, above others? How is the leader dressed? What does she reveal about herself and her values? All of these things will be preoccupations for group members at the early stage. Members who sense that their opinions might not find favour with the leader will suppress those opinions and feelings. Members who identify easily with the leader, and sense common ground with her, will speak up more readily, and disclose more of themselves.

So most of the behaviours we saw as typifying the 'dependency' phase of the group will still be in evidence. The level of comfort will be much higher, because the leader is shouldering more of the burden of responsibility for 'how well it all goes'. But by the same token, the leader will still attract powerful expectations that she will provide safety, care and nurturing, and these expectations will be *strengthened* by the leader's overt assumption of the 'parent' role. By contrast, in the unstructured group, the leader will attract more anger and disappointment from early on, because group members' needs for care, security and 'feeding' are not obviously being met.

Now, it would be natural to think that if a group leader provides structure and focus in the first session, and continues to do so in subsequent sessions, then the group would simply run smoothly in 'dependency mode', and never enter the phase of counter-dependence. And sometimes, this is indeed the case. Yet much more often there are distinct signs that the group is still undergoing a 'rebellion' of sorts, even though it may be less obvious and dramatic than in an unstructured group. As early as the second group meeting, and certainly by the third meeting, someone will directly challenge the leader's authority. Lecture material, a video presentation, or a structured exercise – whatever the leader has been offering to the group will suddenly be challenged. This is especially likely to occur in the case of a 'semi-voluntary' group, as exemplified above, where participants feel 'forced' to attend and are likely to come into the group with an attitude of distrust and resentment. In cases like this, direct challenge from one or two members may start as early as the first session, though it is unlikely that the entire group will join in until later:

> 'Well I don't know about all this stuff you've been showing us. I don't think the parents in that video would know anything about what it feels like to be in our situation.'

'I've been in groups before, and you welfare Johnnies all seem to take the same line. There's a lot of stuff about understanding and empathy, but what I want to know is, what about discipline, eh?'

'Look, nothing personal, but aren't you very young to be telling us what we should be doing in our own homes? With respect, have you ever been married? Do you have kids?'

These challenging statements are really no different from those we noted in discussing the 'counter-dependent' phase of the unstructured group experience. The leader is still being attacked, although typically the 'attack' is on the *content* or *values* with which the leader has tacitly associated herself, rather than with her leadership style *per se*. The third comment listed above does focus on the leader's personal qualities (in a fashion) but not her leadership style as such. Similarly, group members may still confront one another, but these confrontations are more likely to be focused on issues than on personalities:

'I can't agree with what Colin's just said. To me, that's totally wrong, to say that women never "ask for it". Of course they do! And anyone who pretends they don't is just bullshitting!'

So the first and the second phases of the group's development still occur: but because *content* is interposed between leader and group, and between group member and group member, disagreements about content will 'mask' more primitive encounters of personality, and the underlying dynamics of the group are less obvious. If the aim of the group is for participants simply to be exposed to educational material, with the expectation that they will somehow apply it to their own lives and relationships, then this need not matter all that much. Some group members will be greatly affected by what is presented, and others affected very little, or not at all. A skilful presenter will be able to widen the number of those affected, but that is as far as a leader's influence will probably extend. But where the aim of the group is for participants to operationalize the new ideas presented in the group, in the form of actual changes to their behaviour and attitudes, then a structured, leader-dominated group may fail, because it does not tap into the most powerful source of lasting change: the influence of other group members, gained through ongoing, honest working through of the similarities and differences between them. (Similarly, couples who have felt safe enough to face their differences and be honest about their conflicts are likely to end up with a more enriching relationship than those who have avoided this task, and focused instead on the 'out there' tasks of career or childrearing alone.)

Thus, typically, the leader-structured group will progress through the first two phases, but do so in a more comfortable (because more predictable) and less impactful way. Despite this, how the leader handles the group in these phases will still make a marked difference. For example, a structured group in the 'dependent' phase may be assisted if the leader:

- keeps her own presentation of educational material to less than half of the group time, and actively encourages group members to respond to whatever has been presented (a common fault in new group workers is to prepare far too much material, and then spend most of the session 'getting through it', to the detriment of thorough processing and discussion);
- welcomes all contributions and finds something constructive to say about them, regardless of how close they are to her own opinions, or how closely they stick to the 'manual' or preset programme of topics;
- refuses to fall into the common trap of engaging in more and more discussion with a few 'vocal' group members, ignoring the rest (instead, I specifically invite contributions from everyone by going around the group in turn and asking for a quick response from all).

Similarly, when the group begins to show signs of open aggression, it can be very useful for the leader to:

- respond non-defensively to any direct criticism of her ideas or the material she has presented to the group ('I'm glad you feel able to disagree with what was in the video, Krish. That helps other people in the group to feel free to express whatever they think');
- make it clear that while differences of opinion are welcomed, group members must express them in a way which is respectful of each other, and not destructive or disparaging;
- respond empathically and reasonably to attacks based on her age, gender, ethnic background, or professional status ('Yes, well, I can appreciate that it might be quite hard to have someone half your age teaching you about families and relationships. What do other people think?');
- recognize the level of frustration in the group, even if it has not been openly expressed ('We've been looking at some pretty challenging ideas here, and I'm guessing that a lot of you've actually found some of it a bit hard to take, but been too polite to tell me so. Would that be right?').

Much of this, clearly, is very similar to the way the leader would respond in the unstructured group scenario presented earlier in this chapter. In the structured group, I tend to speak more in terms of the 'challenge' or 'difficulty' of the content, and my remarks might refer less to the personality clashes or emotional tensions present. But I would still make a brief acknowledgement of the latter, as if to let the group know that I understand what is going on at a deeper level, even if I am not expecting them to address it directly.

I also find it helpful, in conducting a structured group, to *gradually wind back my own contribution as the group progresses*, session by session taking a less and less overt leadership role, encouraging group members to bring in material or experiences for the group to examine and discuss (rather than seeing myself as the sole provider of these), reducing my own contribution so that I become a facilitator of the group's discussions rather than a 'teacher' or 'expert presenter'. Groups generally find it much easier to cope with this gradual withdrawal from overt leadership, than with the model described in the earlier part of this chapter. And with patience and skill, it can still be possible to get group members to some level of responsible self-disclosure by the latter part of the group's life.

In my experience, it takes a shorter time for a leader-structured group to reach a reasonably non-anxious, reasonably 'open' working stage than it does an unstructured group, especially if the leader employs well-chosen 'warm-up' exercises as a prelude to each session.[7] But this has a cost. Because the group has not had to take responsibility for its own learning, and because the group has not been required to deal with conflict and difference so directly, the level of self-disclosure and interpersonal honesty that it will subsequently be capable of will be considerably less. And so, in turn, the possibilities for true, lasting change in group members will be limited.

What always amazes me about groups is the predictability of their evolution through the early phases, whether the group's 'life' is limited to a single day, or extends over many months. If the group is to meet weekly over a year, the dependency phase may last several sessions, and so may the counter-dependency phase. It is almost as if groups 'know' unconsciously that they can afford to spend a long time in a given phase, or, conversely, that they must transact the first few phases rapidly in order to get something achieved within the 'lifetime' they have been allowed.

Moreover, attentive readers will by now have realized that these same three phases of the group's life correspond quite closely with the first three sessions I described in couple work. In other words, groups, like couples and families, must progress from a state of childlike dependency (including magical expectations of the leader/therapist) through 'disenchantment' (counter-dependency), to 'mature acceptance'. Groups, like couples, must come to the realization that pain, routine and effort are necessary in order to achieve something worthwhile. Those who are not ready to come to terms with this will drop out of the group (just as couples will drop out just before, or just after, the third session because they are not yet ready to transcend either the wish for magic, or the need for angry revenge).

Now, equipped with a map of how groups naturally and instinctively evolve through their opening phases, it is time to take a closer look at how we can use the therapeutic leverage that a mature group provides: the 'power of many'.

Notes

1   'Dependency' is Bennis and Shepherd's (1956) term for this first phase of a group's normal development, followed by 'counter-dependency' and 'independence'. Bion (1961), following the developmental schema of Melanie Klein (see Chapter 3), saw groups evolving through several different 'basic assumption' behaviours, towards an equivalent of the 'depressive position', where the group was capable of working together in a mature way, with realistic expectations and the ability to be creative and nurturing of one another. Bion's own writing is complex and difficult. A clearly-explained introduction to Bion's theory can be found in Stokes (1994).

2   On group members' choice of who to sit next to, see Moreno (1953). Moreno's major works were all essentially self-published for a captive audience of psychodrama trainees, leading to a good deal of repetition. Yet despite some disorganization and self-indulgence, Moreno's work was far ahead of its time, and its principles remain largely relevant today. A readable contemporary introduction to Moreno's psychodrama can be found in Antony Williams (1989). Seating positions, once taken, tend to dictate behaviour. We feel more common ground with the person we sit next to (even if we dislike him/her) than we do with someone we sit opposite (the 'confrontation position'). Warming up the group so that people end up with different seating positions than usual can 'throw the cards in the air' in a useful way and disrupt these patterns.

3   Rogers first used the term 'facilitation' in the title of his paper 'Communication: its blocking and facilitation' (1952). He later specifically employed the term 'facilitator' for group leaders (see Rogers 1970).

4   For a vivid description of how an unstructured group feels from the group member's point of view, see Tennenbaum (1967).

5   By 'pathetic niceness', I mean the kind of automatic social manner that many people adopt in their daily interactions with acquaintances (though not necessarily with intimates). This means that they will reply 'I'm pretty good, thanks' to the question, 'How are you today?', and pretend to be interested in others' concerns when in fact we're not. 'Dirty anger' is the counterbalance to this kind of niceness: a sudden shift into bitterness or accusation after weeks or months of 'being nice' and ignoring real causes of frustration or irritation. One of the things that group therapy can do is to assist participants to try out a way of relating to others that is more authentic than 'niceness' and less punitive

and unfair than 'dirty anger', to voice what they feel at the time (instead of stewing on negative feelings), and to give positive feedback to others only when they genuinely feel it, not in order to 'save face' for the other person.

6   But what if you *do* feel nervous? It is natural that new group leaders will feel some degree of anxiety in response to the group's uncertainty and search for 'someone to blame'. There's nothing wrong with feeling nervous in itself. However, remember that, provided you behave calmly, the group will probably be calmed by your manner, whatever you may be feeling inside. They *need* you to appear in control, and so they will react accordingly.

7   Unfortunately, there proved to be insufficient space within this short book to deal adequately with how warm-ups should be used with groups. Jacob Moreno developed a comprehensive theory of 'warm-up' which went far beyond the superficial notion embodied in the current term, 'icebreaker'. It is not simply that interpersonal 'ice' needs to be 'broken' for people to interact; rather, preliminary exercises should aim specifically to prepare participants mentally, emotionally, and sometimes physically, for the nature of the 'work' they will engage in for the remainder of the session. Thus warm-ups need to be selected for appropriateness to the issues being dealt with, the nature of the participants, and the stage the group has reached, so that at each stage the warm-up feels like a gentle challenge to group members to move just a little further 'out of their comfort zone'. Warm-ups free energy, encourage spontaneity, and generate a wider range of group outcomes than when groups are simply left to warm up 'naturally'. See Blatner (1973: 36–51).

5 The power of many
The group at work

Therapy groups are really rather odd phenomena. Most people in our society find it natural to talk about their personal problems with one trusted individual, not several unknown ones (in many non-Western cultures, it is natural to speak of one's problems with a group – but it would typically consist of close family or community members, not strangers). Initially, therapy group participants usually feel uncomfortable, and for some individuals this discomfort will continue well into the life of the group. This is something they know they 'ought' to do, something that has been recommended to them, not something most of them would have chosen. Yet these strangers, with no bonds of family, no sexual chemistry, and apparently little in common, may find that they communicate with each other more honestly than they do even with their partners or their close friends, and together they may even participate in some of the deepest and most moving experiences of their lives. What is it that makes this possible?

Very simply, *groups harness the power of shared humanity*. When it comes down to it, whatever our differences (gender, class, race, belief, sexual preference), we are all human beings. We all get angry, experience sadness, and feel joy. Not only do we all feel these universal emotions, we experience them in broadly similar circumstances. A major loss will elicit a similar range of responses – though the nature of the loss may vary enormously from person to person. Most of us, if shocked or traumatized often enough, or long enough, will start to become wary, and lose our confidence. Most of us will feel anxious when confronted with something outside our ken. Many people dislike conflict, for various reasons, and avoid it. And most people don't like being misunderstood, or unfairly judged. Once group members start to 'get real' with each other, they are bound to start discovering some of this common ground. And for many, this is a revelation: *Other people can feel the same as I do!*

The thing that participants consistently say, when looking back on a successful experience in a therapeutic group, is that they 'realized they were not alone'. The one thing they valued above all was the sense that others had struggled with the same issues they had. Formal research into the outcomes of group therapy confirms what ex-clients say: whether the group is a psycho-educational group (e.g. anger management, coping with mental illness in the family), a skills development group (e.g. assertiveness training), a support group (e.g. for post-operative cancer patients, or substance abusers in recovery) or a personal growth or therapy group, participants say over and over again that what they gained was this sense of being supported and understood by others with similar experiences. Irvin Yalom calls this factor 'universality'. Of course, participants can, and do, gain much more from a worthwhile group experience, but it is this feeling of being 'not alone' that they will find it easiest to *identify* afterwards.[1]

You might imagine that 'universality' would be most in evidence in groups where participants have all been through a similar experience (e.g. manic-depressive illness, sexual assault, losing a child in infancy). Certainly, 'homogeneous' groups of this kind often feel 'safer' and more comfortable for new participants than groups where participants' reasons for being there are varied. A homogeneous group can make self-disclosure and personal sharing easier, at an earlier stage. Yet even though group members have ostensibly lived through the same sort of traumatic events, their actual experiences will have been filtered through their very different individual personalities and family backgrounds. So while it remains true, as I said a short time ago, that similar experiences generate broadly similar emotional responses, there is still plenty of room for individual differences, and even in homogeneous groups participants are often surprised to find that while many of their basic feelings are shared, there are some which are not. As the group evolves towards matur-ity, *it is likely to be the differences, rather than the similarities, which are the most fruitful source of learning.* Similarly, participants in 'heterogeneous' groups (where there is a wide range of presenting problems) may initially notice *differences*, and often assume that because of the diversity of members' experience, it is unlikely anyone will fully understand them. Yet they will be surprised to discover that there are profound similarities. Whatever the situation, it is self-disclosure that will fuel this process.

If (as I explained in the previous chapter) the group has started well, pro-gressing through its early phases without getting 'stuck', group members should by now be capable of initiating discussion without waiting for the leader to do so. After a few moments of awkward silence, someone (usually one of the 'recognized talkers') will start something, telling others about an experi-ence that occurred to her during the week, or perhaps asking a question of other group members. One or two such 'leads' may be tried out, and responded to only tentatively, before the session gathers momentum. And it usually gets going when someone takes the risk of saying something that is clearly of great personal significance. Now the group really starts to come alive. You can almost feel the air crackle with expectancy. To be sure, heightened anxiety is a component in this, but so.are heightened excitement and emotional investment.

Self-disclosure: the raw material of interpersonal learning

In the previous chapter, I warned against the kind of premature self-disclosure that occasionally happens in the opening session of a group. I was not warning against self-disclosure per se: it is the lifeblood of any group that attempts to harness the power of interpersonal process, and no group can get very far without it. It is simply a question of timing. By the third or 'responsible adult' phase of the group's early life, the group is *ready* for self-disclosure, and it will start to happen naturally. Often participants will edge towards it quite tentatively, sharing 'safer' things first, and testing out the kind of reaction they are likely to get from others. Those who share something personal with the rest of the group must have some assurance that their confidence will be respected, and that others will hear them out attentively, and tentatively share similar feelings or experiences in return.

Women, on the whole, find it easier to handle this process than men, simply because women in our society are socialized into reciprocal sharing as part of 'girl talk'; they are also socialized to show interest and caring when men speak about themselves, where men typically have not grown up with the same expectations of mutual sharing. Some group members may be 'cut off' from their natural feelings, and find it hard to experience much when another group member shares: it is particularly important for the group leader to accept this, at this stage, rather than give these participants the impression that they are 'failing the test' or 'performing inadequately' in comparison with others. In particular, participants whose style is to 'move away' from others may take a long time to experience anything at all in response to another's sharing.[2] It is not necessarily a question of their having no response, rather that they are unwilling to state it.

Participants with non-Western cultural backgrounds may also react to self-disclosure in ways that can appear 'inhibited' or 'emotionally frozen' to a group leader (and participants) unfamiliar with the cultural norms in question. For example, some Asian cultures see the open expression of emotion in public as shameful, and a therapy group counts as 'in public' because the members are not family. It may feel very alien to people from this background to sit with others who are openly talking about their innermost feelings, let alone to contribute to such self-disclosure themselves. When they do so, they may seem 'stiff', awkward or constrained, and it may take them a long time to 'acculturate' to the special expectations of the group environment, even though they may in other ways be thoroughly Westernized and hold responsible jobs in our own society. Yet, when all is said and done, how different is this from the way many 'traditional males' in our own society behave in therapy groups? They too may seem stiff and constrained, they too will often restrict what they express, for fear of being shamed: 'face', conventionally associated by us Westerners with the 'inscrutable Oriental' stereotype, is in fact alive and well in our own culture, too – we simply fail to notice it, because its manifestations seem 'natural'.

How the leader can encourage self-disclosure

As a group leader, I follow tried and true methods of encouraging self-disclosure, which I've learned from watching other group leaders, and being a group member myself. A very typical event in a group where participants are new to interpersonal work is that one member will ask another a question about what she/he has just disclosed. This is part of normal social interaction, where it indicates some level of interest in the speaker, while keeping the questioner (who reveals little or nothing) 'safe'. In a group, the aim is not to be safe, and those who have just spoken 'from the heart' need to be responded to at a similar level of authenticity and risk-taking. So I would typically ask:

> 'Adam, you've just asked Natalie a question about whether she feels that her mum is intruding into her life. That's a valid question, but I suppose I'm wondering whether you've had some personal experience that prompted you to ask that? Does the idea of being intruded upon have some special significance to you?'

Of course, Adam can still pretend that his question has nothing to do with his own life or relationships (although it usually does, in my experience!) If he reacts this way, I do not push further, but simply accept that he may not yet be ready to reveal more about his personal background. However, Adam may also respond positively to the invitation to share a little more of himself, and when he does so, other participants will immediately recognize the difference in energy level and 'realness'.

No participant should be 'forced' into self-disclosure, but those who are prepared to accept the invitation to do so may find that they gain something by taking the risk. Such gentle 'nudges towards self-disclosure' are part of 'resocializing' group members into a new set of norms that, in a safe setting, can provide deeper rewards than ordinary social interaction. To ask a question without revealing the background of experience or assumptions that lie behind it is to take a 'one up' or powerful position in relation to another person, and even though we all do it all the time in ordinary life, it fits less well in a group where safety and trust depend on shared experience of vulnerability.

Offering advice to another group member is a very similar case of a 'socially acceptable' behaviour which in fact keeps the 'advice giver' safe, while keeping the original discloser vulnerable (and often irritated, although she/he may be too polite to show it!) Again, I invite the adviser to show more of him or herself:

> 'Libby, you've made some suggestions for how you think Nicole should handle her situation. I'm wondering where those suggestions came from, in your own life . . . is this something you're familiar with, in your own relationship? Is the advice you gave her something that's worked for you?'

It is extremely common for group members to make generalized statements which totally conceal, or only hint at, the personal experience which underlies them:

> 'Men let you down all the time.'

> 'Broken relationships leave you feeling a bit of a wreck, don't they?'

> 'Women don't have the faintest idea of what's important to men.'

> 'Say if you were suffering from something, say depression or something like that, you'd want to be left alone, wouldn't you?'

Such statements are frequent in the early phases of a new group, because they are, like all the others we've just been examining, 'safe'. The use of the colloquial second person ('you feel') to conceal one's own position ('I feel'), the flat, unqualified generalizations ('all women are irrational'), and the expression of one's own experience in the thin disguise of 'I know someone who . . .' – all these evade personal responsibility, and shift focus from self to less vulnerable targets. And in the process, most of these tactics actually *invite* fight/flight responses from others. It is not productive in a group aimed at interpersonal learning for members to simply engage in these sorts of interactions. By contrast, disclosing one's own history, values, assumptions and significant experiences encourages true understanding, rather than misjudgement, empathy rather than attack, and openness to new ideas, rather than rigid clinging to one's original position. Shared humanity can be perceived much more readily when all participants are prepared to walk away, for a short time each week, from their socially acceptable defensive positions, and encounter one another as equals. They do this more easily because they only know each other in the group context. By contrast, it is far harder for members of a family, or close work group, to do the same, because their relationships are continuous and multi-stranded.

So again, I challenge the generalizations and evasions, gently and only occasionally at first, more persistently and firmly as the group really gets going:

> 'When you say that all women are stupid cows, Tom, you say that as if there's a lot of painful personal experience involved for you. Would you feel able to tell us something about the way you've been treated by women, that has led you to such a strong belief?'

> 'Debbie, you say that broken relationships leave all of us feeling wrecked. Could you speak for yourself, and say "Broken relationships leave *me* feeling wrecked"? Can you say what's different about speaking that way? Can anyone else notice what's different when Debbie says it that way, compared to the way she put it originally?'

Response to self-discolosure

A group member who shares something personal about him- or herself does not need support or response from every single group member. As long as a 'critical mass' of participants responds with some interest, warmth and respect, the discloser will most likely feel relief and a sense that the risk has been worthwhile. Most likely, the disclosure will lead to similar behaviour in others. Already, among those quickest to respond to the initial disclosure, there will be one or two who will, if other things are equal, be willing to do some sharing of their own, because aspects of the original disclosure have 'triggered' strong feelings of a similar nature. Jacob Moreno saw this as part of the ongoing 'warm-up' process, by which each disclosure serves to move the next potential discloser towards 'action' (in a psychodrama group, this would normally take the form of the discloser enacting the experience disclosed, using other group members to play roles of significant others in his/her life).

So successful self-disclosure is likely to lead to more self-disclosure. There are both benefits and risks in this process. The greater the 'spread' of the disclosure (i.e. the more members who disclose), the 'closer' and safer the group is likely to become. Yet by the same token, a group which evolves a comfortable norm of 'parallel sharing' can run into problems of its own. In these groups, members 'tell their stories' at length, eliciting compassion and encouragement from others, but little challenge. It is as if there is an unspoken agreement that everyone who shares will do so at roughly the same level of intensity, and 'not be too different' from the rest. There is another unspoken agreement, too: that nobody should say anything in response to what is shared unless it is sympathetic and affirming. Such groups seem to me to get stuck in a more mature version of the 'dependency' phase. True, they no longer expect the leader to provide for all their needs. But they are still governed by anxiety about 'fitting in' and 'finding common ground', and scared to explore real differences, or risk open conflict.

If this sort of norm evolves, the leader can play an important role in challenging it. While it is completely appropriate for several group members to affirm one another's sharing, and to share similar feelings in return, it is also normal for a *few* group members to feel something *outside* the range of emotions that the group has decreed 'acceptable'. There will be at least one or two members who have felt irritated, frustrated, sad, or critical in response to another member's sharing, yet such is the power of the group norm that they have remained silent. The leader can encourage diversity of opinion, and ensure that those group members who do not respond to a disclosure have an opportunity to speak and a space to voice their 'deviant' reactions. Here, as so often, the most important way the leader can intervene is to make sure everyone in turn has a chance to speak when anything significant has occurred.

'Going around the group': the 'feelings check'

This 'go around the group' technique works at a number of levels, and can be described in different ways, but all of them add up to the same thing. Ensuring that every group member has a chance to express her/his opinion and/or feelings *widens the field of information available to the group*, and brings into the group's awareness a greater range of emotions, opinions and reactions than would otherwise get expressed openly. As we saw in Chapter 3, when the session gets bogged down in repetitive, predictable and unproductive interactions, the best thing to do is to *involve more people directly in the interaction*. 'Going around the group' accomplishes this, and it is probably the most useful and reliable single intervention I use. It brings into the open what might otherwise have been 'secret', withheld, expressed non-verbally, or even unconscious. It raises the level of anxiety, yet as a repeated ritual, it enhances predictability, safety and trust. Everyone is important; nobody is going to be left out.

Most important of all, 'going around the group' stops the session from turning into 'one-to-one therapy with an audience' or 'storytelling in the presence of compassionate witnesses'. Both of these are, of course, very common scenarios in group work, and far more common in practice than the kind of interactional ('here-and-now') model I am proposing here.

'One-to-one therapy in the presence of the group' is so popular because it requires simply that the skills of the experienced individual therapist (whatever his/her approach) be applied in the presence of an audience. The pioneer

Gestalt therapist Fritz Perls, inviting group members to occupy the famous 'hot seat' and 'do some work' with him, provided perhaps the most flamboyant example of this technique. No true 'interpersonal therapy' is involved, although (as we've already seen) any powerful piece of work by an individual group member is likely to 'warm up' others to volunteer for 'work' of their own (a principle Perls had learned from Moreno's psychodrama).

Similarly, 'storytelling with compassionate witnesses' is a model that predominates in leaderless or self-help/support groups (such as twelve-step groups). These groups aim at maintainence, rather than therapy (although of course, significant changes can sometimes occur through participation in them). Such groups can become a vehicle whereby participants perfect an unchanging 'script' which evokes a predictable response from any new audience member, and which may substitute for transformative personal development and self-confrontation.

A somewhat different variant of 'storytelling with compassionate witnesses' has become very influential in Narrative therapy, with its heavy emphasis on the empowerment of participants, and corresponding avoidance of any leader behaviour that might look like 'expertise' or 'imposing one version of reality on others'. In these groups, the emphasis is on the healing power of simply 'telling one's story', and having it affirmed, valued and received with compassion by others. It is particularly significant for those whose whole lives have been profoundly disempowered by oppression, discrimination and judgement, and those who for many reasons have never had the opportunity to talk about their lives freely and at length. Skilled Narrative facilitators hold up a mirror to the strengths and resources which the participants have in fact displayed over their lives, but which the participants themselves have often failed to recognize. This is a challenge, but a very different kind of 'challenge' from that which occurs in a here-and-now therapy group.

Both one-to-one therapy with the group as audience, and storytelling with the group as 'witness', can be moving and valuable processes. But as I have already said in Chapter 4, a group which gets stuck in such a pattern will forfeit its best opportunities for members to learn and grow, not just from interaction with the facilitator, but from each other. So what makes a 'here-and-now' group so different from either of these more widely used models?

Facilitating the here-and-now encounter

In the 'storytelling with compassionate witnesses' model, self-disclosure becomes an end in itself. This is, in a sense, what the group is *for*. Participants tell their stories, sometimes at considerable length, and others bear witness to the suffering they have endured, or to the courage they have shown. One participant's story leads naturally to the next. The content of the stories is a focus of attention, interest and concern. Stories often stay within the same set of themes, with norms of content being set by the first one or two to speak. But if the aim of a therapeutic group is for group members to learn and grow in awareness of themselves and others, self-disclosure becomes *a step on the way to interpersonal learning*, rather than an end in itself. For this reason, the interactional 'here-and-now' group leader does not encourage lengthy stories by individuals about their past lives ('there and then') or about their present lives and relationships outside the group ('there and now'). Some storytelling is inevitable, and essential, but it is how other group members react to the disclosure that really brings the group into the dynamic interactional present. Shifting from storytelling as an end in itself, to examining the reactions of group members to others' disclosures, involves a shift from *content* to *process*.

> One group member, Kylie, tells a story about how she recently left her partner following a one-off violent episode. Two other members, Joshua and Rahnee, begin offering her advice on how to handle her partner's subsequent pleas for her to return to him. Another, Brianna, sits silent but obviously affected. When asked by the group leader what is going on for her, Brianna reveals that she was shocked to hear of Kylie's action, and thinks it was precipitate and unfair, since Kylie's partner has never previously been violent. As soon as she reveals her reaction, Joshua criticizes her for 'not supporting Kylie', and Brianna feels angered and judged by his comments. Kylie herself feels surprised and somewhat disappointed by Brianna's remarks, which she also takes as a criticism of her action.

If the conversation were a social one, an argument would probably develop between these several participants, focusing on the question of whether or not Kylie was 'right' to leave her partner. People would get hot under the collar, and the aggressive interchanges would leave participants feeling angry and/or misunderstood, but confirmed in the views they originally held. This sort of interaction focuses on *content*. Let's look instead at what can happen when the leader helps the group members to focus on process (how they feel, and what that means) rather than on content (what Kylie should or should not have done).

> Leader: Brianna, you've got strong feelings about Kylie's decision, and it's good that you've been able to tell us all about them. But I wonder if you could just put your opinions about Kylie's decision to one side for a minute . . . could you tell the group what actually went on inside of you when Kylie described her situation? What sort of emotions were you aware of? [The leader affirms Brianna's right to her own opinion regarding Kylie's conduct, but then asks Brianna to shift her focus to her own emotional process.]

Brianna: Well, I was just shocked to hear what she'd done. I couldn't believe anyone could be so hasty, and so, so – I don't know, make such incredible judgements about another person, especially when there's been no violence in the past. It seems so unfair. [Typically, Brianna responds with a restatement of her original position, not really answering the leader's question.]

Leader [Trying again in a more explicit way]: Brianna, what were you aware of in your body when Kylie was talking? Can you remember any actual physical feelings?

Brianna: Um, I suppose I felt kind of like someone had winded me. I sort of couldn't breathe for a while, and I felt angry, very angry. It was so unfair.

Leader: Like someone had punched you, so you couldn't breathe? And there was this really strong anger, and it was something to do with being treated unfairly. Could you talk a bit more about that?

Brianna goes on to talk about her own feelings of being treated unfairly by her mother. As a child, she had felt disempowered by her mother's judgements, and unable to say anything, or stand up for herself. So here we have new self-disclosure, triggered not by Kylie's story as such, but by Brianna's *reaction* to it. So far, this looks pretty much like 'one-to-one therapy in the presence of the group', but the leader then turns to Kylie and asks how she has been affected by what Brianna has just said.

Kylie [somewhat reassured]: I thought she must just think I was a bad person, when she spoke earlier. Now I suppose I can see why she would feel so strongly about me leaving Jason.

Kylie's comments are temperate, as if she might still be holding something back, but before exploring this, the group leader decides to check with Joshua, who was also very affected by Brianna's original comment:

Leader: Joshua, what about you? How do you feel now, hearing what Brianna's just said?

Joshua: Irritated. Really pissed off. I think Brianna's doing a bit of a snow job on all of us. She was really judgemental back then, and I think she's still making that judgement, only she's pretending not to.

Leader: So you're still really feeling strongly about that judgement that you felt Brianna was making? Would you be prepared to talk directly to Brianna about what you've just said to me?

Encouraged by the leader, Joshua voices his anger directly to Brianna, and an intense few minutes ensue. Joshua begins to realize that his own fear of 'being judged' is rather similar to Brianna's, and that 'snow jobs' are something that he himself used to do, in order to defend himself against parents he experienced as very intrusive and critical.

Notice how, in this segment of interaction, several group members have 'projected' strong feelings onto others, and then become angry with them as a result. Brianna has projected her fear of being judged onto Kylie, and Joshua has projected his fear of being judged, and his own tendency to 'con' people, onto Brianna. By questioning both of them about *process – how* they are feeling in response to the other person, and what that feeling might mean to them – the leader is eventually able to help both of them to 'take back the projection', that is, to acknowledge the powerful feelings in themselves that they imagined to be felt by the other group member in the first place.

> The leader now turns back to Kylie, and checks how she is after hearing the preceding interactions. Her response shows that she is still holding onto some resentment against Brianna, and so another interaction, this time between Kylie and Brianna, takes place.

Of course, this is only a 'baby step' in a long journey. Joshua, Brianna and Kylie will misunderstand other group members on many occasions, before they will start to recognize how their expectations and assumptions reflect truths about themselves, and may or may not be true of others. But in the process, they will be learning to modify their 'natural' ways of responding to others, and becoming more in touch with their own motives, fears and judgements.

The essence of the here-and-now group is that it is interactive. Group members build up information about one another, not from extensive knowledge of each other's histories and outside lives, but from *how they act within the group itself.* But of course, the way group members respond to one another in the 'here and now' of the group session is highly likely to mirror key aspects of their behaviour *outside* the group ('there and now'), and their reactions to other group members will also reflect assumptions derived from key relationships in their past ('there and then') – especially relationships with parents and siblings. Joshua believes that Brianna is 'judging' Kylie unfairly, because he experienced a mother who 'judged him', and tends to transfer this template onto any woman whose behaviour, tone of voice, or even physical appearance, triggers dormant memories of the first woman who did this sort of thing to him. This is what psychodynamic theory calls 'transference'.

In a group situation, all members will automatically apply ('transfer') such templates to others, and while this will often occur only in a mild and temporary form, for some it will be more powerful and persistent. Age and physical appearance will play a part in this: a woman who is older than most of the rest of the group, and has a calm, accepting manner, will tend to attract 'good mother' transference from younger group members. But age can be overridden by less obvious factors: a youngish man who wears glasses, conducts himself stiffly and offers the occasional critical remark will easily be cast in the role of 'critical dad', even by group members who are ten years older than he is. Transference can occur as a result of extremely subtle cues: a slight curl of the upper lip, a downcast gaze, an accent or a speech mannerism – any of these tiny things may trigger group member A to begin reacting 'as if' group member B were someone else, usually someone in the past, but sometimes a significant person in A's present life (a partner, child, or boss).

So in a sense, any group is potentially awash with semi-conscious and unconscious expectations of others. Again, the important thing is not so much the *content* of these transferences (Kylie reminds Brianna of her feckless mum; Brianna reminds Joshua of his judgemental dad) *but the fact that they are made explicit and talked about, in the immediacy of the moment, between group members.* There is something electric about this process, which makes it very different from even the most moving and involving personal story, and far more dynamic than an intellectual realization, as the result of a therapist's interpretation, or a client's self-insight. In part because this sort of honest talking so rarely occurs in the 'real world', the learning we do through such direct encounters tends to be remembered vividly, and to last long after the actual group is over.

From 'transference' to real behaviour: giving and receiving feedback

When group members relate to each other 'as if' they were really someone else (transference), or see 'hidden' sides of themselves reflected in others' behaviour (projection), we are dealing with perceptions which are to some degree 'warped' or erroneous. Brianna isn't necessarily being judgemental, but Joshua is sure she is, because his own prior experience has 'set him up' to see such judgementalism in others – especially in women. But this is only half of the story. Mostly, when a group member sees another participant in a certain way, and reacts accordingly, there will be *something* in the behaviour of the other to support the interpretation. Only individuals who suffer from deeply rooted, lifelong 'skewing' of perception (such as the paranoid person's conviction that others are harbouring aggressive and malign intentions towards her) will see others in a way which is totally out of touch with the reality. Most people, by contrast, are more likely to pick up something real enough about another person's attitude or behaviour, but then exaggerate its importance, or misinterpret it according to their own existing assumptions and formative past experiences.

So every instance of transference or projection in a group setting is not simply an opportunity for one participant to learn about the distortions in his/her own perception of others. It is equally a chance for another participant to learn more about how he/she 'comes across' – as judgemental, or angry, or a busybody, or a doormat, or critical, or sweet-but-spineless. The more group members feel safe to interact freely, without concealing their immediate reactions, the more others will start to build a picture of them, and while the picture will inevitably be somewhat coloured by biases and personal distortions, a consensus will usually emerge. Hence one of the most valuable activities in an interpersonal learning group, once it has developed momentum, is for a group member to ask others for feedback.

'Feedback' is a term from engineering which has been fruitfully applied to the study of how humans interact in social systems. But within the personal growth context, 'asking for feedback' means simply 'requesting honest information from others about how your behaviour looks to them, what they think of you'. Again, the value of asking for feedback in a group setting is precisely because the norms of a group are different from those of conventional social interaction.

In the 'real world' (which might more accurately be called the 'unreal world'), social codes dictate that we should avoid hurting each other by saying what we honestly think, and encourage us to offer praise and support rather than anything that might be construed as negative. These rules are not without justification, but it is harder to understand those which often prevent us from telling others what we *appreciate* about them, through fear of sounding 'like a used car salesman', or (especially the case with parents and their children) anxiety about giving them inflated ideas of their own worth. In the group, there is more chance that people will tell each other with some degree of honesty what they see – if only because their fellow group members are not friends, work colleagues, or family members, and so there is less to lose by being honest. Moreover, if all has gone well, the group environment specifically encourages interpersonal openness, and rewards it when it happens.

I do not mean that groups instantly or consistently produce high-quality, intensely honest exchanges of information between participants. Some group members tend to confuse honesty with aggressive confrontation (the 'You are so full of shit, Jim!' model, popularized by high-profile programmes for substance abusers such as Synanon); others think it gives them a licence to parade their judgements and prejudices at others' expense, and then, when others protest, to shrug it off with 'That's your problem!' Others again will simply act as they would in the equivalent situation 'out there', and say only nice things, for fear of giving offence. Again, the leader plays an important part here, helping group members to be respectful as well as honest, and again, it is vital that participants have the right to respond to whatever feedback they receive. Equally, it is important that anyone receiving feedback from others in the group should understand that he/she is not required to believe or 'take on board' everything that is said. Not that it is likely most group members would do so anyway! However, there will always be the particularly dependent individual, perhaps prone to low self-esteem, who may feel deeply affected by what he is told, and unable to shrug off what does not 'fit'.

In my experience, asking for feedback from the group is something that tends to occur later in the life of the group, rather than earlier, when participants have already had plenty of opportunity to interact and to observe one another, as well as being socialized into the norm of openness. Earlier, I might suggest it ('Lily, if you liked, you could check with the group and see whether they agree with you about you being a pretty useless person') but once the first group member takes the plunge and requests feedback, others will gradually follow over time. This should never be anything but a voluntary exercise.

Usually, those who request feedback find it a useful and often a validating experience. Sometimes a particular piece of feedback, usually one that is perceived as strongly critical, may 'swamp' the rest in the protagonist's thinking, and it may be important for the leader to point out (if others have not already done so) that there were several positive comments along with the negative one, and to ask what has caused the person to pay so little heed to the former and place so much emphasis on the negative. Some group members can be genuinely surprised by what is said to them: parts of their personality that they had imagined were 'hidden' (because they had never spoken about them) prove to have 'leaked' just the same, and this can be a shock. Some participants will struggle when told by member after member about some behaviour that does not accord with their own prior image of themselves. Such feedback can be a challenge, but, once again, there are always opportunities for the individual in question to explore it further in the group's next session.

> Josephine was told by another group member that she came across as secretive, critical and disapproving of the others in the group. Josephine was shocked, because she had done no self-disclosing in the group, and imagined that others therefore knew nothing about her, and could form no judgements of her. She asked why the others thought she was critical and disapproving, and was told that she 'wrinkled up her mouth when she spoke' (which was true), and that she had a 'whining, dissatisfied tone' in her voice (which was also true). Josephine had also said nothing for entire sessions, and then admitted to being 'a bit irritated' or 'dissatisfied with the group' right at the very end, when nobody could challenge her.
>
> Josephine initially reacted with cold hostility to this feedback, denying its accuracy. As the other group members persisted, she started to weep, and refused to say anything. Those group members who had 'attacked her' (Josephine's word) themselves became distressed, and notably softened their tone towards her, inviting her to 'help us understand you better – tell us the things we don't understand'. Josephine would not

answer these pleas, and eventually left the group for fifteen minutes to compose herself. She returned, but did not speak again until the very end (the very pattern that had been pointed out to her), saying that she was 'extremely angry'. At the group's next meeting, both she and the woman who had confronted her needed to revisit the encounter, and both had strong feelings to express. This time, both revealed more about themselves than previously, and Josephine was eventually able to admit that she had deliberately stayed silent in the group because there were problems in her life that she didn't want the group to know about. She could now see how her taciturn behaviour had created the impression that she believed she was 'superior' to the rest, and that some of her irritation had been at herself, for being unable to participate more fully. One of those who had 'attacked' her softened greatly towards her as a result of this disclosure.

When feelings get hurt

It is almost inevitable, in any group where participants are prepared to risk being honest, that someone, usually more than one person, will become temporarily distressed. It is important that the leader be able to stay calm when this happens, and express empathy without getting pulled into the role of 'rescuer'. Rather, the best course is to gently invite the distressed person to explore her pain. What is it about? What does it remind her of? Does its nature change as she observes it? If the level of distress is too great, or an emotional 'shutdown' has occurred (as in the case of Josephine above), I would normally leave the person alone, with her permission, and turn to other members of the group, who will almost certainly have had strong reactions. Some will 'mobilize' in support of the distressed person (and can be asked about the ways in which they may be indentifying with her), others will want to continue the process of feedback-giving, and perhaps be very frustrated that the distressed individual seems to be 'blocking out the truth'. Still others may be reminded of painful events in their own past lives, and so on. So once more, going around the group is vital. It also gives the distressed individual space to gather herself, and to gain a little perspective.

Sometimes, interchanges between two group members become locked in repeated, angry or hurtful cycles. This is a situation familiar to us from couple therapy, even though these two group members may have been complete strangers to each other before the group began. What such cycles often mean is that instead of the fleeting transferences that occur often between group members, as noted above, these two people have 'locked into' a powerful mutual transference, in which almost anything one does will trigger strong negative feelings in the other – and vice versa. If this happens in couple therapy, I would draw attention to it, and invite the couple to stand aside from the heat of the interaction, and start to look at what, emotionally, might be going on for them (as described in Chapter 3). In a group setting, however, a whole new resource is available: inviting other group members to talk about how *they* are being affected by the predictable patterns of conflict.

Precisely because I have assisted the group to evolve into healthy independence, group members are by now less likely to expect me to 'solve the problem' or 'make everything feel good again' when something temporarily goes wrong between two of their number. Instead, participants will themselves feel implicated and concerned, and their feedback will often provide a new perspective that the group members directly involved in a painful or unproductive interaction may have missed – and one that I, too, may have missed. Group members will often feel free to say things that I might think, but prefer not to say, in the interests of tact and diplomacy. Often, such comments 'hit the nail on the head' for the two members in conflict. If they do not provoke new awareness, and do in fact generate hurt or a feeling of having been slighted or judged, I can always step in to moderate the force of the comments, or indicate empathy for the 'criticized' group member. For me, working with other group members in this situation is a bit like having a 'temporary co-therapist'. I can allow my 'co-therapist' to take risks and be a bit outrageous, and then mediate or moderate if the need arises, without having compromised my own position, which must be to be visibly fair to all parties — The same principle of 'balance' that we talked about in chapter 1.

Examples of wonderfully productive comments from listening group members are:

> 'But you're both saying the same thing! You're really both worried about exactly the same issue, it's just that each of you wants to deal with it a different way!'

> 'When I hear the two of you attacking each other like that, I go straight back to my teenage years. I can remember hearing my mum and my stepdad fighting, and I really hated it. I actually felt scared when you got so heated a minute ago. I felt like I wanted to run out of the group and hide somewhere.'

> 'John, you sound like a heavy parent when you talk to Sylvia. I can almost see you waving your finger! And Sylvia, you sound just like a rebellious teenager. Even the way you sit there with your hair over your face, spitting out comments without actually looking at John – that's so much like a kid!'

Some recurring conflicts between two group members can be sorted out in a full and satisfying way, often through such 'moments of truth' offered by their peers. Other conflicts continue to flicker into life again whenever the anxiety level in the group rises, for whatever reason (and we will look at some predictable reasons very shortly). I have learned to accept that not all participants will prove able to take back all their projections, or gain insight into how they see others in limited, distorted ways. If they gain some degree of insight during the life of the group, this is an acceptable outcome for me. The real, lasting learning may not come until later – but for other group members, witnessing the recurrent conflicts, the learning may come right now. In a group, no event is *ever* the concern only of those directly involved in it!

Departures and 'deaths'

In a long-term therapy group, it is inevitable that sooner or later one or more of the original members will leave (because they are relocating, because they are 'graduating' and feel more content with their lives, or because they feel they are not getting anywhere). Occasionally, the leader may be forced to ask a member to leave the group, when it becomes obvious that he/she is not coping, or is too badly out of step with the rest (if initial selection of participants is carried out thoroughly and sensitively, this should rarely occur).[3] Whatever the reason, when an established member of the group leaves, *the group always has a reaction*. Obviously, the reaction can take different forms, depending on the person who has left, and the nature of his/her relationship to the rest. In my experience, the group 'takes a vacation from intensity' after such an event, or becomes temporarily lethargic and purposeless (as people do when grieving) or 'regresses' to one of the earlier phases of its own evolution (temporary dependency on a leader, or sudden 'James Dean' behaviour).

Group members rarely connect their strange behaviour to the departure of one of their number, and if they are asked about the loss of that individual, they will often deny that they have been particularly affected. Yet the mood *of the group as a whole* says otherwise. Here is another proof that groups have a collective 'life' that exists independently of the motives and thoughts of their individual members. Individual members can truthfully say 'Yes, I miss Jim a bit, but really, to be honest, I didn't feel all that close to him, and it won't make all that much difference to me now he's not here'. Yet, the group as a whole will act almost as if a 'death' has occurred.

Anyone who has ever become devoted to a soap opera on television will probably know what it feels like when a character who has been an integral part of a long-running story is written out of the series. It may seem pathetic or ludicrous to people who do not feel this deep immersion in a fictional world, but what we, the devoted viewers, feel is a profound sense of loss, which may be accompanied by alienation and even anger. How dare the producers do this to us? We were *attached* to that character! She can't just 'die' or 'go off to America' or whatever! We want her to stay around! She has been part of our experience of the show as a whole, and once she has left the show, the show itself becomes diminished or impoverished for us. Some viewers may even stop watching the show in protest. Most will continue, but also continue to mourn the lost character, perhaps for months or even years. It just isn't the same without her.

This is a reasonably parallel situation to what the group (as a collective entity) seems to experience when one of its members 'dies' or 'goes off to America'. It may seem bizarre, it may seem far-fetched, but the group is reacting in just the same way as we do in the soap opera scenario.

Similarly, the advent of a new member, or members, can also disrupt the life of a group for a time. This is natural enough: participants have grown used to each other, and feel reasonably comfortable together. A new member may temporarily shake this equilibrium, raising old anxieties anew. Some new members quickly adapt to the group's ways, and may even fall into a role that is quite similar to one occupied by a former, now departed, participant. Others, by contrast, may find it harder to adapt, and almost from their point of entry, may challenge the group's habits and assumptions. This may throw a group back into the phase of counter-dependency, with unproductive conflict rearing its head. Alternatively, the group may revert to dependency, wanting the leader to 'deal with' or 'put a lid on' the aggressive or challenging new member. Either way, the group will probably enter a time of moratorium, in which previous ongoing issues between group members may take a back seat, while the group puts its energy into dealing with the newcomer.

In an ongoing interpersonally oriented group, members will inevitably come and go, but the group goes on, and the one constant member is the leader or therapist. It is hardly surprising, then, that when there is a change in the group's leadership, this may prove even more difficult for groups to cope with than changes of membership. Everyone is used to their leader's particular style, and, as we saw in the last chapter, the leader's way of caring for, protecting and nurturing becomes something that the group members rely on in order to risk being honest and vulnerable with one another. A new leader will inevitably have a somewhat different way of being in the group, and this will attract a renewed focus on how she/he is similar to, and different from, the old leader. Depending on the level of maturity of the group, and the new leader's ability to be non-anxious about the group's reactions, the group may adjust to a new leader remarkably quickly, or it may take quite some time, with group members mourning the loss of their former leader, and fixating on what they perceive as 'not so good' about the new one. Just as in the group's opening phase, the new leader will again be the focus of attention for a time, and there will be a good deal of overt and covert 'testing' and 'measuring' until a critical mass of group members are convinced that this new authority figure can offer them just as much as the old, albeit in a somewhat different form.

The leader's role in a mature group

In this chapter, we have looked at various examples of the kind of inter-personal 'work' that is possible in a group that has reached maturity. I'd like to conclude with a summary of the ways that the group leader or facilitator can best assist a group once it has learned to work together well.

- The leader should *be aware of the group's energy state*. When a group is functioning at its optimal level, there is energy in the air: expectancy, electricity, anticipation (and yes, some anxiety, too). When the energy sinks, group members begin to shuffle or yawn or even look at their watches surreptitiously. I have learned that my own feelings of tiredness are an infallible barometer. As soon as I start to yawn or feel sleepy, I know that I need to *draw attention to the obvious* ('I've noticed that I'm feeling tired and, looking around, it seems as if most of you have switched off. I wonder what's going on?').
- After every significant event in the group's life (a key piece of self-disclosure, an interpersonal encounter between two or more group members), the leader should 'go around the group' to ensure that the group's full response is available, and to ensure that subsequent inter-action does not become unduly focused on a small minority of the group.
- When group members react to an individual's self-disclosure in typical 'socially acceptable' ways the leader should challenge this by turning to the discloser and asking whether this is the sort of response she/he was hoping for, and what effect the response has had on her/him). A leader should also invite the 'advice-givers' and 'problem-solvers' to talk about what, at a personal 'in here' level, prompted their 'safe' reaction. In this way, I discourage comfortably familiar (but unproductive) interactions, and invite participants to risk being less safe, and thus learn more.
- When a direct interpersonal encounter between two members occurs, the leader should give each participant the chance to speak uninterrupted, as long as they speak honestly, and aren't simply defending themselves against a perceived threat or criticism. In this respect, I would be employing the same skills as I would employ in a couple or family interaction: creating a space for each person to be heard without the other 'rushing in' and short-circuiting the chance that some important new information might be revealed. Yet I

interrupt the speaker myself as soon as I perceive that she/he has wandered away from authenticity, and is simply wheel-spinning, or blaming, as a substitute for honest, self-aware feedback.

- Similarly, the leader should help the other participant to respond as directly as possible to what the first has said, not getting mired in detail, but focusing on the key emotional information that has been transmitted.

- When the group becomes fixated on the behaviour of just one or two members, repeatedly questioning them, worrying about them, or confronting them, the leader should keep in mind that these 'scape-goated' group members may be carrying some feeling that the rest of the group may be keeping outside of awareness. Thus an angry, disruptive group member may be being scapegoated for behaviour or aggressive fantasies that other group members entertain, but do not act upon. Asking the group directly about this is generally the best way of opening up such unconscious processes for productive discussion.

- Whenever any encounter between two or more group members 'gets bogged' in repetitive patterns that do not resolve easily, the leader should invite other group members to offer their responses to the interaction, thus transforming the situation from a stuck 'couple transaction' to a group-level transaction, where new information and emotional authenticity may be brought to bear and help the stuck participants evolve towards something more productive.

- Whenever anything seems to be temporarily going wrong, or getting lethargic, the leader should state the obvious. In most social situations, polite conduct requires that we pretend not to notice when something is going amiss, and 'soldier on', or make stronger efforts to make things 'come right'. This is an example of 'more of the same wrong solution', and it rarely works. Rather, when we have the courage to openly name what is going on, and ask how others feel about it, then we begin to create the energy and resources to find solutions to whatever is amiss.

- Stating the obvious applies particularly to 'temporary interruptions'. When a member has missed the previous session, but is now back, when the group has had a longer interval than usual since its last meeting, when someone has arrived uncharacteristically late, or when the leader has behaved differently than she/he normally would – any of these things, which seem so small and so 'obvious' that we feel embarrassed to mention them, may, at the level of the group's collective consciousness, cause perturbation out of all proportion to their apparent triviality. Group members themselves will rarely talk about them, or connect them with a subsequent feeling of awkwardness, low energy, suppressed resentment, or whatever. It falls to the leader to do so, and a good leader will prepare for each new session by reviewing all the potential changes that the group may have to face this time.

I began this chapter by speaking of the way that groups, no matter what their stated purpose, and almost regardless of their content, seem to 'work' for participants because of the experience of feeling 'not alone'. I hope you can now see how group leaders, too, can feel less 'alone' than in one-to-one therapy with an individual. In a group setting, 'the power of many' is always available to be harnessed for the common good. A group can work well at the level of simple sharing of experience, or acquiring knowledge and practising new skills. But 'the power of many' can go far beyond this level. Participants can still exchange significant experiences and find common ground, they can still learn new things, and begin behaving in new ways. But they can do so through direct, authentic interactions with others, rather than simply through hearing others talk, or 'social learning'. They will start to feel different about themselves, to see new possibilities in their lives, and come to appreciate, in a profound way, that what they originally experienced (in the person of another group member) as 'threateningly different from' may in fact be 'the same as', and that 'comfortable sameness' (also in the person of a fellow participant) may conceal real difference. No other setting but the interactive therapy group can provide quite this experience, in this depth, and at this level of intensity. There is much to gain, and little to lose, by being honest in a well-run therapy group. In a family, it is unfortunately the case that the reverse is often true.

Notes

1   Irvin Yalom's 'therapeutic factors' in group work (among which 'universality' features prominently) are described and analysed in chapter 1 of his classic text, *The Theory and Practice of Group Psychotherapy* (1995: 1–16). Apart from being by far the most comprehensive summary of what is known about group therapy, Yalom's book has the unusual virtue (for such an authoritative text) of being very readable as well. It is the bible for any intending group therapist, whether or not you intend to work in Yalom's 'here-and-now' model (which is described in some detail in chapter 6 (Yalom 1995: 129–38). An alternative account is provided in chapter 4 of Yalom's *Inpatient Group Psychotherapy* (1983: 173–208). Although this book deals with a specialized group, patients hospitalized with acute mental illness, the principles are still applicable to outpatients, and Yalom's description in this book is simpler and clearer than in *Theory and Practice*. Yalom has recently turned to the writing of fiction dealing

with experiences of therapy, and his latest novel is *The Schopenhauer Cure* (2005), which vividly conveys what it feels like to participate in the sort of group that he has spent much of his life leading and analysing.

2   Karen Horney's (1945: 73–95) personality theory distinguished three basic interpersonal styles: people who move 'towards' others, those who move 'against' others (fight), and those who move 'away' from others. Clearly, the last of these corresponds roughly with 'flight' or 'freeze' (in sociobiology), and with the 'avoidant/dismissive' category (in attachment theory). These are the individuals who will typically become the group's 'non-talkers', happier not to draw attention to themselves, and to deal with possible conflict by refusing to be drawn into any interaction at all. The Enneagram (Palmer 1988: 204–36) personality system adds a further dimension to understanding some 'silent' group members. In the Enneagram, point Five is occupied by 'observers', who are more comfortable listening and noticing than contributing. In part, this is because they do not actually experience much of what is going on for them while in the midst of an interaction, but only become aware of their feelings and thoughts afterwards, when the experience is 'recollected in tranquillity' (usually, when they are on their own).

3   I regret that there is insufficient space in this book to deal even sketchily with the subject of how to select participants for group therapy. Fortunately, Yalom (1995: 217–43) deals as well with this topic as he does with almost every other facet of group work.

6 Loyalties and disappointments
The nature of family relationships

Some twenty years ago, I set out to write an account of my own family. I confined my attention to the two generations immediately preceding my own. Although I had personally met only a few of them, nearly all the people I planned to write about had been known by at least one living informant, and often by more than one. Because two of my grandparents were already dead before I was two years old, and I knew relatively little about the other two, I wanted to find out what they were actually like, and how they related to their parents, spouses and children. This caused me to run head-on into the way that my family, like so many others, fractured along the lines of long-ago feuds, and maintained a tactful silence to protect those they had idealized. One living son or daughter would give me an apparently coherent portrait of a now dead parent, but another son or daughter would supply a very different account – equally coherent, equally believable. Mostly, there was some overlap, but at times the two descriptions were so different that it was hard to believe they related to the same person.[1]

I had to conclude, as others had done before me, that although siblings in an intact, biological family may grow up together, they often experience their parents (and, indeed, each other) in very different ways. Their own genetically shaped temperaments will influence how they see a mother, a father, a sister, a brother, a grandparent, an aunt or an uncle. And their temperaments will also shape how other family members see *them*. A shy child will, nine times out of ten, elicit a very different set of responses from others than an outgoing one; an easy-going, unflappable child will 'pull' different reactions in comparison with an intense, sensitive one, and so on. *The interaction of 'nature' (what a child inherits genetically) and 'nurture' (how others treat and respond to her/him) is necessarily, and always, a two-way, circular process.* We see others differently because of who *we* are (as well as because of who they are), and others see *us* differently because of who they are (as well as because of who *we* are). This, in part, explains why it is so easy for family members to believe, with absolute certainty, that they are describing some other family member 'as they really were', when other relatives feel the same certainty about a very different 'truth'.[2]

How disappointments are produced – and reproduced

Human lives start in both hope and disappointment. While many pregnancies are causes for delight, some are unwelcome, even hateful. Yet even then, there may still be some fragile thread of expectation. Often women report feeling 'nothing' for their baby until it is born, and then being touched and even overwhelmed by this miraculous new life that so totally depends upon them to survive. Some babies are given up for adoption, and cared for by those who are not their biological parents, yet here, too, a thread of hope can often be found in both birth mother and adoptive parents, even if that hope must struggle against grim acceptance, anger or harsh judgement. There is something about a life, at its very start, that elicits wonder and invites its carers to invest a baby with their dreams.

Yet such hope and belief are often shortlived. The let-down can come as early as the moment of first contact, when the baby's gender, or its appearance, may spark powerful feelings of disappointment ('I was sure it was going to be a girl', 'I didn't think it would be so dark', 'Good grief, he looks just like his bloody father!'). Even when a baby is at first idealized, disappointment can set in so soon. Your baby wrecks your sleep. It invades every aspect of your life with its insistent, shrill demands. And it simply won't do what you want, at least not nearly as often as you'd like it to. For some caregivers, even these predictable aspects of a baby's nature begin to generate frustration and disapproval. Relatives ask 'Is it a *good* baby?' meaning 'Does it cause you a minimum of trouble?' Temperament, the baby's genetic legacy, often adds further fuel to the consuming fire of disappointment ('I expected her to be quiet and, you know, do what she's told, like I was, and instead she's so headstrong and loud!'). For many parents, disappointment may come much later, as the child begins to find its own individuality, and to make choices and indicate interests that may be alien to those of the parents – or actively destructive to their expectations ('Football's a big part of my life, and he doesn't seem to care about it at all. I always thought we'd share the game, but he's just not interested'). Adolescence is, *par excellence*, the period when this later type of disappointment rears its head.

It is in the nature of most human interactions that once a relationship starts travelling in a certain direction, it is easier (and feels more 'natural') to travel further in that direction. By contrast, to put the car into reverse (as it were) feels alien and difficult. In other words, once we start to see anyone in a certain way, our own reactions to him or her will often ensure that he/she goes on behaving in a manner that will *confirm* our view. An 'easy baby' (placid, often smiling, adaptable and falling easily into routines) will generate positive feelings in its caregivers, and these in turn will confirm the child in its sense that it is loved, worthy, and trusted. This is, of course, the scenario that most readily generates 'secure attachment'. By contrast, a child with a 'difficult' temperament (moody, irritable, and hypersensitive to every change) elicits reactions of disappointment and annoyance from parents or siblings, leading, very often, to some form of *insecure* attachment.

The child takes in these disappointed, frustrated reactions, forming an internal sense of herself as 'bad' or 'a problem'. Naturally, that same child will strive to feel better about herself, and so she may bury the sense of badness deep inside, and consciously form a defiant image of herself as 'unfairly treated'. In turn, her angry defiance will generate even stronger frustration and disappointment from her parents and/or siblings, and later, from teachers, peers and others. The 'chip on her shoulder' grows into a massive log.

This is how families create 'naughty children', who then (often, but not inevitably) go on to careers as 'no-good teenagers' and (sometimes) as selfish, angry, irresponsible adults.

There is, of course, an alternative scenario, in which the child's feelings of 'badness' are turned inwards. In these children, genetic sensitivity will generate depression rather than defiance, or anxiety rather than anger. This child will feel responsible for her own 'badness', and try somehow to cope with it alone – through compulsive, secret rituals (as in obsessive-compulsive disorder), through heroic, if hideously misplaced, attempts to control appetite and body image (as in anorexia/bulimia), or through self-harming in the form of punitive self-criticism, cutting or suicide attempts. But in these instances, too, it is the way others (particularly parents) react to the behaviour that will help to perpetuate it. The frantic attempt to get the anorectic to eat makes her even more resistant to eating, and so on.

The sort of pattern where each participant's reactions to the other strengthens the likelihood of the sequence continuing is called a 'positive feedback loop'. The word 'positive' causes problems for many. The newcomer naturally imagines that 'positive' means 'good', so it comes as a bit of a shock to find that conflicted, troubled relationships are often described in family therapy texts in terms of 'positive feedback loops'. In fact, when used in this way, the term 'positive' simply means 'more of'. 'Positive' reinforcement is a response that leads to *more of* a behaviour, where 'negative' reinforcement results in *less* of that same behaviour (it is a common misunderstanding to see 'negative reinforcement' as the equivalent of 'punishment'; in fact, as many parents and teachers know, punishment often acts as a long-term *positive* reinforcement of undesirable behaviour, even though it may curtail such behaviour in the short term).

In a positive *feedback loop*, 'more of' one behaviour results in 'more of' another behaviour, leading in turn to more of the first behaviour, and so on.

The concept of a feedback *loop* is, to my mind, a more useful and flexible tool than the concept of reinforcement. In a positive feedback loop, we are not asked to think of one person behaving in a certain way, and another person simply 'reinforcing' that behaviour, while remaining somehow 'outside' it and uninfluenced by it. Rather, in a positive feedback loop, both participants act and react, and each is changed, gradually, by the behaviour of the other. The 'dance' that couples do is a perfect example of such loops, as are the repetitive, self-reinforcing interactions that can easily develop between two or three therapy group members.

We could select any one 'bit' of action–reaction, and claim that one person 'started it', but the other can always point to a prior action on the part of the first (perhaps something he/she did an hour before, or the previous day) and say that, therefore, she/he is not responsible. Thus concepts of 'cause' and 'blame' become meaningless. Both parties can always claim that the other is to blame, and that they are 'simply defending themselves' or whatever. Of course, we humans are deeply locked into the habit of seeking 'causes' for things that go wrong, and of blaming someone (usually not ourselves) when they do. The family therapist must find a way of stepping out of such thinking, and the ability to see sequences of behaviour in terms of positive feedback loops is very helpful in assisting us to avoid judgemental, accusatory language, which then becomes part of the loop. We'll see in a later chapter some ways that we can assist families in this respect.

For now, let us take an example of how a 'loop' might evolve over a period of many years. A screaming, tantrum-throwing two-year-old boy becomes an aggressive, door-slamming teenager who punches holes in walls and drives without a licence, and then (perhaps) a violent, intimidating adult who hits and threatens his partner. All of this happens *partly* because the predictable reaction of others to such behaviour is to do something which (quite contrary to their intention) actually makes it continue and worsen. Over time, their attitudes harden and their actions become more extreme. Perhaps a parent, in despair, throws this boy out at the age of fifteen, confirming his inner sense of worthlessness and his outwardly displayed bitterness. Another parent, faced with similar behaviour, might put up with the lack of respect she is shown, arguing that, 'After all, he is my son and I love him'. Later, the boy's adult partner will threaten to leave (but not leave) or 'punish' the violent young man by having an affair – which exacerbates his jealous rage and feeds his suspicions.

These reactions are, in a deep sense, 'natural'. When we are confronted by threatening, aggressive behaviour in another person, humans are biologically programmed to react with 'fight', 'flight' or 'freeze'. Earlier in this book, we observed this programming in discussing the way couples typically interact. When a parent confronts an angry, demanding, punishing child, there are just two 'natural' choices. First, a parent can yell angrily or even physically attack the child (smacking, beating), asserting his parental authority by 'fighting' him (this is actually quite inappropriate, since the parent is a physically powerful adult, and the child is normally smaller and looks to the adult as a trusted person who can supply security and protection). Second, the parent can give in to the child, pleading with him, leaving the room in tears, or withdrawing into hurt silence. These are the human equivalents of what animals do when they 'run away' or 'freeze' into passivity in the face of a perceived predator. These reactions, too, are inappropriate, since a child is not normally a physical threat to a parent (at least, not until mid-adolescence), and should not be in a position to impose his will by force, intimidation or manipulation. Yet both types of reaction often happen, because at some level we humans react to *emotional* threat (even from a physically unequal small child) as if it were a real, overwhelming *physical* threat.

By contrast, remaining calm in the face of aggressive or emotionally manipulative behaviour is not 'natural', nor is standing our ground without 'fighting back'. Nor, indeed, is warmly embracing the child, while simultaneously saying 'No, honey, you can't'. These 'non-natural' behaviours have few animal equivalents – except, perhaps, for those apes who routinely offer to 'groom' others (comb their fur and remove irritating insects) as a way of defusing their aggression.[3]

No wonder, then, that we humans find it so difficult to step aside from a 'positive feedback loop' and initiate a 'negative loop' instead – one that will decrease the aggressive behaviours and angry, hurt feelings in both ourselves and the other person. When we react with anger or passive giving up, we are doing what comes easily and instinctively. When we consciously think about our reaction, and choose what is most likely to help our relationship with the other person, we have to struggle against our own instincts, and against patterns of acting, thinking and feeling which we absorbed long ago from our own parents.

In particular, if as children we ourselves felt 'bad' and acted defiantly, we may well be at a loss to know how to 'step aside' from an escalating conflict with a 'defiant' child of our own. The chances are, our own parents did not know how to do this either, so we grew up with no useful 'model' on which to base our own parenting. On the other hand, if we were compliant children, who suppressed our hostile or wounded feelings in the interests of being seen as 'good', then we may feel equally powerless and clueless when faced with a child who refuses to do what we did – probably much as our own parents felt when one of our siblings 'acted naughty'.

Because the basis of these patterns is instinctive (or 'learned' at such an early age that we do not consciously remember our learning, which in practical terms amounts to much the same thing), most people do not talk about these patterns or really *think* about them (other than to feel bad, and wish things were different). For talking, we typically substitute complaining, and for thinking, we substitute labelling and blaming: 'He's an impossible child', 'Dad's hopeless'. Without intervention, these patterned ways of seeing each other often survive well into adulthood, or even lifelong.

Here is my father, Ian, talking about his relationship with his own father, Albert:

> Well, Dad and I used to *clash*. We never got on. He didn't understand me, and even when I tried to do something for him, he was never grateful. I remember once I offered to take over at the Mill [the family business] for a week or two, while he and Mum went on a holiday. It was during my College vacation, so I gave up my holiday so he could have one. Well, you know what? He just came back, and went back to work the next day, and he didn't say a word. Not a word of thanks! [Ian said these words in a tone of deep disgust.]

My father was in his seventies when he told me this story, and he was describing events that had occurred some fifty years earlier. Nothing that had happened subsequently (including his father's death when Ian himself was in his thirties) had persuaded him to revise his adolescent view of his father. He had developed no understanding of his Dad's emotionally frozen personality that might have helped him to see why Albert might have felt unable to express gratitude to a son who had from the very beginning rejected him, and worshipped Albert's wife – Ian's mother – instead. My own attempts to tell my father what I'd worked out about Albert (who had died when I was a toddler) fell on deaf ears: Ian had been there, and I had not. How could I understand? To him, his dad was 'impossible', whereas his mum was 'a wonderful woman, and that was that'. ('That was that' statements – or their equivalents – are common when adults talk about family-of-origin experiences in therapy sessions. It is their way of signalling that they do not want to look further, or to revisit painful memories.)

How loyalties are produced – and reproduced

As we saw in Chapter 2, children naturally attempt to attach to a parent or caregiver virtually from birth, and these attachments, too, will shape their subsequent interactions within the family. If both parents are able to be fully present for the child, love the child, and care for it together, then the chances are that the child will experience both as valued and important people in its world. However, if the parents are already in conflict with each other (as my grandfather and grandmother were), the existing tensions in their relationship will tend to produce a situation in which a child will be likely to bond more intensely with one, and feel correspondingly more distant from the other.

This is what happened with my father, whose closeness to his mother Ethel automatically excluded Albert. Of course, Albert's own crippling shyness and fits of panicky rage contributed to this alienation, for such processes are always (as we've seen) two-way. But alliances, once formed, tend to strengthen, and the more we cling to one parent, the harder it will be to find common ground with the other. This is yet another instance of the principle that once things have taken a certain course, they will simply continue in that course, unless other possibilities are consciously created.

A child will consistently perceive one parent or caregiver as 'like me', 'safe' or 'understanding', whereas the other may be seen as 'different from me', 'out of reach' or even 'frightening'. In fact, each caregiver will, from time to time, act in ways which contradict these perceptions. Thus a 'distant' parent may occasionally offer closeness, or a 'safe' parent temporarily sink into anxiety or depression, in which she is unreachable. But it is the nature of human emotional bonds that children will overlook such 'exceptions to the rule', and pay much more attention to parental behaviour that supports their existing idealization of one parent, and alienation from the other. Rules (sets of expectations) produce evidence for their own correctness; exceptions create what psychologists call 'cognitive dissonance', and hence tend to be dismissed.

The formation of loyalties is reinforced from the parent's end, too. Adults who are already disappointed in a partner will often seek a substitute closeness in a child. A child is a much more rewarding ally than an adult: he/she looks up to you, believes what you tell him/her, and (at least at first) cannot hurt you back as profoundly as an adult partner can – rather like a pet, really. So parents will, sometimes quite unconsciously, invest emotionally in a son or daughter, or in several of their children, as a substitute for an adult relationship that has failed them. Again, this is what seems to have happened with my grandparents.

> Ethel, my grandmother, soon felt disappointed in Albert, once they were married and living together. He was very far from being the masterful yet sympathetic man she had read about in her romance novels. He could not articulate his feelings, retreated into himself, had little confidence, and exploded whenever anything out of routine was asked of him. Faced with disenchantment, Ethel, like so many women before and since, idealized her sons instead, notably her eldest, Dick, and her youngest, Ian (my Dad). On them she lavished the love and belief she would once have had for Albert.
>
> By contrast, each of Albert's daughters – there were three of them – clung almost as fiercely to their father as the sons did to their mother. They admired his practical skills, and saw his caution and frugality as virtues (where Ethel saw them as mean-spirited and withholding). To them, his withdrawn personality seemed 'natural', and the two younger

daughters both went on to become similarly withdrawn as adults. In old age, they fiercely defended him against all charges of being 'difficult' or 'obnoxious', insisting that those who laid these charges were totally mistaken, and had not seen 'the Dad we knew'. In fact, because they had approving, loving expectations of him, they had elicited different responses from him from the hostile, defensive ones elicited by their brothers, who had less positive expectations.

What was happening here was not simply a case of parent–child alliances. Genetic similarities were involved as well, for both of the two younger girls shared their father's unsociable, anxious temperament, just as both Dick and Ian shared their mother's outgoing, cheerful personality. These genetic similarities made the alliances more likely, and almost certainly strengthened them. However, the eldest daughter, Gwynneth, is a clearer case of a child-to-parent alliance operating without much genetic component. Gwynneth loved and admired her father lifelong, despite being outgoing, sociable and confident – the exact opposite of him. And although she was genetically similar to her mother in many ways, she grew up resenting her. Shared genes do not automatically bring closeness, nor do different genes automatically lead to antagonism or difference. The enormously strong alliance between Ethel and her eldest son seemed almost to require Gwynneth to forge the opposite alliance with the 'left out' parent – her father.

Clearly, cross-gender bonds (when parent and opposite-sex child feel deep, unconflicted affection for one another) are also involved in such alliances, yet once again, this is not so simple as it appears. When a couple have two children of the same sex one after the other, these offspring do not automatically *both* bond with the opposite sex parent. Instead, the alliances seem to work unconsciously towards 'balance', so that a first son may bond with his mother, as predicted, but then a second son may bond more with his father, and the third with the mother again. This is, in fact, almost exactly what happened in my grandparents' family.

> Dick, Ethel's eldest son and first child, bonded with her, as we have seen. But her second child, Ted, seemed to feel an instinctive sympathy for his father, Albert, while retaining a strong affection for his mother. It might be said that he was not 'allied' with either, but moved easily between the two. The third child was Gwynneth, and, as we have seen, her alliance lay with her father, following which the fourth, my own father Ian, repeated Dick's pattern of feeling close to his mother, and distant from his father. The fifth child, another daughter, repeated Ted's and Gwynneth's alliance with their father, while the last daughter, Cherie, managed to like and admire both parents, rather as Ted, the second, had done. Laid out like this, a family of six children exhibits a pattern of alliances that almost

recall the patterned genetic variations Mendel observed in generations of bean plants.

More important, for practical purposes, than these complexities, is the fact that parent–child alliances are kept in place by the same 'inertia' that we have already seen operating in other family processes. Once a child is allied with a parent, that alliance tends to continue and even strengthen. When families present for therapy, the alliances will soon become apparent, often indicated quite blatantly in where individual family members choose to sit. Those who feel close will sit close (often right next to one another); those who feel distant will sit as far away from each other as the seating in the room allows.

> Eighteen-year-old Deena sits next to her mother, and when asked about how the latter might unwittingly be contributing to the family's problems, replies curtly that her mother is the one she can always turn to, a wonderful person who is her closest friend. She ignores the invitation to see her mother as a person who might have faults as well as virtues, making a statement of her own loyalty, and disregarding the more problematic and conflicted experiences that her brother sometimes has with their mother. Her brother Daniel, sitting directly opposite his father, carefully defends his mother too, reserving his honesty for the father who has angered him. His statement foregrounds his disappointment with his dad, with loyalty to his mum in the background.

And, as we saw in Chapter 4, seating pattterns will not only mirror existing alliances and antagonisms, but also confirm them, and invite them to manifest themselves in open agreement or disagreement. Hence, changing family members' seating positions, a tactic adopted by Salvador Minuchin in the family therapy model he popularized in the 1970s, can be a powerful tool for change, giving family members a temporary, but potentially transformative, experience of seeing each other differently. Part of the rationale for early family therapy's preference for dramatic, surprisingly 'concrete' interventions like this one was precisely the fact that families so readily become 'stuck' in dysfunctional patterns of interaction that they lose the ability to perceive that things can ever be different, and require experiences that are novel, colourful and surprising to 'shock' them out of their self-confirming mindsets – and behaviour sets.[4]

Generation to generation

One reason why the alliances and loyalties that we have been examining are so strong in their effects is that they nearly always resonate with similar patterns of alliance and loyalty in previous generations. A father finds it 'natural' to bond with his eldest daughter because, in turn, his own father bonded with his own older sister. A mother finds her husband disappointing and unworthy of her, and turns to her son instead; her own father found his daughter a more equal companion than her mother. And so on.

> Ian, my father, had, as we saw, a distant and hostile relationship with his own father, Albert. The two men did not understand one another, and were never close. In fact, Albert had had a distant relationship with his own father, Petherick, and had always felt close to his mother. In an exact reversal, my father hero-worshipped his mother, Ethel – a woman whose strong loyalty had been for her father, Richard. The pattern is clear: for Ethel, males were trustworthy and lovable; females were more problematic. She took this template into her relationship with her own children.

As we saw in Chapter 2, Murray Bowen, the great theorist of intergenerational family process, suggested that individuals came to adulthood with a certain level of 'undifferentiation'. That is, we are all, to varying extents, prone to simply react to stressful situations (e.g. the distress of another family member) in ways that 'feel right' because of our own emotional programming. To Bowen, the ability to consciously reflect upon a stressful situation, to make thoughtful choices about how one wanted to respond, was what distinguished human beings from animals. But, as Bowen realized, most of us can activate this conscious reflection only some of the time. The potential of our cerebral cortex (the multi-folded 'new brain' that makes us distinctively human) is often swamped by instinctive reactions (Bowen called this 'emotionality') that are dictated by the more primitive parts of the brain which we share with creatures such as reptiles. Fight/flight/freeze reactions, for example, are dictated by the 'old brain', not the cerebral cortex, and our sophisticated rational intellects are surprisingly slow to prompt us to stop and look at whether these instincts are really serving anybody's best interests.[5]

We observed other instinctive reactions at work in therapy groups (Chapters 4 and 5). When groups become sluggish and uncooperative in the wake of losing or gaining a member, or after a holiday break, they are reacting as if governed by some sort of 'shared old brain'. Leaderless, a group has no equivalent of the cerebral cortex that each of its individual members possesses. It cannot 'reflect' upon its actions, or make good decisions based on rational evidence. And this is so, even though individual members may all be of very high intelligence and perfectly capable *individually* of logical, rational thought. In many ways, it is the leader, facilitator or therapist who must function as the group's equivalent of the cerebral cortex and help the group to think about what it is doing, rather than simply reacting. In time, the leader may need to do this less, as the individual group members learn to take over the leadership role and provide this 'thinking' function for the group. But probably the group will always depend upon the leader's 'new brain' role to some degree, especially when its members regress to primitive modes of thinking and acting under the pressure of intense anxiety.

Like groups, but even more so, tightly bonded social systems such as families are particularly prone to generate instinct-based reactions. Anxiety, Bowen thought, travels around families very rapidly, and as soon as a key family member becomes distressed or anxious, others around him or her start to feel their own level of anxiety rise. This in turn leads to 'instinct-driven' responses, which are not thought about, but simply 'acted upon'. Thus if a son or daughter becomes depressed or withdrawn, one of the adults (often, but not always, the mother) will respond by moving in closer to him or her, in an attempt to help or comfort the distressed young person. As with a therapy group member who insistently 'rescues' another in order to defuse his own anxiety, this is not necessarily helpful at all (especially if the young person is already locked into a pattern of being overly dependent on the mother, and has failed to learn to stand on his/her own feet). Another family member, perhaps the father or stepfather, will react in a different, but equally 'instinctive' way, maybe by becoming harshly critical of the young person, and demanding that he/she 'get off their butt and start to act responsibly'. Rather than facing up to, and thinking about, their own anxiety, both these adults 'naturally' focus on the distressed young person, and see him or her as 'the problem', and try to 'do something' about it, to reduce their level of tension.

This combination – one parent empathic, but over-close and over-responsible, the other detached, but over-critical and unempathic – is a classic pattern that develops in response to almost any 'problem behaviour' in a family's children. It can be found in response to anything from 'naughtiness' to schizophrenia, from asthma to attention deficit hyperactivity disorder, from drug abuse to depression. Not surprisingly, 'polarised parents' fail to achieve anything except (usually) to make the problem worse. The child or young person gets a confusing, 'split' message from his/her caregivers. The adults themselves become increasingly locked into their positions, each angry with the other for failing to see the 'obvious truth' of the situation, each failing to see what the child needs from them. Each parent will feel alone, the only one who *really* understands what the child needs. The conflict between them will raise the general level of anxiety in the family, and in turn the 'problem' young person will respond to this, often by becoming even more distressed or withdrawn or aggressive. The family 'solidifies' around this triangle, and soon starts to feel as if things have always been this way, and can never be any other way.[6]

Needless to say, the triangle is not really new: it was already the case that the young person was 'allied' with one parent against the other (in the way we explored above), and the symptomatic behaviour simply pushes each of the parents into more extreme, intensely held positions around it. Of course, in families where a parent, or sometimes a step-parent, is able to take on the same role as the facilitator in a therapy group, and serve as the 'new brain' for the whole family, things can gradually improve. But the families that we see in therapy often do not possess such adult leadership, or must be assisted to develop it. Instead, the adults who 'lead' the family group are themselves driven by the level of anxiety they have brought with them, largely unaltered, from their own childhoods.

Bowen's theory proposes that the child who is on the receiving end of 'undifferentiated', anxious behaviour from her parents generally goes on to become an adult whose own behaviour exhibits roughly the same level of 'undifferentiation'. As we saw in Chapter 2, individuals mysteriously 'know' to select a partner whose level of inability to think while anxious matches their own, and so the stage is set for a new generation of the family, in which the now-adult child will react to her own children in a way not dissimilar to the way her parents reacted to her. Not just genes, but patterns of feeling and acting, repeat in families.

Most educated people assume that such intergenerational 'repeats' can be accounted for by the psychological concept of 'social learning': this means that as small children we observe our parents' words and actions, and naturally 'model' ourselves upon them. Everyone with young children is well aware of this sort of imitation: as soon as children learn to speak, out of their mouths come exact repetitions of our own exclamations ('cute' and lovable if the phrase repeated is 'Oh dear, oh dear, oh dear!', less so, perhaps, if the phrase is 'Shut your face!'). Actions, too, are modelled directly upon ours, and so, often, is the expression of feelings. Yet there are puzzles and complications which social learning theory has to stretch hard to deal with. Why does a child 'model' *one* parent's behaviours, but leave the other caregiver's behaviours quite alone? Why would some children 'model' the words and actions of the parent who is mostly absent (usually the male partner), when it has the constant presence of the other (usually the mother)? Only the cross-generational alliances we examined earlier in this chapter can really make sense of the former, and only genetically determined temperamental similarities can really make sense of the other. And why, above all, do children apparently 'observe' and 'store' behaviours in memory, without activating them at all in childhood, only to find that those same behaviours well up unchanged, twenty years later, when they themselves become parents of young children?

As we have seen, Bowen's theory proposes that small children automatically and unconsciously absorb the level of anxiety that their adult caregivers feel. Bowen did not (as far as I am aware) spell out the next step, but to my way of thinking it would be this. The children would then experience the same need to 'channel' this anxiety that the adults do, and it would make sense to me that they would typically adopt the adults' own behaviours as a way of doing so. Their choice of *which* adult to 'learn from' would be dictated by the complex interaction of the same factors as we have been describing in this chapter: genetic temperament, child–parent alliances, and birth order. Some of the behaviours would not manifest themselves until the child reached the age at which the anxiety would 'kick in' – the age when that child had itself become a parent. Behaviour needs an appropriate 'stage' on which it can be 'performed', after all.

Invisible loyalties and denied bonds

As we saw earlier in this chapter, many adults cling fiercely to idealized images of one of their parents (occasionally both) and in this way display 'loyalty' in its most obvious form. However, the process we have just been examining shows us a different form of loyalty. In this 'invisible' loyalty, individuals find themselves acting just like an adult model, even if that 'model' was someone they detested, even if the model was someone they hardly knew. This sounds like the opposite of idealization, yet in a curious way it is the same. Both loyalties are driven by patterns learned so far back in our childhoods that they seem almost 'instinctive'. The term 'invisible loyalty' was coined by a contemporary of Bowen, Hungarian-born Ivan Boszormenyi-Nagy, who made a special study of the ways in which patterns of feeling, thought and action repeat themselves across generations, even when (in fact, *especially* when) one generation has little or no contact with those that came before it.[7]

Here we come across another of those family processes that seem contrary to the logic of social learning theory. It makes sense that close acquaintance with an adult family member could lead to 'modelling' one's behaviour on his/hers. But how would *lack* of knowledge produce a repetition across generations? There is something here that is a kind of collective equivalent to 'denial' within an individual. When an awareness within ourselves is too painful, too uncomfortable or shameful, we 'deny' it (not only to others, but also to ourselves). We simply tell ourselves 'I am not like him. I am completely different. In fact, I hate him. So how can I resemble him in any way?'

Families do the same sort of thing, only at the level of their collective 'consciousness'. Families will often 'cut off' from a family member whose conduct has been deeply distressing to live with, abusive, shameful or intolerable (alcoholism, mental illness, criminal behaviour, and sexual invasiveness are among the most common examples). They refuse to have contact with him/her, and do not speak of him/her. Of course it is perfectly justifiable for a family to refuse contact with an individual who has acted abusively or destructively in the past and continues to do so, apparently without remorse or shame. But, the 'cut-off' typically extends further: family members will not tell their children about the individual, or what he/she was like. If asked, they will either pretend ignorance, or flatly refuse to speak further ('Well, that's that'). The refusal to name the reality of the situation goes beyond justifiable self-protection, into denial, and a kind of 'airbrushing' of the past in order to ensure a 'clean' future. In these circumstances, a child will sometimes grow up exhibiting some level of genetic similarity to the 'disappeared' family member, causing his/her parents enormous fear that he/she will 'turn out the same'. The fear cannot be spoken about, and as time goes on, it looms larger and becomes even less possible to acknowledge ('because if we told her, it would be sure to make her worse'). The fear and the secrecy drive parents into more rigid, extreme attitudes towards the 'problem child' (who perhaps would not have needed to be a problem, had it been possible to talk openly about the original 'problem') and trigger his/her own potential for destructiveness or selfish, entitled behaviour. And so on. Thus the child's 'invisible loyalty' to the 'liquidated' relative comes into being in a context of cut-off, denial and ignorance. Withholding knowledge can be as destructive as imparting knowledge before children are old enough to cope with its impact, and families typically err on the former side rather than the latter.

Family 'denial' of this kind extends to all kinds of 'secrets', of every degree of 'shamefulness'. Most of them are very different from the one above, where a relative may have to be disowned because of his/her continuing potential for real, invasive damage. Adoptions, out-of-wedlock pregnancies, rapes, suicides, early infant deaths – all can be, and often are, concealed from children as they grow up, and not acknowledged even between the adults who have experienced them. Shame is the great destroyer of truth in families, and one of the family therapist's key tasks is to somehow find a way of lifting its burden.[8]

Alternatively, it may be the 'difficult' family member him/herself who severs the connection, living a lonely, drifting existence in cities on the other side of the country, emigrating to another part of the world, or even living quite close by, but with no visits, no contact of any kind. This family member tells him/herself, 'I'm better off without them. They've treated me like shit, they've ruined my life, I'm not going to have anything to do with them ever again.' This family member may then go on to raise children without contact with, or knowledge of, his/her original family. He/she may vow, 'I'm not going to treat them the way I was treated', and consequently go to the other extreme, producing children who grow up feeling entitled to have whatever they want, whatever the cost to others. Thus another generation of 'problem children' grows up, as a direct result of the emotional cut-off in their parent's generation. 'Invisible loyalties' have come into being once again.

Bowen argues that when 'cut-off' occurs, family members remain as closely meshed together as ever, despite perhaps living worlds apart. The shadow of the unresolved conflict lies as heavily on the one who leaves as on those who stay behind. The fact that it cannot be spoken about does not mean that it cannot be *felt*. The family has found no way to face up to the conflict and work through it by thinking, and then acting in a rational, planful way. Instead, faced with overwhelmingly painful feelings, they have simply acted out of the instinctive behaviour patterns that they share with wolves, birds and lizards.

New generations of family members grow up, ignorant of a conflict that may have occurred in their parents' generation, yet aware nonetheless of discomfort, of 'no-go areas', or questions that must not be asked. They inherit their parents' level of denial, and grow up 'knowing' that whatever it was that happened must have been so terrible that it cannot be spoken about. They take this frightening awareness into their own adult relationships, finding themselves facing their own 'no-go areas'. And it is in these circumstances that the most eerie family phenomena of all seem to occur.[9]

> My mother's grandfather George Edward died suddenly of a heart attack at the age of 43. The sudden death shocked his young family. Despite an apparently successful legal career, he left his family with little money, and his son Victor, my grandfather, had to leave the private school he had been attending, abandon his hopes of becoming a doctor, and earn his living as a low-paid journalist. Victor married Eva, my grandmother, and they had two children together, but his marriage disappointed him, and when he left Australia to fight for King and Country in 1915, he fell in love with another woman. His marriage survived, but the betrayal could not be openly talked about, and as a child my mother knew only that 'something had happened during the War' which had caused permanent distrust between her parents. Victor never settled back into civilian life in Australia, drank heavily, and died suddenly in a car accident at almost exactly the same age as his own father had. His two children were traumatized, as he himself had been, and his son (my uncle) who was only nine at the time, began truanting from school. He joined the army at the earliest possible age, the same age as his father Victor had been when he was forced to leave school and go to work. He fought with distinction in the Second World War, and married overseas, never returning to his own country except for two brief visits. Though he wrote to his mother and his sister (my mother), his emotional life was completely separate from theirs. At around the same age at which his father, and his father's father, had died, he retired from the army, and began drinking heavily.

This dramatic example (and I have left out several even more telling details through lack of space) illustrates the way that cut-off emotions (shock and traumatic grief) may create the necessary conditions for a repetition of trauma, which in turn sends more 'shockwaves' into the next generation. My point is this: it may not be possible to avoid trauma, but facing up to it, talking about it, and trying to live with it, is more likely to decrease its impact than the 'natural' reaction of walling it off in silence as a 'taboo topic'. By trying to protect themselves from additional distress, families in fact generate even more distress, and over a much longer time period. Once again, I think inherited temperament has a fair bit to do with this. Particularly sensitive people (and my family on both sides is full of them) feel trauma more deeply, and find more difficulty in facing distressing emotions (including shame). More resilient families, experiencing the same initial traumas, might manage them better, talk about them more openly, and hence face less destructive consequences.

Why families get so stuck

In this chapter I have tried hard to show just how complex family patterns are, how multi-layered and multi-determined. For me, this makes it easier to understand why families get entrenched in negativity, taking 'the way they perceive it' for 'the way it has to be'. Family patterns are sustained by the interaction of three, four, five or more people, some ageing, some adults in the prime of life, some infants, some children, some adolescents, all growing and changing, and locked into alliances and enmities which, like paving in a 'herringbone' pattern, interlock and support one another.

In part, this seems to be why only a minority of families seem to benefit from 'understanding how the past is alive in the present' (those therapies derived from, or related to, psychoanalytic approaches):

> Faced with my account of the three-generation repeating pattern of traumatic loss, cut-off and alcohol abuse in my mother's family, my relatives seemed sceptical, quizzical or simply bored. Few of them seemed able, or willing, to take in the implications of the pattern, and dismissed it as 'reading too much into it all'. 'Anyway,' as one relative told me, 'it all happened a long time ago: it's got nothing to do with us'.

Similarly, if we simply explain to parents how their 'natural' behaviour is unwittingly sustaining their child's behaviour problems, only a proportion will be able to process the information and use it to alter their own behaviour. More common is the response 'I don't see why I should change! It's *her* problem! Why can't you help her to learn a bit of respect? In practice, attempts to promote straightforward behaviour change on the basis of insight ('If what you're doing isn't working, are you ready to face the challenge and do something different?') are far less successful than a carefully orchestrated TV therapy, with a master performer like Dr Phil, might suggest.

To return to analogies used earlier, families, like therapy groups, operate at the level of survival instincts whenever their existence seems threatened. Well-meaning attempts to promote change around distressing, painful issues seem to strike many families as 'threats to their existence'. To use language which family therapy would now consider old-fashioned, they 'resist' change, and 'maintain the status quo', as if unwilling or unable to understand the longer-term implications of their inflexible clinging to established loyalties and disappointments.

Beyond blame and shame

Near its beginning, family therapy probably had more in common with group therapy than at any other time. Pioneers such as Virginia Satir and Carl Whitaker challenged whole families to openly express their feelings, explored the parents' past in the presence of their children, named unhealthy parent–child coalitions, and generally expected the family to relate like the members of an 'encounter group' (a popular modality at the time). This way of working could yield high-octane interactions, but it was hard work for the many therapists who did not possess high levels of energy, and the ability to manage multiple, intense interactions. Moreover, many families simply were not up for something so confronting, or willing to commit to sustained work over quite a number of sessions. Lots of families refused to bring all family members to sessions, and others dropped out very early, leaving family therapy with a bad name.

Increasingly, family therapy became characterized by a search for ways to 'work around' this type of resistance. Quite deliberately and consciously, some leaders of family therapy made a decision to 'step aside' from the complexity of meanings and emotions as defined by families themselves, and instead to use language strategically (i.e. consciously and deliberately) to redefine realities and invite change in patterns of behaviour. And, despite a procession of 'revolutions', new metaphors, and new ideologies over the past twenty years, family therapy practice continues to make *strategic use of language* to 'unstick' families from the kinds of dysfunctional patterns we have been exploring in this chapter.

First, family therapy abandoned the wording that located problems 'inside' individuals. Instead of talking about somebody 'having' depression, or 'having' an eating disorder, or a drinking problem, they paid attention to how these problems were *maintained* (or even 'nurtured') by the interactions that the individual had with other key people in his/her world. Avoiding notions of 'cause' and 'effect' (which would identify someone as having 'started it all', and lead automatically to blame), family therapists instead spoke of 'inadvertent' behaviour. Where family members felt controlled and dominated by 'the problem' in their midst, it made sense for the therapist to suggest that the problem might be a friend, rather than an enemy. This was sometimes called 'reframing' and later 'positive connotation' (seeking out ways in which 'problem' behaviour in one or more family members might actually be assisting the family to deal with, or avoid, other problems). Any 'weakness' could be framed as a 'strength' or a virtue (and so we have therapists commending a withdrawn, passive man for 'protecting your wife from your anger'). Any 'symptom' could be seen as a 'solution to a problem' (and so the Milan Associates might commend an anorexic girl for keeping her parents' marriage together, 'sacrificing herself' to distract them from their conflicts through their fears for her life).[10]

Family therapists began to invite families to talk about their strengths and achievements, rather than their perceived weaknesses and failures – the 'solution-focused' approach. If the weaknesses and failures so dominated everyone's awareness that they demanded centre stage, then therapists began to talk about them as entities external to the individual, so that they no longer compromised the identity and esteem of the person who experienced them. Thus therapists of a Narrative persuasion would ask 'How long has fear been in the driver's seat of your life?' or 'Can you tell me any victories you've won in your struggle with anorexia over the past three years?' We will return to the advantages of these uses of language in Chapter 8.[11]

Where more traditional approaches would endeavour to explore the destructive effects of long-established loyalties and enmities, but by doing so risked reinforcing blame and shame, family therapy came increasingly to avoid such 'head-on' collisions with the family's way of seeing things. Family work became less to do with bringing family members together to openly acknowledge and work through their problems and misperceptions, and more to do with inviting families to play a very different game, in a different playing field altogether. Though much less radical than many family therapists, the next chapter will show my own blend of both the 'old' and 'new' approaches. For paradoxically, despite how strongly 'set' many family patterns can be, to change them is not impossible – if we are simply prepared to throw our weight on to the other side of the yacht, to counter the wind in the sail, which would otherwise capsize us.

Notes

1 See Crago (unpublished, 1998), an 'emotional history' of my family of origin.
2 For temperament research, see p. 49, n. 8. On genes that 'pull' certain responses from caregivers, see Reiss *et al.* (2000). On the various 'temperament styles' ('easy', 'difficult', etc.), see Kagen *et al.* (1997).
3 Frans de Waal's (1989) studies of the conflict resolution behaviour of apes make fascinating reading in terms of both their similarities to, and differences from, their human equivalents.
4 See Minuchin (1974: 138ff.). Many of Minuchin's 'dramatic' tactics evolved during his period of working with ghetto families (Minuchin 1967).

5   Bowen used the term 'emotionality' to mean, roughly, 'instinctive anxiety' (see Kerr and Bowen 1988). This, along with his obvious valuing of rational thought, led some of his critics to assume that he was 'scared of emotion' or 'had a masculine preference for intellect over emotional expression'. This was not the case. Rather, Bowen believed that what was important was the ability to feel whatever one felt, but also stand back from that feeling, and not simply act impulsively on it. Bowen's understanding of the 'old brain' and its functions was derived in the main from Paul MacLean's work (see MacLean 1978, 1990). More recent brain research (on humans) has confirmed and greatly extended the sorts of insights that were available to Bowen in the 1970s; see, for example, LeDoux (1998).

6   Triangles were a key concept in both Minuchin's (1974) structural family therapy and Bowen's (see Kerr and Bowen, 1988). However, there are some differences in how each understood the nature of triangles, and also differences in how each proposed that they should be dealt with in therapy.

7   On Ivan Boszormenyi-Nagy, see p. 9, n. 9.

8   In my article 'The not to be opened letter' (Crago 1997), I examine some of the dilemmas that face the therapist dealing with intergenerational 'secrets', and suggest a way of responding to them without necessarily arguing for the secret to be revealed.

9   Earnshaw (1998) has greatly extended Freud's concept of the 'repetition compulsion' and the notion of 'anniversary reactions', collecting a great deal of biographical material to show that traumatic events in one generation typically 'shadow' the lives of the next, as soon as the adult son or daughter reaches the age the parent was when the trauma occurred. This effect occurs regardless of whether or not the son or daughter knows of the parent's trauma.

10 Selvini Palazzoli *et al.* (1978)

11 For solution focused therapy, see de Shazer (1985) and Cade and O'Hanlon (1993). For introductory papers on the key concepts of narrative therapy, see p. 171, nn 8 and 9.

7 'All those people in the room!'
Getting started with families

An adult therapy group may comprise eight or more people, yet when a family of four or five straggles in, the room seems somehow more crowded. There's an immediate sense of 'Oh wow, all these people!' The air is heavy with expectation. Polite, well-bred families betray their tensions in small signs, often non-verbal. Families too desperate to care about appearances act out their tensions immediately and dramatically: kids refuse to sit down, or insist on swapping seats, parents try to control them and get treated with scant respect in return, adult partners sit as far apart as possible, or cling to each other as if for dear life. Whatever way they present themselves, families demand our attention, and yet distract each other, and us, from getting down to work quickly and easily. We are likely to feel awkward, shambling, even incompetent, at least for a while. Where on earth do we begin? If we wade in and start asking questions, are we likely to do more harm than good, maybe even cause 'an explosion'? These are common fears in counsellors coming to family work for the first time. So how do we get something under way without making things worse?

A therapy group starts without a history. While each individual group member has a reason for being there, and a legacy of dissatisfaction or distress in his/her own life, the group has not yet evolved any *shared* experiences of suffering, conflict, or trauma. Couples and families, by contrast, come into counselling with a shared history, an 'agenda' of pain, disappointment and anger. This agenda is what they will naturally 'warm up to' when they start to speak. So we cannot begin a family session simply by providing an initial statement, and then 'sitting back and seeing what happens', as we might be able to do with a therapy group of motivated, voluntary clients. Just as with a couple, our first task in meeting with a new family is to provide some basic structure, a structure which can contain the high anxieties and very different 'realities' likely to be present, either overtly or not far below the surface. In order to do this, we must be prepared to act firmly and clearly from the beginning. And in many cases, 'from the beginning' means from the initial telephone contact.

Getting started: who should attend the session?

Before we can do family therapy, we have to get families to attend sessions together, rather than send one of their number to be 'fixed'. In the early days, some family therapists insisted that every member of the household attend, from infants in arms to aged grandparents, or boarders in the family home. They wanted to convey the novel idea that the work was going to address the family as an entity, rather than simply focusing on the one or two family members identified by others in the family as 'the problem'. This tactic, while critical in gaining leverage with some types of family problems (e.g. drug-abusing young people), was probably unnecessarily confrontational for many families, and led to a high drop-out rate, and clients leaving with a sense that they, the 'innocent parties' were being 'blamed' for the problems experienced by one of their number. This was especially the case where that family member had a mental illness. Feelings of shame, and corresponding blaming of others, are fundamental to many of the families we see in counselling, and over the years family therapists have learned to be more flexible, and less confrontational, as a way of avoiding the crippling effect of such feelings.[1]

Typically, one parent (usually the mother) will ring with a request that I see her child or teenager individually, 'to sort out his problems' or 'because I think she really needs help and I'm at the end of my tether'. I generally respond by asking some questions that try to gauge the extent of the difficulties, and how long-standing they are. I then routinely ask whether she (and her partner if there is one) would be prepared to meet with me before I see the young person, 'so I can get some background information, before I see your son/daughter'. Most parents are reasonably happy with this request, and many are relieved to get the chance to tell 'their side of the story' first. If the parent indicates that her partner may not want to attend, I do not push for this, but simply say 'Well, then, if you just come by yourself, that will still be very useful, and maybe later it might be important for me to get his point of view.'

I use this initial phone call, and the subsequent meeting with the adult or the adult couple, to start an assessment of the problem – how severe it is, how long it has been going on, what it might mean. But I am also trying to assess whether it might make sense to work with the parents/caregivers alone, 'coaching' them on how to help the child, or whether it is important to begin by seeing the whole family together, before deciding whether to continue with the whole family, with the adults by themselves or (in comparatively rare cases) with the child alone. Why would I want to see the whole family before deciding how to proceed? Because so much more *information* is available to me: 'action information', not just reported information. In a family session, the family cannot help but tell me about themselves, whether they want to or not, and whether they use words to do it or not.

Why would I rarely think in terms of individual therapy for the child, at least as an initial option? Firstly, because being sent to 'see someone' is likely to be stigmatizing, and if young people are already facing distressing feelings, it would be better if they were spared the additional distress of feeling that their problems were so 'bad' they 'had to see a counsellor'. Second, because children rarely ask for help directly, and are thus mostly 'involuntary' clients, ambivalent or even actively hostile to the idea of being 'seen' by me or anyone else. It seems fairer to me that, if they do need to be involved, they be involved alongside of those who actually perceive the problem – usually, their caregivers. Finally, without an in-depth knowledge of the child's or teenager's family, its current dynamics, and its past history, individual therapy, even with a relatively willing young client, is often hamstrung. Working with a young person's reality alone often means that we miss key pieces of information about what the problem means (in terms of the family as a whole) and how it is maintained, inadvertently, by other family members.

I must admit that I personally feel less anxious about seeing a whole family if I have first met with the adults, established a beginning relationship with them, and got an initial sense of what may be going on. I can then go into a 'whole family' session with more confidence, and clearer ideas about what I need to find out, and what sort of structure I need to provide. If a key family member is unwilling to participate (it is often the father, but sometimes it is an adolescent identified as 'the problem' who refuses to attend), then I like to know this beforehand, and rather than try to 'fight' it by trying harder to get that person to come to the session ('more of the same wrong solution'), I simply go along with it, and make sure that, when I meet with the rest, I remember to ask things like:

> 'If your son was here, what do you think he would say about where the problem lies?'

> 'If your stepdad was here, do you think he would be happy with what's going on, or do you think he'd want things to be different?'

Getting started: providing a structure for the initial session

Providing a structure for a first family session will usually involve:

- joining with the family (establishing a minimal working relationship with them) before getting into 'the problem';
- deciding which family member to engage with first;
- seeking information from all family members, and being prepared to

interrupt (as with a couple) in order to allow everyone a chance to contribute fairly;

- declining invitations from one or more family members to join with them in animated discussions of 'who is most to blame' or other distractions from the problem;
- being prepared to alter what we are doing, if it isn't working;
- deliberately asking about things that are outside the family's own 'agenda' (often this will mean asking about successes, good times, and previous partial solutions to long-standing problems);
- working towards some minimal common ground, where all family members who are capable of understanding the situation can agree that something needs to be addressed or needs to change.

'Joining' and 'warm-up'

In some respects, 'joining' is the family therapy equivalent of 'establishing a working alliance' in individual psychotherapy. The counsellor must honour each family member's reality sufficiently for them to feel 'I'm probably going to get a fair hearing here', and indicate some empathy for their perspective. This is the basis on which the counsellor may later be permitted to ask difficult questions or to challenge perceptions. The 'joining' phase of the family session might also be seen as equivalent to Moreno's notion of 'warm-up': by engaging with each family member about topics that are not directly linked with the presenting problem, the counsellor gives each one the opportunity to acclimatize her/himself to the counselling environment, to speak about things that are emotionally 'neutral' or positive, and to realize that other aspects of his/her life – not just 'problem behaviour' – are going to be considered important by the counsellor.[2] Talking initially about something non-threatening, even fun, can particularly assist children who may be anxious at being blamed, or worried that the adults may 'blow up' into angry exchanges or outpourings of distress.

In attempting to engage young people, I try to avoid asking them about school (unless they specifically volunteer it), but I do ask what type of music they like, what movies they've seen recently and what they think of them, what computer games they play, or what sports they follow. All of these things offer me insights into what matters to them, and opportunities to ask 'dumb' questions about things they know more about than I do (current music, and sports, are two topics on which I am genuinely ignorant). If children seem reticent and give minimal answers, I don't persist for too long, instead suggesting that they may feel more like talking later, and that I won't pressure them to speak unless they want to. Initially silent or surly children will often spark up once a sibling or a parent says something they disagree with! Again, this is the principle of *going with the resistance*, rather than 'fighting' family members to do things my way. By calmly accepting that someone does not feel like talking right now, and refusing to be flustered or authoritarian in response, I can give the message that such feelings are natural, and that everything will be all right anyway – in much the same way as this message is conveyed by the therapist's 'non-anxious presence' during the first and second phases of a therapy group's early development.

Engaging with the problem: getting information

When it is time to engage more directly with the problem that has brought the family in to see me, I must decide *who to speak with first*. This is made much easier if I have already spoken with one parent on the phone, or seen one of the adults, or both, in a prior meeting. I can then say to the other family members:

> 'Well, I've had a chance to talk to your mum [or whoever] a few days ago, and she's told me a few things about the situation . . . so now I'm interested in hearing from everybody else about what you all think is going on, and what can be done about it.'

When summarizing what I have already been told, I substitute try hard to be as diplomatic as possible! If loaded, judgemental terms have been used by a parent or caregiver, I substitute factual descriptions:

> 'The way your Dad sees it, one of the things your family is facing is that Jason has been getting into some trouble at school, and he seems to have lost interest in his after-school job too. I got the impression that everyone wants the best for Jason, but that when they try to talk to him about it, he gets angry and leaves the house.'

From my early family therapy training, I learned to avoid turning directly to the 'problem person' in the family, and asking them for their response to such accounts from their caregivers. Instead, I turn next to the family member I think might most capable of seeing things more objectively, without taking sides. An older sibling (sometimes, surprisingly, a younger sibling) is often such a person, and I can ask this young person for his/her ideas about the situation. I might add 'That's what your mum said . . . I wonder is there anything else you think I should know? Maybe something you've noticed, but that she didn't mention?' I wait until a couple of family members have supplied their perspective on the problem before directly asking 'Jason' for his thoughts.

Needless to say, the neat 'formula' I have just supplied is just that – a neat formula, which doesn't always work, and which may need to be altered to fit particular families and particular problems. There are occasions when it *is* necessary, right from the start, to ask the 'identified patient' (as family therapists used to call the 'person with the perceived problem') up-front, especially if I have the strong impression that he/she has been systematically marginalized in the whole dialogue. There is thus an element of 'rebalancing' in the order in which we might solicit information from the various family members. Although I generally agree with Jay Haley's rule that parents should always be asked first (to establish that they are, or should be, in charge), I think even this rule may need to be broken occasionally.[3] Sometimes parental authority has so far broken down that an older child is the real 'authority' in the family, and that position may need to be acknowledged through involving her or him very early in the questioning process. Indeed, it is not unusual for caregivers (particularly if they have a disability, or have themselves been neglected or traumatized in their growing-up years) to function more like children than like responsible adults.

Gaining information from all family members is easy when children are old enough to be able to hold their own in an adult-level conversation, but when they are either too young to fully understand what they are being asked, or unable to articulate their responses and make themselves understood, then different forms of engagement and information-gathering need to be employed. Toddlers and younger preschoolers can often be introduced to the toy box early in the session, or provided with art materials, and, with uncanny accuracy, the ways that they choose to interact with these non-verbal media will often tell us much of what we need to know about the family, and their perceived place in it.[4] Even the youngest family members will have their own ways of 'telling' us what is important to them, and what other family members may be unwilling to voice openly.

Pre-verbal children are very like pet animals in their sensitivity to the emotion of others. Babies will start to wail loudly, and older children suddenly begin a loud interaction with a sibling, in direct response to something that has just been said (or not said).

> Natasha and her husband William had seen me several times, bringing their eight-month-old baby with them. The little girl rolled around on her blanket and amused herself most of the time, but as soon as Natasha began touching on painful childhood memories of sexual abuse, the child began to fuss loudly, and would not be comforted when William (a very involved and caring dad) picked her up. Only Mummy would do, and of course, holding and soothing her child made it very difficult for Natasha to continue to experience the intensity of emotion she had begun to feel. Instead, she became distanced and matter of fact, as if to say 'Well, that's enough of that for today'. Some would say that the little girl had 'protected' her mother; perhaps it would be more accurate to say that she

simply responded instinctively to her mother's rising anxiety, by displaying anxiety of her own. The *effect* of her fussing, though, was to defuse her mother's anxiety. [This tiny example vividly demonstrates Bowen's principle about how families *instinctively* react to anxiety, and how a child's distress can deflect from adults' problems.]

Younger school-age children, not yet inhibited by social norms, will also 'blurt out' the most amazingly accurate things about their parents and siblings, precisely the things that the older members of the family have carefully avoided saying. While I do not favour immediate 'interpretations' of such behaviour ('I think what Patrice is trying to tell us is . . .'), which can come across as a bit 'know it all' on our part, I do think that we can sometimes wonder aloud about what the child's behaviour or words might mean, or store up the information to introduce in a less immediate way later, when the emotional temperature has gone down a bit.

Observing young children's informal play during a session shades into structured assessment exercises for the whole family which require interaction and participation in response to a common task. For example, the 'family interactive art exercise'[5] requires all family members to use a range of media provided (colours, scissors, magazines for cutting up) to produce a joint picture of the family, say, or a collage of a 'family day out'. Families are deliberately given minimal instructions as to how these tasks are to be accomplished, and this enables the therapist (and/or observers) to notice who takes charge, who is responsible and who avoids responsibility, who monopolizes attention, who gets marginalized, who distracts, who attempts to mediate or problem-solve, and so on. Alliances and stand-offs are also clearly revealed by such exercises, which remove some of the developmental differences in maturity and articulacy between adult and child family members.

Of course, much of the same information will be revealed by families in subtle and unsubtle ways during a normal 'verbal' session. Just as in a therapy group, it will often be significant who sits next to whom, and which family members choose opposing seating positions. Often, one or two family members will attempt to dominate, and others will prefer passive withdrawal rather than open conflict, while others again attempt to 'hose down' incipient conflicts. In this sense, family members' unexamined, unrehearsed behaviour towards each other will more vividly reveal their underlying dynamics than what they actually put into words.

Asking about the problem

Yet it remains important in a first session to fill out our picture of the presenting problem itself. We may already have a sense of how long the problem has existed, and who it mainly affects. Now, we need to find out more exactly:

- Who is most involved in the problem? Who is least involved?
- How do those directly involved interact around the problem? ('So, you and your Mum have fights about how much you're prepared to eat at mealtimes. Who starts the fights? What exactly happens? Who else gets involved? How long do the fights last? How do they typically end? What do people feel like afterwards? How long is it before the same fight starts up again?')
- Have there been times when the problem does not occur, or gets resolved easily?

These types of questions are basic to most forms of family therapy, whatever 'school' a practitioner may belong to. They direct family attention to facts, rather than to discussions of who is to blame, and they raise consciousness of predictable patterns. From family therapy's early days, practitioners have found that gathering factual data cooperation is an excellent way of gaining family members' cooperation, while simultaneously avoiding unnecessary levels of anxiety at an early stage in the family's work. Factual questions of this nature (particularly favoured by Bowen's followers) lead naturally (in first, or later, sessions) to 'scaling questions' and 'relative influence questions', of the type used by brief and solution-focused therapists:

> 'How much of your life would you say this problem of your weight dominates?'

> 'What proportion of your thoughts do your "down feelings" take up?'

> 'On a scale of one to ten, where '1' would mean that you had pretty much total control over how often you wash your hands, and 'ten' would mean you had no control at all, where would you place your own level of control over this handwashing thing?'

> 'Which other family members do you believe that your Dad's temper most affects? Which family members do you believe are least affected?'

It is generally much easier to get family members to agree on the harmful *effects* of a problem (which everyone can deplore) than to gain agreement on 'who is most responsible' or 'to blame' for the problem!

In this way, we attempt to *work towards some measure of agreement, some common goal*, even though family members may be polarized around other aspects of the problem situation. A general agreement that everyone would like to see things improve, or that everyone would like to lessen the harmful effects of the problem on the whole family, is often a relief to the family, whose entire experience of the problem to date may feel like continuous conflict, blaming, defence, distress and helplessness.

Noticing the unnoticed: asking about exceptions and successes

Like couples, families tend to evolve patterns of interaction that carry negative meanings for them, and their perceptions then become dominated by those meanings, so that they produce more and more evidence to support what they are convinced they see. Evidence that contradicts their preferred meanings tends to be dismissed, or not even seen at all. Because families create such powerful, multi-stranded patterns, it is even more vital than it is with couples for us to draw attention to 'exceptions' to the beliefs they have constructed around destructive 'feedback loops'. Entire schools of family therapy (notably the brief, solution-focused and strength-focused approaches of Steve de Shazer, Bill O'Hanlon and Insoo Kim Berg) assert that we simply need to look persistently for the strengths, successes and 'sparkling moments' which families have in their shared histories, yet which are often completely omitted when they are telling us their stories. These stories are typically organized around the problem, full of negative judgements, pessimism and frustration. By altering the focus of the story, and the language in which it is told, we can invite the family, right from the beginning, to participate in a different construction of their joint reality.

Quite apart from this goal, enquiring about 'exceptions' or 'unique outcomes' is fully justified simply as part of a full assessment process. Thus we might ask:

> 'Have there been times when the problem seemed less pressing than it does now? What did you notice about those times? Was anyone doing anything different? Were the family's circumstances different?'

> 'Have you ever tried anything that you thought might help with this problem? What did you try? How long did you try for? What degree of success did you have when you tried?'

If some partial successes have been reported, we might ask:

> 'What do you think it might have been that persuaded you to stop trying this way of approaching the problem? What got in the way of your persisting?'

If families do come up with some clear 'exceptions', I often draw attention to them by saying something like:

'What you've just told me actually sounds pretty important. I'm not too sure just what it means now, but maybe in time we can discover that. At any rate, it makes me wonder whether you might have discovered something, back then, that had the potential to help you with the problem. Maybe you lost sight of it, but perhaps it might be worth taking another look at, to see if it still has something to offer?'

Some families, presenting a story of unremitting loss, conflict, illness and accident, inadvertently include little references to things which we can see are actually significant triumphs of the human spirit. When this happens, simply drawing attention to these things may in itself be enough to kickstart the family into perceiving its own history with more pride, and less distress:

> Agnes, a defeated-looking middle-aged woman whose family had experienced multiple, serious problems over many years, brought her adolescent and early adult children in to see us. Her husband, a surly recovering alcoholic, had flatly refused to come. In the first two or three sessions, Agnes described the succession of tragedies that had overtaken her and her children: one of them born with a developmental disability, another developing multiple sclerosis, a third getting pregnant as a teenager and having to give up her baby for adoption. She herself had suffered for many years with depression, while attempting to cope with all of this and keep the family together while her husband continued to drink. Although we did not specifically ask her to tell us about the family's achievements, we did realize that the father's giving up drinking might itself be an important milestone. When we asked about what had enabled him to make this tough decision, and what had changed in the family as a result, Agnes revealed that in fact, things had made a definite change for the better some years before his decision to give up alcohol. This led to our asking about other things that had changed for the better over the past 20 or so years. There proved to be several momentous changes, none of which had been mentioned in the family's initial presentation of the problems facing them. We made a very large 'timeline' in the form of a wall chart, and hung it on the wall in front of the family, adding new 'turning points' and details about their significance. Over the subsequent sessions the children joined Agnes in pointing out things that should go on the chart. The family ceased seeing us after some ten sessions, reporting that most of their problems were now under control. Agnes sent us Christmas cards for many years afterwards, giving us reports on the family's continued progress.

While this sort of story is impressive and inspirational, simply drawing attention to 'success stories' as well as 'failure stories' does not always lead to such smooth progress towards better outcomes. As I mentioned when discussing couples, sometimes too much emphasis on successes and achievements can come across to clients as an unwillingness to hear their pain, a determination to 'cheer them up' no matter what. It can even propel some families into renewed crisis, as if to let us know, loud and clear, just how bad things are. In this, as in any other intervention, we must once again remember that if clients fail to embrace our approach, we need to rethink what we are doing, and listen to them, instead of simply persisting.

In the first session or two, however, what I mostly do is simply 'balance' the negativity of the family's account by asking about potential positives. Later, when I know more about what is going on, I may (or may not) use the evidence of 'exceptions' and 'success stories' as the basis for an intervention like the one we used with Agnes. I might also choose to use colourful sets of cards such as St Luke's *Strength Cards, The Bears, Angels with Attitude* or *Stones*,[6] to bridge the gap between the older family members and young children whose language is undeveloped. Picking up one of these cards, with their strong visual and tactile appeal, is also easier for whole families whose ability to articulate feelings about self and others may be undeveloped. These tools are generally very effective in shifting the focus on to a family's resources and positive qualities; like all strengths-based and solution-focused approaches, however, they will occasionally backfire badly, when clients' self-esteem is so low that being reminded of their positive qualities may make them feel worse, not better.

Why this problem? Why now?

As the final stage of engaging with the presenting problem, I try to find out what it means that this particular problem has been seen as so significant ('Why this problem?') and what it might mean that the problem began when it did, and has now reached proportions serious enough to drive the family to seek professional help ('Why now?'). I might want to do this by asking questions like:

> 'Is there anyone else in the family [I usually explain that I mean the extended family, on both parents' sides] that has had a similar sort of problem? What does this mean to you, that your own child is showing the same sort of behaviour as this person?'

> 'You've said that he's very anxious, and he's agreeing with that. How would you rate the level of anxiety in the family generally, compared to his? Is it half as high as his? Or a quarter as high as his? Or lower still?' [This allows the family to triumphantly tell me that it is in fact higher.]

'The problem is about eating and weight. Now, none of the rest of you has an eating disorder, but I wonder if perhaps food and exercise and weight are something that some of you would think about a fair bit, even though you don't have any problems in that area?'

'You've told me that her problems started to get bad about two years ago. What other sorts of things were happening in the family around that time?' [Adults often do not mention the deaths of significant family members, so I sometimes ask directly: 'Were any children born around that time? Did anyone in the family die around that time?']

Of course, symptomatic behaviour may erupt in direct response to a 'secret' – such as an affair, which is not only unknown to the children, but also unknown to the partner. It is highly unlikely that such a secret would be revealed when the counsellor asks such a question, but sometimes this information is disclosed much later, when the counselling relationship is more solid, and (perhaps) only the adult family members are present. However, even when the secret is kept, there is often a certain sense of unease and tension which I might notice, and note for future reflection or enquiry.

More commonly, symptomatic behaviour in a young person is a consequence of some significant change in the family's way of life: the separation of the parents, the repartnering of one, or both, of the parents, one parent's loss of stable employment, the serious illness or injury of one parent, and so on. These changes, obvious to us, may not be nearly so obvious to family members. Some problems start to settle down as soon as it is recognized that the young people's behaviour simply signals a high level of family anxiety, and indicates that perhaps their needs are being neglected as parental energy is withdrawn to cope with overriding stresses.

Asking, 'Why this problem? Why now?' may lead naturally to, or proceed simultaneously with, the construction of a genogram. I do not now routinely draw up a genogram, as I used to do for years, with every couple and every family. There are times when it is simply not necessary: straightforward family presentations – which I call 'level one' presentations in the next chapter – often do not require it. More significantly, families which are already prone to determinism can, in my experience, interpret genogram information as indicating that 'There's nothing we can do about the problem – it's fate'. Often they will insist on this interpretation, despite my strenuous argument that knowing about family patterns actually permits family members to choose, instead of being swept along by 'fate' or 'our genes'. Finally, some families will make their opposition to 'delving into the past' so clear from the start that I find it better not to insist. (In such cases, the adults will often have concealed certain things from their children, and they are not yet ready to 'go there' in their offspring's presence, and to challenge this directly is to risk having the adults pull the family out of counselling prematurely.)

However, with these exceptions, drawing up a genogram is still a valuable assessment tool. To do it properly takes at least one session, and often more, and so I sometimes delay it until the family has 'attached' to me sufficiently to allow me this lengthy enquiry into the past, the relevance of which is only gradually going to become clear. My own tendency when I began drawing genograms as a neophyte counsellor was to fasten excitedly on to family patterns, particularly dysfunctional personalities, repeated negative interactions, and emotional cut-offs. I think I betrayed my own fascination with 'pathology', a fascination few of my clients shared! I have subsequently learned to ask deliberately about the 'up' side even of dysfunctional and painful situations in the family's past:

> 'Sounds like your Dad had a fair bit to answer for, and he never really was prepared to admit it. Did anything good come out of it all, as far as you were concerned?'

> 'What you've told me is that you and your sisters often felt sort of alone, without much support or guidance. Did you find strength in each other? Who else did you turn to, when your parents weren't able to give you what you needed?'

> 'So you resented all of that pressure to do well at school, and rebelled a bit by not caring about your grades. But I'm guessing that at the same time, you were learning a lot, in your own way, even if it wasn't through formal school work. What other things were happening in your life at that time?'

> 'Hmm. Your Mum obviously had a very hard time when she was growing up . . . and you copped some of it. Yet from what you've told me about your grandparents, it sounds as if she actually managed to do a lot better with the three of you than her parents managed to do for her. Would that be right?'

Again, this sort of commentary and questioning forms part of our attempt to bring some balance and optimism into otherwise 'problem-saturated' accounts of the past. And again, I would drop it if it became apparent that the family were taking it as a glib dismissal of their problems.

Hopefully, by the end of two or three sessions, I will have more of an idea of what it means that this problem has developed at this time. I may, or may not, share my understanding of this with the family at this stage. If I do, I will try to be tentative about it. There is a great deal more to be learned, and some of it may reveal my early guesses to be 'wide of the mark'. But at least I now have a hypothesis to guide me as I sit with the family in future sessions.

'Problem kids': born or made?

My final aim in the assessment phase of family therapy (and genogram work is often useful in clarifying this) is to get a sense of how much of the behaviour of the 'problem child' is genetic in origin. I am clear that some children (around 10 per cent, according to Thomas and Chess's landmark studies[7]) are indeed born not with 'bad' genes (a massive, judgemental oversimplification), but with a bundle of genetic potentials which makes them particularly *vulnerable to things going wrong* in their environment. Such children will give problems right from the start (difficulties feeding, sleeping, tolerating changes, etc.). I have little doubt that, for such children, loving, patient, intelligent, consistent parenting can make a huge difference. As we saw in chapter 6, many 'difficult' children will not receive that sort of parenting. The challenges they present will be more likely to elicit frustration and anger than calm acceptance. And all too often, these same difficult kids are born to parents who are themselves emotionally vulnerable, and consequently insufficiently secure and confident to be able to supply the 'secure base' their difficult children so desperately need if they are to maximize their potential for coping.

So when a parent contacts me about the problems they are experiencing with one or more of their children, I want to find out, over the first couple of sessions, whether I am most likely dealing with one of these truly challenging children, who would create heartaches for any parent, or with a child whose bundle of genetic potentials is more in the normal range, but where the problems the child is now experiencing have been gradually, unwittingly, 'built' by a sequence of unproductive interactions with parents, as discussed in Chapter 6. I ask, 'What was he/she like as a baby?', 'Has he/she always been this way? Or did it start somewhere?'

Additionally, I want to gain an impression of the strengths and weaknesses of the parents themselves, through whose eyes the child's problems are being presented. Is this girl an uncontrollable 'monster' only because her mum feels so out of control of her own strong feelings that she cannot see her daughter's behaviour in perspective? Is that boy really deeply depressed, or is Dad feeling his son's withdrawn behaviour as an additional load to carry in his own depressed state? What do these parents instinctively and naturally 'do right' with their child? What do they 'do right' with other children, although not, perhaps, with this one?

And then there is the behaviour of the 'problem child' him/herself. What do I notice about him or her in the room? Do I pick up shame and embarrassment, or defiant, disruptive conduct? Is a supposedly 'hyperactive' child able to keep still? Is a child with an 'attention deficit' in fact able to concentrate for twenty minutes on a drawing or a computer game? I am trying to match up my own direct observations with what I have been told (by the adults), and gradually starting to get a sense of where this child, together with this problem, stands on a continuum from normal to extreme. All of this is the business of 'assessment', as I see it in a family context. Then, I want to notice how others react to the child, what happens between him/her and his/her siblings. Does the child seem more aligned with one adult, or the other? How do they treat him/her? Dismissively? Angrily? With resignation and disempowerment? Of course, I could present family members with pencil-and-paper instruments to test my perceptions of these matters. My own approach is less precise and orderly, but I suspect that what I deduce from my observations and questions is not very different from what a test would show.

As I have already made clear earlier in this book, I do not see genetics and parenting as an 'either/or' polarity. Rather, I suspect that parenting inadvertently reinforces genetic heritage, making it more likely (rather than less likely) that problems will occur with children who are already genetically vulnerable. But it can be very affirming for parents to be told:

> 'Your kid has been difficult from the beginning, and only a saint could have coped perfectly with that sort of behaviour. So what's happened isn't 'all your fault' at all. But even though he's older now, and he's got into some worrying habits, how you handle him can still make a difference. The real question is, how ready are you to try something different from what you've been doing?'

The 'third session phenomenon' revisited

Families, like couples and groups, go through an equivalent of the 'attachment and disenchantment' process over their first few sessions. Like couples, families often come back to a second session reporting that 'things are a bit better', even though really all they have done is meet me and tell me about the problem. Like couples, families often run into some sort of 'crisis' between the second and the third sessions, although with families, this is most likely to take the form of some temporary worsening of the presenting problem:

> 'We nearly didn't come today. Tom threw another of his little hyssy fits last night, a really bad one. I just didn't know what to do, and I think he's actually started to get worse since we've been coming here.'

> 'Leanne went off with her "friends" last Friday, and didn't come back until Sunday, stormed around the house in a mood, and then went out again. I think she's "on" something.'

Exactly as with couples and groups, it is important that we remain calm when confronted with this information, and take it seriously, but not too seriously. Although the reported behaviour is only that of one family member, *we are in fact being told something about how the whole family feels about having to see a counsellor.* Remember, just as with a group, when one member of a family acts in a certain way, and the energy of others gets tied up in the threat he or he/she seems to pose to the rest, then we can assume that that one person is actually expressing something on behalf of the whole family (or group).

Rather than side with the parents and siblings against the 'family scape-goat', we need to step aside from their urgency and rising anxiety, and think about what message the family, as an entity, might be trying to convey. Are they, for instance, telling us in an indirect, metaphorical way, that they feel full of rage at us, for failing to magically fix Tommy in a single consultation? Rationally, of course, they would not remotely be thinking this way. But at the level of the 'self' of the whole family, a 'self' about as mature and rational as that of a three-month-old infant, they may well feel this kind of irrational, total anger. Or are they telling us that they would really prefer to 'get out of here', instead of having to talk about such painful feelings with a stranger and wash the family's dirty linen in public? Is Leanne's 'mood' an unconscious way of communicating the whole family's depression and dissatisfaction at our failure to 'hold' them adequately?

I am not suggesting that I would make such an interpretation directly after the young person's behaviour has been reported, or do it in such an obvious way. But I would certainly consider saying something a bit later, something like:

> 'I guess I'm wondering if all of you are feeling a bit down today. After all, you're here to get something done about Tommy [Leanne], and so far they're still doing the stuff you're worried about. I'm wondering if maybe you might feel a bit let down, a bit frustrated that I'm not helping you?'

Whether we 'interpret' the problem behaviour in this way or simply turn it over in our minds, it is important that we be able to react in a non-anxious way. These days, people are quite accustomed to helping professionals (particularly alternative health practitioners) saying 'the problem is likely to get worse before it gets better' or predicting a 'healing crisis'. I sometimes choose to do this with families, indicating that they can expect 'two steps forward, one step back' for a while, and explaining that this is a natural process, because families get used to being the way they are, and may find any change, even if it's for the better, uncomfortable. Some families seem curiously reassured by this, as if it lets them, as well as me, off the hook: nothing has to change overnight, and we can feel less pressured and less anxious, taking a bit of time to allow the family to explore how it might feel to be together in a rather different way, and to find a solution that is right for them.

Family therapy: a pragmatic business

Unlike couples, families rarely present for counselling with complaints of 'lack of communication', 'drifting apart', or 'betrayal of trust'. Instead of these relational concerns, with their sense of existential longing and the desire for self-actualization, parents of young people typically ask for help with much more defined, practical problems. Their kids are 'hanging around with the wrong sort of friends', are using drugs and denying it, have disappointed them by their lack of interest in school work, play up every time they come back from their Dad's place, or sit around smoking pot instead of going out and getting a job. Sometimes their kids seem scared of normal kid life, won't go on school camps, and seem withdrawn and depressed, or they are engaging in rather peculiar behaviour, like 'having' to wash their hands twenty times instead of just once. Instead of self-actualization through relationship (which is what couples today have learned is their 'right'), parents tend to be more pragmatic. They want the 'problem fixed'.

Of course, very serious betrayals of trust can be present behind the façade of these 'behaviour problems': past (or even present) sexual abuse of the child concerned; frightening violence in the adult relationship; and children neglected because an adult caregiver has a mental illness, abuses drugs, or in some other way is unwilling or unable to give proper attention to the children's needs (see below). These kinds of problems are typically presented not by clients themselves but by welfare and child protection agencies and courts, who require families to attend counselling because it is already clear that something is very seriously wrong, and that intervention is needed if the children are to remain in the custody of their parent(s). Yet even involuntary clients will often focus on their children's behaviour, or their difficulties in getting a partner to help with these children, rather than initially acknowledging their own very considerable struggles in living.

Compared with group or couple therapy, family therapy is thus, at least in its inception, and often all the way through, a pragmatic business. Huge and frightening spectres may loom over it, and must be acknowledged and engaged with if they bear directly on the safety and emotional well being of the children. But even if we must deal with violence or the effects of present or past abuse, we are still going to be in the business of helping struggling caregivers to find workable solutions to behavioural problems in their children. These are the problems that are in the foreground for them, or at any rate, the problems they find it easier to acknowledge. Second, we will often be working towards enabling these caregivers to separate out their own issues from their children's, and (ideally) making it possible for them to work therapeutically on these issues of their own, so that they will be better able to care for, and respect, their children as beings separate from themselves.

In line with family therapy's pragmatic nature, it generally makes good clinical sense to start with what the family itself perceives as the main problem: the behaviour of one or more of their children. As this is tackled, it is often possible to see more clearly how much the adults' own difficulties are contributing to the children's, and if we can make some progress towards improving things on the 'kid behaviour' front, then adults are often more willing to trust us to help *them*. Getting to this point may take a few sessions— or many months.

Solutions that work, but can't be implemented

Viable solutions to most parenting problems are widely available in our society. Self-help books and parenting courses basically teach what emotionally secure, responsible parents do anyway: supportive feedback rather than criticism; firm limit-setting, combined with warmth and affection; calmly standing your ground in the face of escalating anger from a young person; building in 'quality time' with your child amidst the busyness of the day; engaging your child in active problem-solving, and offering real choices rather than simply telling the child what to do; ensuring that both parents (whether living together, separated or repartnered) take a common line on key issues, and so on. These messages are dramatized and reinforced daily, through mass-audience daytime television shows such as *Oprah* and *Dr Phil*. If these sensible, workable rules were followed, I suspect that 80% of the problems presented to family therapists would simply disappear. But even though they 'know' what would work, many parents and caregivers are unable to put these rules into practice, for a variety of reasons:

- Given that most serious behaviour problems in children have slowly evolved over years, any parenting strategy that aims to modify them must be applied consistently over a considerable period of time. Many parents simply give up on a strategy when it does not produce results quickly.
- Generally speaking, if parents' own self-esteem is low, or if they have powerful unmet needs, it will be far harder for them to be patient and calmly tolerant while their children gradually learn to act prosocially, and they are more likely to become angry when the children seem to 'reject' their help.
- It will also be difficult for such parents to engage their children in productive discussions of their problems; talking things out calmly

does not come naturally to them, and they become frustrated at a conversation that doesn't quickly produce compliance.

- When a child develops problems, particularly of the 'acting out' variety, it is much easier, and less shameful, to blame the child than to consider altering one's own behaviour in order to help that child. To embrace changed parenting strategies is to 'lose face', to give up an entitlement to righteous anger.
- Many parents are overwhelmed by the pressures of their lives, and are themselves in sore need of care, love and consistent 'parenting'. They cannot give what their children need, because their own needs are clamouring for attention first.

In a very real sense, then, *the work of the family therapist is not to supply the solutions, but to get parents to a point where they are willing to try them, or contemplate trying them*, and then to offer them the parents support while they learn to be firm, calm and consistent instead of impulsive, emotional and unpredictable. At one extreme of the spectrum (parents whose ability to parent adequately has been severely compromised by the deficits of their own upbringing, or the unresolved issues in their own personalities), the work of the family therapist may be to 'parent the parents', so that they can be proper parents to their own children.

Notes

1   Carl Whitaker, in particular, was famous for sending families away if one or more family members were missing from the first session. Such a scene is dramatically described in his session-by-session account of a single family in therapy, *The Family Crucible* (Whitaker and Napier 1978). A very different approach to handling first-session dynamics and 'joining' with a real family is described by Lang (2000). On 'aggressive outreach', to get families of drug abusers to attend sessions, see Stanton *et al.* (1982: 71–102). On the dynamics of shame and blame, a useful introduction can be found in Furlong and Young (1996). The difficulties of engaging families presenting a son or daughter with a mental illness led to the 'psychoeducational model', in which workers now go to great lengths to assure families that schizophrenia is a purely medical problem, for which they, the parents, are not responsible in any way. However (and paradoxically), family members are then coached to reduce levels of 'expressed emotion' around the young person, in order to decrease the risk of relapse, thus accomplishing at least some of the aims of 'family therapy' without invoking either the name or the systemic principles. See Falloon *et al.* (1982).

2   For a provocative perspective on asking 'frivolous' questions in the first session of couple therapy, see Madden (2005).

3   Haley (1976). Haley's book, incidentally, contains one of the clearest and most practical 'how to' accounts of structuring a first session with a family (pp. 9–47). Despite its age, it is still well worth reading.
4   See Scott (1999).
5   See Koslowska and Hanney (1999).
6   Available from St Luke's Innovative Resources, 137 McCrae St, Bendigo, Victoria 3550, Australia; www.stlukes.org.au.
7   Thomas *et al.* (1963) and Thomas and Chess (1980).

8 Beyond blame and shame
Three levels of family work

In looking back at the families I have seen over the years, I have come up with some tentative ideas about three different levels of difficulty, and three corresponding stances a counsellor can usefully take. I have concentrated on families who present problems with children, rather than on families who present an adult problem which impacts on children. This is only because it is less likely that the latter type of family will voluntarily present, or be referred, for family therapy. In practice (as we've already seen in Chapter 6) children's and adults' problems are inextricably linked, and there is little use in trying to decide which 'came first'.

Level-one families

Level-one families are comparatively straightforward to work with:

- Parents seek help before they reach the point of despair. Hope is still alive, or can readily be rekindled.
- At the assessment stage, parents can give me a convincing picture of the personality and behaviour of their child or teenager. Their account 'hangs together' and is neither idealized nor denigratory. They can acknowledge the strengths of their child or teenager, while being realistic about his/her faults.
- Parents readily accept the idea that it is up to them, as adults with responsibility, to implement strategies that will assist their child or teenager, rather than insisting that the 'work' must come from the young person, because he or she 'is the one with the problem'.
- They feel pain rather than shame: what is going wrong in the family hurts, but the pain is not felt as 'humiliation' (an indicator of a very fragile ego).
- The situation makes them angry, but they do not direct all of their

anger at someone else (blaming is another way that people protect a fragile sense of self). They have some recognition that this is a shared problem.

- Adults can hear, and implement, straightforward advice on how to tackle their problem, provided the ground is carefully prepared, and the timing is appropriate.
- Change for the better is generally greeted positively by everyone in the family. There is no major 'backlash', and no new symptomatic behaviour suddenly erupts in a different family member.
- The family is robust enough to be able to implement changes without being pulled off course by the anxieties of relatives, or by other helping professionals and organizations. We do not usually need to involve the family's wider social network in planning and intervening.

Paradoxically, level-one families have less need for 'family therapy' than others – even though, if offered it, they can usually make productive use of the sessions. In many instances, I see the whole family only once or twice, and then work mainly with the parents. This applies also to single parents, where the other biological parent never comes into counselling, or is only peripherally involved. What this points to, I suspect, is a family where at least one of the parents experienced secure attachment as a child and has been able to offer secure attachment to their own children. Much of what I do is 'coaching' parents to act differently with their children (and partners), but I can only do so if I am reasonably confident that their account of those children, and others in their world, is accurate. The way that the non-attending family members behave when the parent starts to change will soon tell me whether or not this is so!

> Shumaila came to see me on her own, to talk about problems with her late adolescent daughters. She had recently been divorced from her husband, and the children continued to live with her, but saw their father regularly. There had been a range of common 'teenage problems' since the separation, including 'laziness', lack of motivation at school, and suspected drug use. The younger daughter had actually run away for a short time, about a year before, and the threat that she might do so again hung heavily over Shumaila. Shumaila, an extremely competent receptionist for a large medical practice, was resentful and bitter at the way she 'did everything for her kids' but 'got nothing back in return'. They allowed her to cook, clean, wake them in time for work or college, provide them with clean ironed clothes, and generally act as their slave – despite the fact that the elder daughter had a well-paid job.
>
> Shumaila spent some eight sessions complaining about how unappreciated and unsupported she felt, talking also about how she had

been her mentally disturbed mother's main carer during her growing up years, a role which, she recognized, had been partly wished on her by cultural expectations ('The eldest daughter is the one who has to look after her parents if they are ill'). During this time, my questions as to whether she would consider withdrawing some of the support she gave her children met with a blanket response: 'I could never do that. They are my kids. I have to look after them. I just wish they would be a bit grateful. I feel so tired, so exhausted all the time. Sometimes I wonder if life is worth living.'

After two months, Shumaila seemed to reach a point of crisis, where she hinted that something needed to change. I asked her whether she was desperate enough to try something that would seem risky, and contrary to her own values as a parent. She sighed and said she would try anything. I suggested she draw up a list of all the things she did for her kids, and then think about which of these responsibilities she would feel least worried about handing back to them. Next session, she produced a list, and said she thought she could try withdrawing three 'services'. I argued that this was asking too much of herself, and that she might be better to experiment with withdrawing only one initally, and see how she coped. We discussed the guilt she would probably feel as a result of failing to 'do her duty' by her kids, and she assured me that although she would certainly feel guilty, this would not stop her. We also discussed the possible 'backlash' from the kids – resentment, disrespectful comments, and possibly increased drug use, which Shumaila dreaded.

The result of this initial experiment was quite positive. Shumaila had felt relief, and very little guilt. There had been no reaction more dire than some grumbling from her younger daughter. The elder one had almost seemed pleased to be told that more was expected of her. Shumaila was willing to try withdrawing further services over the next couple of months. Steadily, she realized that she felt less helpless. Both her children complained, but she stood her ground, and began to notice that her daughters seemed more appreciative of the things she still did for them. This made her feel good. Open affection returned to her relationship with both girls.

Over succeeding sessions, Shumaila recovered much of the self-esteem she had lost during four years of separation and single parenting. She was able to act more assertively towards others in her life, including relatives, her ex-husband, and male friends, and felt less like a 'doormat that people walk all over'. She delightedly informed me that her daughters had both urged her to 'go out and meet a nice man', and that they did not want her to stay single for their sake.

It would be easy to see my work as individual counselling, since I met only with Shumaila. However, I was guided by family therapy principles: if

Shumaila could gradually change her behaviour towards her daughers, and could persist in that change, then she could reverse the direction of the 'feed-back loop' that had been operating, in which the girls had been becoming more and more irresponsible, as Shumaila took on more and more responsibil-ity for them. It's also important that I 'held' Shumaila's frustration, disap-pointment and helplessness for almost two months, until she came to a point where she was sufficiently fed up to try something different. Had I offered her the same strategies in the first few sessions, she would not have been able to implement them and I would have had ground to make up as a result.

Level-one interventions: cautious encouragement

Much of what I do with level-one families I would describe as 'cautious encouragement'. 'Cautious' because even with families where hope and goodwill remain alive, slipping back into old patterns of thinking, feeling and acting is always possible, and when this happens the impact of the 'negative' event can temporarily be more powerful than the progress the family had begun to make. John Gottman's groundbreaking research[1] is highly relevant here: one 'negative' interaction seems to count as the equivalent of four or five 'positives'; conversely, it takes a great many satisfying and hopeful inter-actions to counter the effect of a few negative ones. However, although level-one families are vulnerable to this effect, the counsellor's non-anxious presence and quiet encouragement can make a real difference to their willingness to persist in working towards change.

Thus, with level-one families I would do some or all of the following:

- Ask (at assessment) about times in the past when the family had coped better with the problem, or when temporary solutions to it were found ['exception' or 'unique outcome' questions].[2]
- Highlight these successes by asking more questions, and showing a lively interest. ('How do you think things might have been different in the family if you'd been able to go on doing what you did for that week?')
- Sympathetically explore the reasons why previous 'potential solu-tions' to the problem were aborted. ('What do you think was the main thing that got in the way of you continuing to do that?
- Cautiously test the family's willingness to attempt new solutions or persist with previous potential solutions. ('How risky do you think it might be for you to try something like that again? What do you see as the main thing that would stand in the way of you persisting with that idea longer than a few days? Is there anyone in the family that you think might lose out?')
- Offer suggestions for things they might do differently ('experiments'),

but build these suggestions as much as possible on families' own ideas, making sure that they are credited as the originators. ('What you came up with last session sounded pretty useful to me. Would it make sense to you to try that out, only maybe adding an extra bit, where you tell Kylie in advance what you're planning, and why you would like to trust her more?')

- Frame new behaviour as 'experimental'.[3] ('This is just something you're trying on for size. Whether it works or not isn't the purpose of the experiment. The purpose is to find out more about the problem, and what stops you all from solving it.')

- Ask in detail (if working with parents alone) about possible ways their child/adolescent may respond to new behaviour on their part. If they are vague, suggest likely scenarios, based on previous client families facing similar situations. Ask how parents think they would respond to such reactions from the young person, and what they might need to keep them 'on track'. (I usually offer them the opportunity to phone me if they sense that they may be pulled off course by the young person's reaction. Few actually do phone, but the offer seems to steady them in their resolve. As attachment theory would see it, I thus act as a 'secure base' for their explorations of new territory.)

- Offer praise and warm encouragement when parent, young person, or both are able to make a 'breakthrough' to new behaviour, and ask questions about what made the breakthrough possible. ('What do you think it was, inside of you, that made you able to do something so different from what you've always done in that situation? What might it be about your Mum that made her able to respond so gently, instead of biting your head off?')

- Accompany praise for 'breakthroughs' with caution about possible 'slipping back' or 'backlash'. ('Now that you've had this success, and you feel so good about it, do you think you might find yourself slipping back into your old ways? Sometimes new behaviour feels very strange at first, and people like to go back to the old ways because they feel more comfortable and familiar. Do you think that's a possibility for you? If that happened, how do you think your parents might react? How do you think you might feel?')

- Teach family members about a 'three steps forward, two steps back' process towards lasting change: slipping back is to be expected, and the important thing is not to be drawn off course by it.

- Ask about the effects on all family members of any change for the better. ('How have Kylie's changes impacted on you? Have any of you noticed any down-side to what's been happening? Does anyone maybe feel that they've lost out, or become a bit invisible, while all this has been going on?')

- Ask (when change is firmly established) what advice the family might give to other clients facing similar problems.

Level-two families

Level-two families are trickier to work with, in the sense that, while change is still possible, it is less likely that it will come about through straightforward 'coaching'. These are the families that gave rise to many of the creative strategies of early family therapy, as therapists realized that the families would remain unchanged by insight, and would negate direct attempts to alter their behaviour.

- These families may indicate a strong desire for things to be better, but have difficulty imagining how this could come about. While hope may not be 'dead', it seems to have receded into the far distance.
- Parents or caregivers tend to be strongly polarized in their perceptions of the problem child, and there is little evidence of common ground. Thus one will typically defend, excuse and collude, while the other will blame, attack and distance. While both will say they love their child and feel concern for him/her, their behaviour says that they are more invested in maintaining their own rightness, as part of an ongoing battle with each other.
- Sometimes the only common ground caregivers can occupy is when they join forces to attack someone outside the family who they can agree has acted abusively or unfairly (and this can easily be the therapist!).
- Parents and caregivers in these families may find it difficult (at least initially) to accept any degree of responsibility for solving the problem with their child or teenager. Rather, they make insistent demands, either that the young person change, or that the other caregiver change.
- The young person's difficulties are felt as 'shaming', rather than as 'painful' to both the young person and the caregivers.
- The family often has a history of attempted solutions which failed because they were not pursued for long enough, or because one caregiver sabotaged the other's attempt to implement new strategies. (This can normally ascertained by careful, persistent questioning at the assessment stage.)
- Straightforward advice from the counsellor is thus highly likely to be treated the same way as previous attempts to resolve the problem, and may not be appropriate.
- Changes for the better within the family, particularly those that are

instigated by the 'problem' young person, may be ignored as of little significance (an interesting parallel to what happens with the 'dismissive' style of attachment in infancy).

- Alternatively, changes for the better within the family may elicit a 'backlash', in the form of a worsening of symptoms or problems in a *different* family member. For example, an adolescent who has dropped out of school gets a job and develops pride in his work. Parents continue to complain about how he 'ruined his chances of doing well academically'. Meanwhile, it is discovered that a younger brother has started using marijuana on a regular basis. Thus 'comfortable discomfort' is restored.

- When changes for the better start to occur, they may be held back, or even undermined, by the unwitting actions of other systems that are interacting with the family: schools, legal practitioners, medical or psychological specialists, child protection agencies, etc. These other professionals intend, of course, to be helpful. Yet around difficult families, professionals and agencies often develop anxious, knee-jerk reactions, punitive behaviour, or extreme cynicism, which end up 'putting the brakes' on change.

Level-two responses: circular questioning

Because of the strong forces which restrain change in level-two families, an accurate picture of the 'problem' young person may not emerge from speaking with the adults alone, and it is also important to observe how that young person interacts with others in the family, rather than simply how she/he presents when meeting alone with the counsellor. Individual therapy with the young person will be inadequate if it is not informed by an accurate understanding of how the whole family interacts, and may fail completely. A common scenario is that the 'problem' young person can develop a strong alliance with an individual professional, but that this alliance actually ends up working towards cut-off and confrontation, rather than greater understanding and reconciliation.

In family sessions where positions are polarized, and 'separate realities' are very separate indeed, family members may have quite limited information about what others think and feel, and distorted and misleading perceptions of each other can often develop as a result (this is the kind of thing that led some members of my own family of origin to come up with such different assessments of each other, as mentioned at the beginning of Chapter 6). 'Circular questioning', a technique developed by the Milan Associates in the 1970s, was invented specifically to deal with such families, and is both an assessment tool and an intervention in its own right.[4] Each family member is asked not to speak about his/her own opinions or beliefs but to say what he/

she believes *another* family member's opinion or belief would be, with regard to the problem or some other relevant family issue. For example:

> 'Greg, what do you think your Mum thinks about your sister's eating problems?'

> 'Lisa, what do you think Catherine thinks about Greg's "habits"?'

Such questions can be extended in all kinds of directions, for example, to incorporate an element of 'forced choice':

> 'Greg, do you think your Mum is more in favour of your sister getting on top of her problems with eating, or do you think she's more in favour of the eating problems winning the battle?'

> 'Leonie, do you think Catherine thinks that Greg's habits are more of a positive thing for him, or more of a negative thing for him?'

Circular questioning is a sophisticated skill, which is ideally learned while doing co-therapy with a worker experienced in its use. Unfortunately, its very popularity has led to its adoption as a discrete 'microskill', and it is sometimes so taught to students outside of family therapy training courses, with minimal acknowledgement of the systemic understandings which give it meaning.

Level-two responses: seeking help from the family's 'helpers'

It can also be important to ask specifically, at the assessment stage, about who else has been involved with the family in addressing the problem, and who is most invested in helping with it. These people may need to be involved either at the start or later. Sometimes, it is another professional (a school counsellor, a teacher, a priest, a child protection worker), or even one or more whole agencies who have had long-standing or recent contact with the problem young person. We will say more about the process of involving other professionals when discussing level-three families.

It is important to find out who lives in the family home, and who is in daily contact with the family around the problem. One family I saw had been through several different 'treatments' with a variety of medical and psychological professionals without anybody realizing that the maternal grandmother, who lived close by, played a major role in the way the family coped (or failed to cope) with their developmentally delayed and volatile son. Liaising with 'helpers' or 'advisers' within the extended family may not be too difficult, and grandparents, aunts, uncles or cousins who have been heavily involved with the family will often agree to come in for a session on their own, or join the clients for an expanded session. Such expanded sessions can be intense, and full of anxiety for all concerned, since in the extended family's daily life, key emotional communications between relatives nearly always take place via private phone calls and meetings, and the information is passed on only selectively to others in the family. Setting up a session like this, in which communication is 'out in the open', challenges all present, and needs careful handling by the counsellor.

Many of the skills involved are similar to those required for handling a therapy group (see Chapter 5): ensuring everyone gets a hearing, not allowing the discussion to become hijacked by two or three of those present, and working with participants to clarify meanings and assumptions, so that what is heard corresponds with what was communicated. If the session can be managed so that anxiety does not run too high to prevent useful dialogue, and so that previously 'secret' matters can be discussed more openly, then there is often a sense of relief, and a sense that things can now move forward.

> Cindy and Reg had been married for twelve years, and had two children, who were initially presented because of problems concentrating at school, and physical symptoms for which no medical cause could be found. After several sessions with parents and children together, Cindy and Reg were seen on their own, and disclosed that both drank 'more than we should' and that this sometimes led to reciprocal violence. There followed several months of couple work, during which time the children's symptoms improved somewhat, but did not go away entirely. It was clear that the couple had exhausted their goodwill towards each other, and that bitterness and reciprocal blaming had taken its place. Couple counselling was getting nowhere. While they spoke of separation, there was always a reason why it could not take place, with Cindy dissolving into tears at the thought of supporting herself (even though she had qualifications and had worked before her marriage).
>
> Eventually, we suggested that the couple invite their parents in to a 'special session', since by now we knew that both Cindy's parents, and Reg's father [his mother had died ten years earlier] were heavily involved in the ongoing saga of Cindy and Reg's marriage. The atmosphere at the first joint session was electric with tension. Within half an hour of the three older adults hearing the truth about the marriage from both sides (instead of only from their own son/daughter), it was clear that a dramatic shift was taking place. 'Is this true, Cindy?' said her father, after learning for the first time that Cindy had a drink problem [in her regular phone conversations with her parents, she had only talked about *Reg's* drinking problem]. Reg's father was quieter, but similarly shocked to hear a version of events in which his son emerged as an alcoholic who was capable of angrily assaulting his wife when she belittled him in front of guests.

> Only two expanded sessions were held, but within a few weeks Reg had moved out, Cindy had got a job, and both had been able to agree fairly amicably on arrangements for them to share the children. Subsequent individual sessions with both Cindy and Reg showed that their gains in maturity had been maintained [the children were doing better, too].

I do not wish to suggest that all extended family sessions yield such rapid and positive results. But they nearly always generate a powerful process. Instead of the partial truths that have sustained the polarized responses of individuals within the family, more of the truth is now open for discussion, and the polarized perceptions and responses are called into question. While it may not be possible for an emotionally honest cross-generational dialogue to develop in the room, families are rarely left unchanged by what has happened.[5]

Level-two responses: encouraging caution

In level-two families, the principle of *neutrality towards change* is particularly important. With a level-one family, we might say:

> 'Well, you're all in agreement that your daughter has had very serious medical problems, and that you have had to stay very close to her, and exercise a great deal of responsibility for her. But you're also telling me that she's getting bigger and more able to look after herself, and you resent having to do so much for her. You're wondering how safe it might be to let her take more responsibility for herself. You've agreed that it's a bit scary to allow her to take care of her own medication, but you're telling me that you can see the point of it. So let's talk about how you might go about it, and what the risks might be.'

With a level-two family, we might need to say something more like this:

> 'You've emphasized to me how serious your daughter's medical problems are. As I understand it, her condition is life-threatening. And this has been the case ever since she was born. And I've got a sense that you've both been incredibly responsible parents. In many ways, you've sacrificed your own lives for her, and it's paid off, because she's survived, and she's actually doing better now, and the doctors seem pleased with her. She's getting bigger, and she can understand things better. You're also telling me that you resent having to look after her so much, and stay so closely tied to her. You feel like you don't have any life of your own. John, you said that perhaps she could be trained to take care of her own medication, but Mary, you said that the

thought of giving her that responsibility terrified you.' [A lengthy summary, but necessary in order to reassure both caregivers that they have been fully 'heard' by me, before I go on to offer them my own ideas about the threatening subject of change.]

'I guess what I'm thinking is that the two of you have been in this situation for many years, and it's been the whole of your life, really, during that time: looking after your daughter, and making totally sure that if she ran into a crisis, one of you would always be there, and she could get help in time. That's been so much a part of both of you that I'm wondering whether you should think very carefully about whether you want to change it. For example, I wonder what you would both lose, if you went that route – training her to self-medicate, I mean. What parts of yourselves and your values would you have to give up, or change, if you decided to do that? What would it feel like for you, to maybe put yourselves first, rather than her? Would it seem somehow disloyal to all your principles? You've both told me again and again that the greatest thing you can do in life is to help someone else, and you've both told me that looking after yourself seems some-how selfish and unworthy of you.' [This is a condensation. I would not normally ask all of these questions one after another, but would get a response to each before proceeding to the next.]

We might term this attitude, 'encouraging caution' as opposed to the 'cau-tious encouragement' we used with level-one families. Needless to say, when we as workers take a position that is neutral towards change, or even actively argue its risks, we also need to be careful to say only what we can genuinely stand behind. As we saw in Chapter 3, such statements should actually pro-ceed out of *empathy*: deep empathy for the way that so many human beings (including ourselves) get stuck in the conviction that they have no choice, and no way out. 'Restraining' or cautioning statements frequently bring a puzzled response from clients (who automatically assume that we are 'on the side of change' because that's our job). Occasionally, their response is an angry one. Psychodynamic therapists have to be prepared for clients to be angry with them when they deliver interpretations that hit a 'sore spot' by openly naming something that the client has felt to be unspeakably awful, and so has kept out of conscious awareness. Interventions that actively restrain change, or warn against its risks, may be a kind of family therapy equivalent to this. I see them as speaking to the 'unconscious of the system', as contrasted with the 'unconscious of the individual'. Level-two parents may even join forces to blame *us*, rather than re-examine their own restraints on change. But more commonly, if such interventions are done gently and non-anxiously, what happens is that families feel curiously understood, and then *find themselves experimenting* with change after all – not necessarily changes of the kind they had previously been fearfully contemplating, but changes that are likely to be productive for them nonetheless.

Level-two reponses: getting the language right

A key aspect of successful work with level-two families is to use language that does not imply blame. As we've already seen, these families are all too prone to both shame and blame; it is vital that we avoid saying anything that sounds shaming to them. Consequently, I have learned a variety of ways of phrasing sensitive matters so that agency is less obviously implied:

> 'So you've *found yourselves* being critical and negative around your son?'

> 'Sounds like the two of you have *got stuck in a situation where* there's been a lot of bad feeling between you.'

> 'Could it be that you've *inadvertently* started to notice all the things that she gets wrong?'

> 'When he acts that way, and it feels like he wants to get into a fight with you, do you think it would be possible to *decline that invitation*, or do you think it's *an invitation that you sort of can't refuse?*'

Many of the most creative uses of this sort of language (including some of those I have just listed) I learned from Michael White, in the years before he began to call his work 'Narrative therapy'. We will look at some further applications of Narrative practices in our next section, on level-three families.

It is even more important to watch our language when responding to family sessions with therapeutic letters. Letter writing is a subject of its own, which I do not have space to go into here; but, like many family therapists, I have found over the years that letters can communicate to families more clearly than is possible in the hurly-burly of sessions, and that they can also be used to offer messages about the risks of change in ways that are provocative without being affronting:

> 'Sol, you've told me that your own father never took any interest in you. You grew up feeling the pain of his lack of interest, and his disrespect. You never got openly angry with him, because you felt that you'd lower yourself by doing that. You told me about that time he tried to take the strap to you, when you were a teenager, and you just laughed at him. You felt kind of 'above' him. So when he died, you

didn't feel any grief. But now you've got a son of your own, who seems to be doing things that fly in the face of everything you stand for, everything you've worked for in your life. Tom just doesn't seem to care, and he acts disrespectfully and dismissively towards you. Maybe, without meaning to, or even realizing what he's doing, your son is giving you a chance to fight him openly, in the way you couldn't do with your Dad. Probably, this idea of mine is going to strike you as pretty odd. I'm not expecting you to agree with me, but I'd certainly be interested to hear what you think, next time we meet. And I'll be asking Tom what he thinks about it, too.'

Level-two responses: greeting change conservatively

When changes begin to occur in level-two families, it is important to continue to greet these changes very conservatively. After all, these systems have been used to things being 'comfortably uncomfortable' for many years, and any alteration in this situation may well cause perturbations that cannot be foreseen. At the point where families begin to report changes, it is useful to engage families in an exploration of what the risks might be if change continues, and whether the benefits of continued change do or do not outweigh those risks. Hence those questions (again best employed with whole families, rather than with subsystems such as parents alone) which ask:

> 'Who in the family do you think might be most pleased if Catherine continues to put on weight?'

> 'Who in the family do you think might be most upset if Catherine continues to put on weight?'

Again, these questions have their greatest impact when asked of all family members in a conjoint session. In the same way that young children can often blurt out things that older family members have learned to suppress, so they can produce amazingly accurate answers to some of these questions:

> 'Sharon [aged nine]: I think Grandma will be most upset. I think Grandma thinks Catherine's special, and she likes her to stay always the same. Grandma always says, 'That child doesn't have a problem. It's you [pointing to her parents] that has the problem!'

Circular questions within conjoint sessions are perhaps the closest we can get, with a level-two family, to the kind of 'interpersonal encounter' that an adult therapy group can achieve. My sense is that while level-one families can often benefit from 'straight talk' because they have sufficient self-esteem and basic trust to do so, level-two families rarely feel 'safe' enough to even engage in this exercise, let alone make productive use of it. Circular questioning is a way of facilitating both sharing and feedback between family members, but it does so indirectly, and without the element of confrontation and fear that a direct interpersonal encounter normally entails. And of course, when family member A hears B state a wildly inaccurate version of what A thinks, it is usual for A to want to correct the misperception, revealing in the process a good deal that may previously have been kept silent.

Sometimes, families will claim that they can't think of any risks. If so, we need to *suggest* several risks which they need to take seriously, all based on what we have learned about how and when things have gone wrong in the family in the past. When a family suggest benefits they think will follow from change, I sometimes turn the supposed benefits around, and say:

> 'You're telling me that things will be wonderful once Jason comes off drugs completely. But from what you've told me, there might be a flip side to that. Yes, it would be great if Jason could get clean. But I guess I'm wondering whether the two of you [parents] might find yourselves talking about different subjects, once you don't have Jason to worry about any more. Wouldn't there be some difficult stuff that might come off the "back burner"? How do you anticipate that you'd cope with that?'

In summary, with a level-two family it pays to remain cautious about change well into the change process itself. If this can be done in a way that is both honest and respectful, then the chances are that changes, once set in motion, may continue. If we become too enthusiastic about change too soon, then we are likely to *find ourselves inadvertently sabotaging* the very thing we'd hoped and worked for! The family will react to our open encouragement as a shaming criticism ('This is what you should have been doing all along'), and will *find themselves doing the opposite*, as if their collective 'mind' were the mind of a toddler who has just learned to say 'no!' and enjoys the power it gives him.

Level-three families

Because most of my family work has been done in private practice, where families voluntarily present for help, I have worked with relatively few level-three families. My knowledge of them is less extensive, and less immediate, and now, looking back on the families I failed to help years ago, I can see that in fact these were often level-three families, and that I was unable to keep them in counselling because I failed to appreciate their fragility, or the level of support they required. So how are these families different from those we have looked at so far? In my experience, level-three families:

- Have lost sight of hope completely. They do not expect to change, and have accustomed themselves to chronic dysfunction and, in some cases, chronic despair (which may be masked by apparent insouciance, endemic drug and alcohol use, or both).
- Tend to be referred by others (schools, doctors or courts) rather than self-referred. Often they are long-standing clients of various health and welfare agencies, and the scope and duration of their difficulties makes agencies keen to transfer the burden of anxiety and responsibility to someone else.
- Sometimes have their children or adolescents taken away from them because they are seen (by others) as abusive and/or neglectful. Alternatively, they present one or more of their children to welfare services, desperate for someone else to take the responsibility for them.
- Live with high levels of shame, not only due to immediate family problems, but often reflecting generations of poverty, unemployment, sexual abuse, mental illness and substance abuse, and sometimes marginalization because of their ethnicity or culture. (Similar families do exist at high socioeconomic levels, where cultural difference, poverty and unemployment are not factors, but high levels of dysfunction are still passed from generation to generation.)
- Typically blame out ('It's the welfare') or blame in, in a hopeless, giving-up way ('I'm just no good at looking after kids. My Mum was the same. None of us are ever going to be any good at it!').
- Fail to 'digest' temporary successes and achievements, so that a pervading sense of failure persists and the memory of success cannot be retained as a basis for hope. In fact, temporary successes may even 'remind' these families how bad and hopeless they actually feel. This makes a straightforward strengths-based approach problematic. (Again, I am reminded of the insecurely attached child who is unable to react with pleasure when his mother reappears, but instead ignores her, or 'punishes' her by angrily yelling at her.)
- Find it very hard to accept a realistic degree of responsibility for their children's difficulties, and consequently fight stubbornly against any suggestion from inside or outside the family that changing their own attitudes or behaviour might impact positively on their offspring. Again, parents feel these suggestions as a shaming criticism, not as constructive support.
- Often exhibit values and beliefs that locate power, control and agency outside the individual self. This can be due to cultural difference (as when the family belongs to a culture that thinks 'collectively' rather

than individually, and whose traditional beliefs teach acceptance of one's lot, rather than struggling to better oneself). It can also be the result of generations of isolation, poverty, disability or mental illness, which can produce, within Western cultures, attitudes and values very different from those of the employed, urban, able-bodied, relatively stable majority.[6]

What level-three families need

While it is beyond the scope of this book to offer authoritative guidelines on how to work with level-three families, here are some principles that I have (painfully) learned to follow when interacting with such families:

- Level-three families are governed by shame, to a level even beyond level-two families. Whatever we do with them, we need at all times to avoid creating more shame.
- Since such families tend to locate agency and power outside the self, and even outside the immediate family, restoring a sense of control over their situation, and pride in themselves, may well require working with several families, or even a whole community, at once. It may be easier for the *community* to empower itself than for any individual or nuclear family within it.[7]
- Since problems and difficulties in living bring shame, which family members defend against by angry blaming out, or depressed blaming in, problems and difficulties are better framed as 'outside' the self. Hence 'externalization', pitting 'the person' against 'the problem'.[8]
- Since such families are often embedded in a network of relationships with other professional helpers, agencies and government instrumentalities (such as police, probation/parole services, juvenile justice, and child protection), effective intervention must acknowledge the importance of these agencies, and seek to involve them actively in planning any intervention. If this is not done, then it is not unlikely that the professionals will unwittingly undermine or defeat the tentative moves towards change that may arise out of the empowerment process.
- If change for the better does start to occur, it is vital that it be investigated, celebrated, codified and publicized, so that the family cannot simply slip into forgetting that it has occurred, but is constantly reminded of it by a wider community.

In this sense, I see the process of change agency with level-three families as almost the polar opposite of the process with level-two families. The type of conservative, cautious attitude to change that is often quite realistic and helpful with level-two families may be experienced by level-three families as denigratory or degrading – a statement that we, the professionals, 'don't believe they can make it'. Yet when change occurs in such families, it needs far more than straightforward encouragement, as in the 'coaching' model that is appropriate to level-one families. News of the change must be kept alive long enough for its impact to be felt properly. Only what is dramatically different, *and recognized as such by others outside the immediate family*, is likely to be strong enough to counterbalance generations of entrenched pessimism and cynicism.

Much of the most successful work with such families has been characterized by ideas now associated with the Narrative therapy movement, although (as the endnotes to this chapter attempt to indicate) some of its concepts and practices have a history that considerably pre-dates Narrative therapy. These practices include:

- externalizing problems (ultimately a logical development of early family therapy's insistence that problems did not lie within individuals, but in interactions and social systems);
- helping clients to explore social and cultural influences on negative beliefs about self;
- creating client-chosen advisory panels which can serve as alternative, positively oriented reference groups;[9]
- planning conjoint meetings (including not only family meetings, but also large community meetings) in such a way that all present can speak uninterrupted, and are simultaneously restrained from responding with critical and aggressive comments and questions;[10]
- reconceptualizing counsellors and therapists as *witnesses to both suffering and hope*. Much of what counsellors do is reflecting back clients' stories in ways that enhance awareness of previously hidden 'strengths' and resources, but simultaneously make it difficult for clients to reject or dismiss these reflections. Again, I see the strategic use of language as crucial to this project.

White and his colleagues see Narrative practices as the living out of an ideology which combines social constructivism with a strong commitment to what might be termed 'community psychology', 'social justice' or 'liberation theology' (depending on one's perspective). Narrative ideology has generated a powerful sense of belonging and trust among its adherents, and an equally strong implication that one cannot utilize the approaches without sharing the underlying beliefs. I personally believe that White and Epston's enduring contribution to family therapy has been their ability to engage meaningfully with level-three families, to go 'beyond shame and blame' and to create a way of working that can turn the 'despair' of such families into 'empowerment'.

Indeed, Joanna Macy, who popularized 'Despair and Empowerment' workshops in the peace movement of the 1980s, worked in a somewhat similar way. She encountered people deeply mired in pessimism about the state of the international arms race, and found that only when their sense of helplessness and hopelessness had been fully voiced and fully heard was it possible for them to begin to experience tentative glimpses of hope, and to take back some sense of control over the demoralizing juggernaut of government and the military-industrial complex.[11]

Much the same process needs to happen with level-three families, I believe. We cannot simply go to them with hopeful questions about the positive things they have done in the past or are doing now, for such questions will appear to dismiss their long histories of pain and hopelessness. Instead, our first step is to listen to them, at length and in depth, and then show them by our responses that we have heard their stories, and been moved by them. Our second step, very often, is then to connect them with others who can equally hear their stories, and share their own similar experiences, and offer solidarity and support in their distress. When we facilitate such 'temporary communities', we are in fact doing a form of group work, rather than a form of family therapy. Yet it is a very different form of group work from that described in Chapter 5 of this book.

Instead of working hard to get individual participants to offer honest responses to each other and then to examine what these responses might show them about themselves, we must (in systems severely afflicted by blame and shame) ensure that they listen to others' stories, and tell their own stories, rather than interact directly. That kind of honest interaction might come later, outside of the formal meeting of the temporary community. It is by no means impossible that it might eventually start to happen within the formal meetings, but this would probably occur only when most members of the temporary community had recovered sufficient pride and sense of agency to be able to interact directly without causing slight, offence, or renewed feelings of blame and worthlessness.

Successful family work at level one, and sometimes even at level two, often leads to couple work – because parents reach a stage of willingness to take back responsibility for their own part in their children's difficulties. In a similar way, successful family work at level three often takes the form of group work, or at least, of 'consultation with temporary social systems', the full treatment of which is, unfortunately, beyond the scope of this book.

The resurgence of 'multi-family therapy' in recent years is a case in point. While multi-family therapy seems largely unconnected with Narrative therapy's 'outsider witness practices', it effectively accomplishes similar ends. In multi-family therapy, several families facing similar problems (a family member with a degenerative illness, a family member with a drug problem, etc.) are invited to participate in what is essentially a form of group therapy. Participating families learn from other families that they are 'not alone' (as in any form of group therapy), and stories of pain and miscomprehension can be shared with cathartic effect. Yet the work of multi-family groups goes well beyond this. Family members see their own problems in a new light when confronted with the evidence of others, who may struggle with worse, or lesser, degrees of distress. They come to feel safe enough to offer feedback to each other, the children of one family, for example, offering suggestions on the way the adults in another family are handling children of their own age and with similar difficulties. Somehow, expanding the unit of treatment beyond the single nuclear family (with its shut-in intensities) seems to enable even 'rigid' and highly defended parents and young people to move into greater levels of self-awareness, and greater willingness to take some responsibility, and initiate experiments with new behaviour.[12] It is a further example of the principle that involving more people in our interaction can 'unstick' an impasse.

Defeats and victories

Shortly before writing this final chapter on family work, I experienced a painful failure with a family I'd begun to see about six months earlier. The work had started promisingly, and we'd been able to get some improvement in the situation of one of the family's two very stuck adolescents. I had warned the family against the possible effects of this small change continuing, and the boy had reacted by becoming more resolved not to give up his step towards responsible adulthood. But, under the spell of this improvement, I had started to treat this level-two family like a level-one family, and to press the adults to examine the pain of their own families of origin. Both, though prepared to go along with a certain amount of this, indicated clearly that they did not see it as relevant to their current problems with their son and daugher. I reacted by becoming more rigid and more confrontational. Suddenly, both the father and the mother, previously deferential and polite, became angry and dismissive of my attempts to help them. I had lost their confidence, and nothing I could say would bring it back. The family's behaviour had fatally hooked my own tendency to become idealistic and hopeful about change, and then, faced with evidence of human frailty, to judge and denigrate. I had ceased to be a 'non-anxious presence' for this family.

I tell this story not in a spirit of masochism, but as a proof of the fact that, however experienced and skilled we may think we are, some clients will always touch our weak spots, and we will fail to help them. It is a painful lesson, but a necessary one. Family work is never easy work, and sometimes it defeats us. No wonder family therapy is the least popular option among newly trained counsellors and therapists! But when it succeeds, it succeeds in a way that offers rewards beyond the ordinary, and I have had my share of these too. We can sometimes intervene to help a parent and a child regain understanding and trust – reversing a cycle that might otherwise have become toxic and lasted lifelong. We can sometimes enable couples, whose continuing relationship is simply causing their children unnecessary pain, to dissolve their union and start to rediscover themselves and their children in a fresh and more hopeful way. And we can, most movingly of all, sometimes facilitate understanding and forgiveness between adults and their ageing parents, enabling the wounds of the past to be healed, and the older generation to die with peace and dignity, instead of in lonely, frozen pride.

When suddenly the emotion in the room softens and the interaction drops down into authentic, heartfelt feeling, instead of the desperate cut and thrust of 'blame and defend', the frustration, the hard work and the anxiety of family therapy all seem worthwhile. After all, we humans are social creatures, not isolated individuals. Family therapy addresses the breakdown of social bonds at the most profound, complicated and painful level. For me, there is no exhilaration to match the restoration of these bonds, no satisfaction in living richer than this. Family therapy is hard work, but it is work which, if it succeeds, will affect not just those in the room with us today, but generations unborn, whom we will never see.

Notes

1 See Gottman (2000).
2 The term 'exception' was popularized by Steve de Shazer, although he actually acknowledges Wallace Gingerich and Michele Weiner-Davis as having originated the concept; see Steve de Shazer (1985). 'Unique outcome' is the term preferred by Michael White; see White (1989c).
3 This very useful term comes from Michael White's work in the years before he and David Epston created Narrative therapy; see White (1989b).
4 See Selvini Palazzoli *et al.* (1980). Other key developments of circular questioning technique can be found in Penn (1985) and Tomm (1988).
5 An excellent, clearly written introduction to the project of 'multigenerational family therapy', in which adult clients and their parents attend joint sessions, is Freedman (1992); see especially pp. 214ff.
6 'See p. 10, n. 10.
7 This concept, now associated mainly with Narrative therapy and the work of the Public Conversations Project (see n. 8 below), probably owes a good deal to the activist community work of Saul Alinsky much earlier in the twentieth century. See Alinsky (1971). See also the network therapy approach of Speck and Attneave (1973).
8 'Pitting the person against the symptoms' was described by Michael White as early as 1984, though he did not then call it 'externalizing'; see White (1989a).

A very clear explanation is given by David Epston (1998) with a respectful but robust response by Bill O'Hanlon, an originator of solution-focused therapy. See also Carey and Russell (2002).

9   See Carey and Russell (2003).
10 White (2003). See also the work of the Public Conversations Project in the USA, movingly exemplified in Roth (1993).
11 See Macy (2003).
12 See Asen *et al.* (2001). Further examples of multi-family therapy, or parents-only groups, with particular populations can be found in Blyth *et al.* (2000), Lemmens *et al.* (2003), Paterson *et al.* (2002) and Cameron (2005).

Some principles of interpersonal intervention

Much lies ahead for those of you who have begun working with couples, families or groups (and hopefully, with all three). As in any form of counselling and therapy, what counts is not so much knowing *what* to say, but *when* to say it, and you cannot learn that from any book, but only from hard experience, reflected upon honestly with supportive colleagues. However, it makes sense to conclude with a brief restatement of some principles that we have returned to again and again, in various forms, in earlier chapters.

Interpersonal work harnesses 'the power of many'

Some years ago, Bryce Courtenay wrote a bestseller called *The Power of One*, an inspirational story of one man's triumph over adversity. Such narratives are always popular, for obvious reasons. This book, by contrast, has been about a less popular option, which I call 'the power of many'. When we multiply the number of clients in the room, we create possibilities that are not present when we work with an individual alone. We gain access to more information, because we *see* how people interact with others (rather than simply listening to their descriptions of how they interact) and because we have immediate access to how others (not just ourselves) are affected by them. The level of energy is often much higher. We have more potential points of therapeutic leverage to explore. And when people get together, and start to feel safe to relate honestly, sharing dreams as well as fears and angers, they begin to generate possibilities for creativity: new connections, new ideas, new strategies. While the latter outcome is most obviously evident in a large-scale group (such as a community consultation, multi-family group, or professional workshop), it is always potentially present in work with smaller client units: couples, families, and therapy groups. Working simultaneously with more than one client is also demanding: the level of anxiety is generally higher (especially at the outset), it is not as easy to build a comfortable bond as it is with an individual client, and there are more choices and possibilities at each step in the process. The vast majority of counsellors and therapists will always choose to work one-to-one for these reasons. But for those who want to embrace the challenge of interpersonal work, the rewards are great.

Be a non-anxious presence

Because interpersonal work often involves high levels of anxiety, we must be a non-anxious presence. Crucial to staying non-anxious is our ability to *think* about what is going on, rather than simply *feeling* and *reacting*. Thus we need to be 'differentiated' from the emotional intensity of what surrounds us, and if we can do this, then the level of anxiety in our clients will automatically decrease, and they will increasingly be able to think for themselves. Generally speaking, the more people are in the room, and the more densely interwoven their patterns of interaction, the higher the level of anxiety that will be felt, and the harder it will be for us to remain free of anxiety. Maintaining the ability to think rather than react in the face of systems that are both large and highly anxious is often more than can reasonably be asked of a single worker. A co-therapy pair can 'steady' each other and rescue each other from emotional entanglements. The next step up is the presence of a team of two or more, who may be behind a mirror, or in the room with the clients, but who are less directly involved in the interaction than the counsellor, and who can thus 'stand back' to some degree from the light and heat that will be generated. Network therapy, multi-family therapy and community consultation all call for teams of workers who can offer one another a 'secure base' as they individually struggle to retain some objectivity in the presence of the group's tensions. While today's reflecting team operates very differently from the unknown 'experts' hidden behind the one-way mirror of early family therapy, the team still help to supply a non-anxious presence.

Make full use of the people in the room

Interpersonal work is interactive work, not individual work before an audience. When working with two or more people simultaneously, it makes sense to use them as resources for each other's learning. Couple work where one dominates and the other's opinions and feelings remain unexplored is not useful. Whenever the energy stays focused on a single participant, or on the blaming, painful interaction of two participants, we can be sure that important information is being ignored, and perhaps a more important issue is being avoided. This is equally true of groups and families. So, as interpersonal workers, we need to *use all of the people available to us in the room*. Initially, this often calls for a planned *warm-up* phase (see below); later, it will involve our ability to draw participants' attention to the way that interaction has narrowed down, and deliberately invite contributions from all present. We must understand that nobody becomes a 'deviant' or 'scapegoat' within a social system *unless other members of that system permit him or her to occupy that role.* 'Difficult' group members and 'problem teenagers' say something significant about, or on behalf of, the others in their system, and we need to address this significance, rather than attempting to tame or expel them.

Planned warm-up facilitates productive interaction

Just as car engines must 'warm up' in cold weather and athletes 'warm up' before strenuous physical exercise, so therapeutic groupings 'warm up' to the anticipated rigours of the session. Planned warm-up can assist therapy groups to prepare themselves more fully for a productive session, encouraging spontaneity and openness in graded steps. In contrast, couples, families and work teams (where there is shared history and intense bonding) tend to warm up 'naturally', but this warm-up is almost inevitably focused on perceived problems: it means that the ensuing dialogue will be 'problem-saturated'. Although the concept of warm-up is rarely applied to 'natural systems' such as couples and groups, it probably should be. Fifteen minutes at the start of the first session, devoted to discussion of non-problematic areas of their lives, may result in the couples and families accessing a wider range of feelings, and a broader perspective on their joint lives, during the ensuing problem-focused discussions. Sometimes I find it works better to hear a couple's or family's account of their distressing situation first, and then, in the second session, ask them to engage with some form of warm-up that broadens their frame of reference to encompass achievements and pride, as well as complaints and pain.

The larger the grouping, the more need there is for planned (worker-instigated) warm-up. When appropriate warm-ups are employed at the start of any group process, the group is more likely to access the full range of its resources, to interact more energetically, and to be more invested in the process and its outcomes, than if the warming-up process is left to chance. Seating positions that group members will take as part of their 'natural warm-up' may need to be planfully altered if interactions are to be more productive. This applies equally to families.

Provide necessary structure and leadership

Implicit in the preceding point is the principle that when more than one person is in the room with us at a time, we must exercise leadership and create structure, in order to facilitate outcomes that are more than simply replications of the spiralling, negative interaction that couples and families experience outside counselling. Similarly, in group work with unrelated participants, we must create minimal structure, and hence minimal safety, in order to allow group members to 'attach' to us and to each other. What clients need from us are rules of interaction, 'gatekeeping' to allow everyone a fair hearing, and intervention to prevent participants being hijacked, detoured or manipulated by others, with the consequent loss of the original intent of a communication.

The larger the group, in general, the greater the need for leadership and structure on our part. The facilitation of large-scale community meetings, or of groupings of several families around a common issue, demands a high-energy *involvement* from the facilitating team, regardless of whether or not that team takes a high-profile, charismatic role in proceedings. A team can be low-key, empathic and reflective, but it still requires high concentration and energy to generate this kind of response.

People bond around similarities, but learn from differences

We are instinctively (and perhaps genetically) drawn to people who seem 'like us'. We bond readily with them, and feel safe with them. Couples, therapy groups, and larger communities come together readily when they have a common interest, or perceive that they have common features. Structured exercises that ask participants to work on a common goal, or which recognize common ground, tend to generate solidarity, mutual trust, and energy directed outwards at improving the situation of all. The lower the level of ego strength and the higher the level of shame in participants, the more sense it makes to place people together with others on the basis of shared problems and shared pain. They can gain esteem and empowerment from feeling solidarity with 'alike' others, and through being witnessed and affirmed on the basis of shared experience.

However, perceived similarities are often illusory, and as we risk showing more of ourselves, we perceive differences in people we initially thought were 'like us'. This is a natural development in every couple relationship; it also occurs in therapy groups, and between parents and children in a family. Differences are, for the most part, initially perceived as threats. They trigger biologically rooted processes of fight, flight or freeze. To act on this sense of threat is part of our instinctive programming. However, when we can reflect upon and enquire about perceived differences, instead of automatically responding to them as threats, we can learn much about the other person and about ourselves. The role of interpersonal intervention is to help people to 'stay with' threatening differences, to gain more information about them (e.g. by asking the 'different' person about him/herself), and to acknowledge what parts of a perceived 'threatening difference' might also be unacknowledged parts of the self. If people can stay with this process through to its conclusion, they can reach a sense of deeper commonality with the 'different' one, and enjoy a relationship that is richer for having faced up to potential conflicts, instead of simply denying them, or acting them out in angry, punishing interchanges. 'Same' thus gives way to 'different', and 'different' eventually gives way to 'same' – but at the more profound level of common humanness.

When things get stuck, broaden the social context

A basic principle of family therapy since its beginnings has been that when a situation seems 'stuck' and unresolvable, the best thing to do is often to involve more people. This is a practical application of the notion that while a problem may appear intractable when viewed within a narrower social context (say, a father–son relationship), as soon as that context is broadened (say, to include the mother, a second son, or a grandparent) then the problem takes on a different aspect, and new possibilities are created for comprehending and resolving it.

This principle potentially applies to many variants of interpersonal work. 'Going around the group' to elicit the reactions of all participants is a fundamental technique in group therapy. Involving the referring person, or an extended family member, in sessions can generate fruitful new possibilities in family work. Even in couple counselling, we can access, and planfully refer to, our own direct reactions in response to the couple, turning a 'stuck' dyadic interaction into a three-way interaction. And when one partner is involved with someone outside the relationship, broaching the idea of inviting the lover into a session will often decisively resolve the whole stuck situation. In family work, broadening the context might mean bringing in family of origin, or it might mean bringing together as many as possible of the family's professional helpers and help systems to discuss why the family is having such a hard time. Alternatively, we might choose to involve other families, as co-participants in a multi-family 'group', again creating new possibilities for solidarity, understanding and challenge between participants.

Search for meaning, but don't impose it

Broadening the context may not mean physically involving more participants. Instead, it might mean enquiring into the history that lies behind the presenting problem. Being mindful of why *this* particular problem has occurred at *this* time will take us beyond the apparently 'closed' world of the nuclear family into a wider world of extended family patterns, a world of significant social events (wars, abuse, poverty, loss of status and dignity, loss of family members, loss of community, loss of culture) which have impacted on the family in the past, and which may have been influential in bringing about its current state and preoccupations. Acknowledging these wider contexts can make a big difference to some clients. When the past is restored to a meaningful place, the present can feel different, and people can feel free to change. But other clients do not find understanding the past helpful. For them, talking about the past may even *inhibit* change by eliciting fatalism, shame and blame. In these cases, I sometimes think that intergenerational perspectives may assist us, as workers, to understand, but should be avoided with clients, in favour of frameworks that permit them to move more freely.

Help people connect with solutions that are already known to them

Human beings are almost always clever enough to figure out solutions to their long-standing interpersonal problems. In many cases, these solutions have already been tried, but abandoned prematurely because they feel threatening to the 'comfortable discomfort' in which most of us live: fear, loyalty, anger, idealization and grief get in the way of change. Interpersonal intervention needs to concentrate on the *process* of blocked interactions, not their content, unpacking the painful feelings that lie behind the endless wrangles and bitterness. Emotionally more secure clients can learn to express their own feelings, and hear those of others, more clearly, leading to enhanced understanding and decreased threat. Clients whose early life experience has left them very distrustful, shamed and inadequate may not be able to do this via direct interpersonal encounter. For them, the damage to trust and self-esteem must first be repaired, a process that might come, lengthily but profoundly, through individual therapy, or less lengthily but still profoundly, through the experience of deep connection to others who have had similar experiences: the soothing experience of feeling accepted and understood (similarity) must come before the challenge of confronting difference.

References

Alinksy, Saul (1971) *Rules for Radicals: A Practical Primer for Realistic Radicals*. New York: Vintage.

Asen, Aia, Dawson, Neil and McHugh, Brenda (2001) *Multiple Family Therapy*. London: Karnac.

Bennis, Warren and Shepherd, H.A. (1956) A theory of group development, *Human Relations* 9 (4): 415–37.

Berger, Kathleen Stassen (1988) *The Developing Person through the Life Span*, 2nd edn. New York: Worth.

Bion, W.R. (1961) *Experiences in Groups, and Other Papers*. London: Tavistock.

Blatner, Howard A. (1973) *Acting In: Practical Applications of Psychodramatic Methods*. New York: Springer Publishing.

Blyth, A., Bamberg, J. and Toumbourou, J. (2000) *Behaviour Exchange Systems Training: A Program for Parents Stressed by Adolescent Drug Abuse*. Melbourne: ACER.

Bobes, Tony and Rothman, Barbara (2002) *Doing Couple Therapy: Integrating Theory with Practice*. New York: Norton. (Originally published in 1998 as *The Crowded Bed, An Effective Framework for Couple Therapy*.)

Boszormenyi-Nagy, Ivan and Krasner, Barbara (1986) *Between Give and Take: A Clinical Guide to Contextual Therapy*. New York: Brunner-Mazel.

Bowen, Murray (1978) An interview with Murray Bowen, in Murray Bowen, *Family Therapy in Clinical Practice*. New York: Aronson.

Cade, Brian and O'Hanlon, Bill (1993) *A Brief Guide to Brief Therapy*. New York: Norton.

Cameron, Dorothy (2005) Multi-family Groups [for people with dementia], *Context*, 77 (February): 23–6.

Carey, Maggie and Russell, Shona (2002) Externalising: commonly asked questions, *International Journal of Narrative Therapy and Community Work*, 2: 76–84.

Carey, Maggie and Russell, Shona (2003) Outsider witness practices: some answers to commonly asked questions, *International Journal of Narrative Therapy and Community Work*, 1: 3–16.

Casey, James (1989) *The History of the Family*. Oxford: Blackwell.

Crago, Hugh (1997) The not to be opened letter: family secrets, hidden knowledge and violated prohibitions, *Australian and New Zealand Journal of Family Therapy*, 18(2): 99–108.

Crago, Hugh (1998) A family in time. Unpublished manuscript.

Crago, Hugh (1999a) What happens at the third session? Unpublished manuscript.

Crago, Hugh (1999b) *A Circle Unbroken: The Hidden Emotional Patterns that Shape Our Lives*. Sydney: Allen & Unwin.

Crago, Hugh (2003) Who should be a family therapist? A personal view of selection for training, *Australian and New Zealand Journal of Family Therapy*, 24(3): 141–9.

De Shazer, Steve (1985) *Keys to Solutions in Brief Therapy*. New York: Norton.

De Waal, Frans (1989) *Peacemaking among Primates*. Cambridge, MA: Harvard University Press.

Dicks, H. (1967) *Marital Tensions: Clinical Studies towards a Psychological Theory of Interaction*. London: Routledge & Kegan Paul.

Dumont, Louis (1977) *From Mandeville to Marx: The Evolution and Triumph of the Modern Ideology*. Chicago: Chicago University Press.

Earnshaw, Averil (1998) *Time Bombs in Families, and How to Survive Them*. Sydney: Spencer Publications.

Epston, David (1989) *Collected Papers*. Adelaide: Dulwich Centre Publications.

Epston, David (1998) Internalising discourses versus externalising discourses, in *'Catching Up' with David Epston: A Collection of Narrative Practice-Based Papers Published between 1991 and 1996*. Adelaide, Dulwich Centre Publications. (Originally published in 1993 as a contribution to S. Gilligan and R. Price (eds), *Therapeutic Conversations*. New York: Norton.)

Falloon, I.R., Boyd, J.L., McGill, C.W., Ranzani, J., Moss, H.B. and Gilderman, A.M. (1982) Family management in the prevention of exacerabation of schizophrenia, *New England Journal of Medicine*, 306: 1437–40.

Freedman, David S. (1992) *Multigenerational Family Therapy*. New York: Haworth.

Freud, Sigmund (1974) *Introductory Lectures on Psychoanalysis*, ed. James Strachey and Angela Richards. Harmondsworth: Penguin. (Originally published in 1916–17.)

Freud, Sigmund (1977) *Three Essays on the Theory of Sexuality*. Trans. James Strachey, ed. James Strachey and Angela Richards, Harmondsworth: Penguin. (Originally published in 1905.)

Furlong, Mark and Young, Jeff (1996) Talking about blame, *Australian and New Zealand Journal of Family Therapy*, 17(4): 191–200.

Gottman, John (2000) *Marital Therapy: A Research-Based Approach. Clinician's Manual*. Seattle: Gottman Institute.

Grant, Jan and Crawley, Jim (2002) *Transference and Projection: Mirrors to the Self*. Buckingham: Open University Press.

Haley, Jay (1976) *Problem Solving Therapy: New Strategies for Effective Family Therapy*. New York: Harper & Row.

Hargraves, Terry and Anderson, William T. (1992) *Finishing Well: Ageing and Reparation in the Intergenerational Family*. New York: Brunner-Mazel.

Hellinger, B., Weber, G. and Beaumont, H. (1998) *Love's Hidden Symmetry: What Makes Love Work in Relationships*. Phoenix, AZ: Zeig, Tucker.

Hendrix, Harville (1988) *Getting the Love You Want: A Guide for Couples.* Melbourne: Schwartz & Wilkinson.

Hildebrand, Bruno (2004) Fallrekonstruktive Familienforschung und Familientherapie: die Sequenzanalyse in der Genogrammarbeit, *Familiendynamik,* 29(3): 257–87.

Holbrook, David (1973) The Problem of C.S. Lewis, *Children's Literature in Education,* 10 (March): 3–25.

Hoang, Lê (2005) 'I thought we came for therapy!' Autobiography sessions in couple therapy, *Australian and New Zealand Journal of Family Therapy,* 26 (2): 65–72.

Holmes, Sophie (2002) Contribution to Glenn Larner *et al.*: What are the core learnings of family therapy? *Australian and New Zealand Journal of Family Therapy,* 23(3): 128–37.

Horney, Karen (1945) *Our Inner Conflicts: A Constructive Theory of Neurosis.* New York: Norton.

Jacobs, Michael (1998) *The Presenting Past: The Core of Psychodynamic Counselling and Therapy,* 2nd edn. Buckingham: Open University Press.

Kagen, J., Snidman, N., Arcus, D. and Resnick, J.S. (1997) *Galen's Prophecy: Temperament in Human Nature.* New York: Basic Books.

Karen, Robert (1998) *Becoming Attached: First Relationships and How They Shape Our Capacity to Love.* New York: Oxford University Press.

Kerr, Michael and Bowen, Murray (1988) *Family Evaluation: An Approach Based on Bowen Theory.* New York: Norton.

Klein, Melanie (1975) Some theoretical conclusions regarding the emotional life of the infant, in *Envy and Gratitude, and Other Works, 1946–1963.* London: Hogarth Press. (Originally published in 1952.)

Koslowska, Kasia and Hanney, Lesley (1999) Family assessment and intervention using an interactive art exercise, *Australian and New Zealand Journal of Family Therapy,* 20 (2): 61–9.

Krause, Inga-Britt (1998) *Therapy across Culture.* London: Sage.

Lang, Moshe (2000) *The Answer Within: A Family in Therapy Re-examined.* Melbourne: ACER.

Le Doux, Joseph (1998) *The Emotional Brain: The Mysterious Underpinnings of Emotional Life.* London: Weidenefeld & Nicolson.

Lemmens, G., Verdegem, S., Heireman, M., Litaer, G., Van Houdenhove, B., Sabbe, B. and Eisler, I. (2003) Helpful events in family discussion groups with chronic pain patients: a qualitative study of differences in perception between therapists/observers and patients/family members, *Families, Systems & Health,* 21: 37–52.

Lidchi, Victoria Gabrielle (2003) When can mediation contribute? An application to therapy, *Australian and New Zealand Journal of Family Therapy,* 24(2): 102–8.

Lorenz, Konrad (1952) *King Solomon's Ring: New Light on Animal Ways.* London: Methuen.

Lukas, Susan (1993) *Where to Start and What to Ask: An Assessment Handbook.* New York: Norton.

Luthman, Shirley Gerhke and Kirshenbaum, Martin (1974) *The Dynamic Family.* Palo Alto, CA: Science and Behavior Books.

MacKinnon, Laurie K. (1998) *Trust and Betrayal in the Treatment of Child Sexual Abuse.* New York: Norton.

MacLean, Paul D. (1978) Why brain research in lizards?, in N. Greenberg and P.D. MacLean, *Behavior and Neurology of Lizards.* Washington, DC: NIMH.

MacLean, Paul D. (1990) *The Triune Brain in Evolution.* New York: Plenum Press.

Macy, J.R. (1983) *Despair and Personal Power in the Nuclear Age.* Philadelphia: New Society Publishers.

Madden, Michael (2005) Five useful questions in couple therapy, *Australian and New Zealand Journal of Family Therapy,* 26(2): 61–4.

Markowitz, J.C. (ed.) (1998) *Interpersonal Psychotherapy.* Washington, DC: American Psychiatric Press.

Maturana, Humberto and Francisco Varela (1992) *The Tree of Knowledge: The Biological Roots of Human Understanding,* 2nd edn. Boston: Shambhala.

McGoldrick, Monica, Gerson, Randy and Shellenberger, Sylvia (1999) *Genograms: Assessment and Intervention,* 2nd edn. New York: Norton.

Minuchin, S., Montalvo, B., Guerney, B.G., Rosman, B.L. and Schumer, F. (1967) *Families of the Slums: An Exploration of their Structure and Treatment.* New York: Basic Books.

Minuchin, Salvador (1974) *Families & Family Therapy.* Cambridge, MA: Harvard University Press.

Moreno, J.L. (1953) *Who Shall Survive.* New York: Beacon Hill.

Palmer, Helen (1988) *The Enneagram: Understanding Yourself and the Others in Your Life.* New York: HarperCollins.

Paterson, Rosemary, Luntz, Helen, Perlesz, Amaryll and Cotton, Sue (2002) Adolescent violence towards parents: maintaining family connections when the going gets tough, *Australian and New Zealand Journal of Family Therapy,* 23 (2): 90–100.

Penn, Peggy (1985) Feed-forward: future questions, future maps, *Family Process,* 24 (3): 299–310.

Pitt-Aikens, Tom and Thomas Ellis, Alice (1989) *Loss of the Good Authority: The Cause of Delinquency.* London: Viking/Penguin.

Reiss, David with Neiderhiser, Jenine L., Hetherington, E. Mavis and Plomin, Robert (2000) *The Relationship Code: Deciphering Genetic and Social Influences on Adolescent Development.* Cambridge, MA: Harvard University Press.

Rogers, Carl R. (1942) *Counselling and Psychotherapy.* Boston: Houghton Mifflin.

Rogers, Carl R. (1951) *Client-Centered Therapy.* Boston: Houghton Mifflin.

Rogers, Carl R. (1952) Communication: its blocking and facilitation, *Northwestern University Information,* 20: 9–15.

Rogers, Carl R. (1967) *On Becoming a Person: A Therapist's View of Psychotherapy.* London: Constable.

Rogers, Carl R. (1970) *On Encounter Groups.* New York: Harper & Row.

Rogers, Carl R. (1980) *A Way of Being.* Boston: Houghton Mifflin.

Roth, Sallyann (1993) Speaking the unspoken: a work-group consultation to re-open dialogue, in Evan Imber-Black (ed.), *Secrets in Families and Family Therapy,* (pp. 268–291). New York: Norton.

Satir, Virginia (1967) *Conjoint Family Therapy: A Guide to Theory and Technique.* Palo Alto, CA: Science and Behavior Books.

Scott, Elizabeth (1999) Are the children playing quietly? Integrating child psycho-therapy and family therapy, *Australian and New Zealand Journal of Family Therapy,* 20(2): 88–93.

Selvini Palazzoli, Mara, Boscolo, Luigi, Ceccin, Gianfranco and Prata, Giuliana (1978) *Paradox and Counterparadox: A New Model in the Therapy of the Family in Schizophrenic Transaction.* New York: Aronson.

Selvini Palazzoli, M., Boscolo, L., Ceccin, G., and Prata, G. (1980) Hypothesising – circularity – neutrality, *Family Process,* 19(1): 3–12.

Shaddock, David (1998) *From Impasse to Intimacy: How Understanding Unconscious Needs Can Transform Relationships.* Northvale, NJ: Aronson.

Shorter, Edward (1975) *The Making of the Modern Family.* New York: Basic Books.

Siegert, Richard J. and Ward, Tony (2002) Evolutionary psychology: origins and criticisms, *Australian Psychologist* 37(1): 20–9.

Speck, Ross V. and Attneave, Geraldine (1973) *Family Networks.* New York: Pantheon.

Stanton, M. Duncan, Todd, Thomas C. and Associates (1982) *The Family Therapy of Drug Abuse and Addiction.* New York: Guilford.

Stiefel, Ingeborg, Harris, Poppy and Zollmann, Andreas (2002) Family constella-tion: a therapy beyond words, *Australian and New Zealand Journal of Family Therapy* 23(1): 38–44.

Stokes, Jon (1994) The unconscious at work in groups and teams: contributions from the work of Wilfred Bion, in Anton Obholtzer and Vega Zagier Roberts (eds), *The Unconscious at Work: Individual and Organisational Stress in the Human Services.* London: Routledge.

Stone, Laurence (1977) *The Family, Sex and Marriage in England 1500–1800.* London: Weidenfeld & Nicolson.

Tennenbaum, S. (1967) Carl R. Rogers and non-directive teaching, in Carl R. Rogers, *On Becoming a Person: A Therapist's View of Psychotherapy* (pp. 299–313). London: Constable.

Thomas, Alexander and Chess, Stella (1980) *The Dynamics of Psychological Develop-ment.* New York: Brunner-Mazel.

Thomas, Alexander, Chess, Stella and Burch, Herbert (1963) *Behavioural Individuality in Early Childhood.* New York: New York University Press.

Tomm, Karl (1988) Interventive interviewing: Part III. Intending to ask lineal, circular, strategic, or reflexive questions? *Family Process* 27, 1: 1–15.

Wilber, Ken (1986) *Up from Eden: A Transpersonal View of Human Evolution*. Boston: Shambhala.

Whitaker, Carl A. and Napier, Augustus Y. (1978) *The Family Crucible*. New York: Harper & Row.

White, Michael (1989a) Pseudo-encopresis: from avalanche to victory, from vicious to virtuous cycles, in Michael White, *Selected Papers* (pp. 115–24). Adelaide: Dulwich Centre Publications. (Originally published in 1984.)

White, Michael (1989b) Negative explanation, restraint and double description: a template for family therapy, in Michael White, *Selected Papers* (pp. 85–99). Adelaide: Dulwich Centre Publications. (Originally published in 1986.)

White, Michael (1989c) The externalizing of the problem and the re-authoring of lives and relationships in Michael White, *Selected Papers* (pp. 5–28). Adelaide: Dulwich Centre Publications. (Originally published in summer 1988–9.)

White, Michael (2003) Narrative practice and community assignments, *International Journal of Narrative Therapy and Community Work*, 2: 47–55.

Williams, Antony (1989) *The Passionate Technique: Strategic Psychodrama with Individuals, Families and Groups*. London: Routledge.

Yalom, Irvin (1983) *Inpatient Group Psychotherapy*. New York: Basic Books.

Yalom, Irvin (1995) *The Theory and Practice of Group Psychotherapy*, 4th edn. New York: Basic Books.

Yalom, Irvin (2005) *The Schopenhauer Cure*. New York: HarperCollins.

Zeldin, Theodore (1994) *An Intimate History of Humanity*. London: Sinclair-Stevenson.

Index

Related books from Open University Press

Purchase from www.openup.co.uk or order through your local bookseller

AN INTRODUCTION TO FAMILY THERAPY
SYSTEMIC THEORY AND PRACTICE
SECOND EDITION

Rudi Dallos and Ros Draper
University of Plymouth; Institute of Family Therapy, UK

This popular introduction to the theory and practice of family therapy offers a comprehensive overview of the core concepts and ideas that have developed in systemic theory from the 1950s to the present day. Thoroughly updated with the latest research and developments, and illustrated throughout with lively examples drawn from clinical practice, this user-friendly guide provides practical resources and suggestions for improved therapeutic practice.

New to this edition:

- A new chapter on systemic formulation
- A new chapter on practice development 2000–2004
- Increased coverage of the evidence base for the effectiveness of family therapy
- Stronger focus on attachment and psychodynamic perspectives
- Comprehensive references to key people, events and texts

Written by experienced authors, this essential resource is key reading for students and practitioners of family therapy as well as those from the fields of counselling, psychology, social work and the helping professions who deal with family issues.

Contents
Preface – Introduction – The first phase – 1950s to mid-70s – The second phase – mid-1970s to mid-1980s – The third phase – mid 1980s to 2000 – Ideas that keep knocking on the door – Systemic formulation – Current practice development 2000-2004 – Research and evaluation – Reflections and critique – Postscripts – Appendices – Index.

360pp   0 335 21604 8 Paperback £24.99   0 335 21605 6 Hardback £60.00

ATTACHMENT NARRATIVE THERAPY

Rudi Dallos

This book captures a groundswell of current interest in the application of attachment theory ideas to systemic practice. It offers a creative leap forward by throwing new light on narrative and systemic theory. It proposes that Attachment Theory offers a developmental model not only regarding the content but also the structure of narratives. This can equip researchers and practitioners with new ways to look at motivation for therapy in terms of families' abilities and fears about talking and developing stories about their lives and problems.

The book sets out a framework for practice – Attachment Narrative Therapy – that is summarised in terms of a four-stage approach to working with families, couples and individuals. Clinical examples are employed throughout the book along with personal reflections. This is not offered as a prescriptive model but as an aid and guide to practice that can draw on elements from attachment, systemic and narrative therapies. By exploring aspects of the different approaches, it points to gaps in current theory and practice and offers useful integrations and developments. Moreover, the book is based in both research and practice: evidence-based practice and practice-based evidence.

For the practitioner, there are therapeutic guides outlining the applications of core 'techniques' and frameworks for clinical practice as well as extensive reading guides offering connections to related theory and practice.

Attachment Narrative Therapy provides an innovative approach for all those interested in developing their therapeutic practice.

Contents
Introduction – Attachment stories – Biology and stories: Attachment theory – Interacting stories: Narrative systematic therapy – Attachments in family contexts – ANT – an integrative model – Re-authoring lives: Clinical applications – Discussion – Index.

2006   160pp   0 335 21417 7 (Paperback)   0 335 21418 5 (Hardback)